The Idea of Social Activity for Older People

Polish Studies in Economics

Edited by Ryszard Kokoszczyński

VOLUME 17

Halina Nadobnik

The Idea of Social Activity for Older People – Local Policy Implementation

PETER LANG
Berlin · Bruxelles · Chennai · Lausanne · New York · Oxford

Bibliographic Information published by the Deutsche Nationalbibliothek
The Deutsche Nationalbibliothek lists this publication in the Deutsche Nationalbibliografie; detailed bibliographic data is available online at http://dnb.d-nb.de.

Library of Congress Control Number: 2025033904

ISSN 2191-8848
ISBN 978-3-631-93818-8 (Print)
ISBN 978-3-631-93819-5 (E-PDF)
ISBN 978-3-631-94249-9 (E-PUB)
DOI 10.3726/b23164

Published by Peter Lang GmbH, Berlin (Germany)

info@peterlang.com

This publication has been peer reviewed.

www.peterlang.com

To my grandmother
Halina

Contents

Figures and Photographs 9
Tables 11
Acknowledgements 13
Introduction 15

CHAPTER 1
The context of social activity for older people
at the local level 23

CHAPTER 2
Theoretical framework 69

CHAPTER 3
Research design 93

CHAPTER 4
Results and conclusions 117

Bibliography 217
Appendices 241

Figures and Photographs

Figure 1:	The development of paradigms and theories within gerontology	24
Figure 2:	The changing perception of city in urban studies	44
Figure 3:	Ambiguity-conflict matrix: policy implementation processes	68
Figure 4:	Glocal space	89
Figure 5:	Coding process and applied codes	111
Figure 6:	The stages of the analysis	251
Photograph 1:	Halls of VIVA Older Citizens Fairs. Visitors marching from stall to stall, established by firms, travel agencies, public bodies, or non-governmental organisations	123
Photograph 2:	Leaflet from a company offering gas valves recommended for use in the homes of dependent people with memory impairments	123
Photograph 3:	The members of older citizens' club produce charity greeting cards. They do it during VIVA Older Citizens Fairs	157
Photograph 4:	Photographs of leaflets collected during the VIVA Older Citizens' Fair. They advertise a tourist office dedicated to older people, which offers domestic and foreign trips. Their clients are active older people	172

Photograph 5: Fragment of a leaflet of the University of the Third Age, organized by the Poznan University of Life Sciences 178
Photograph 6: A tour of the Museum of Applied Arts in Poznan, organized as part of the Older Citizens' Days 179
Photograph 7: A tour of the Museum of Applied Arts in Poznan organized as part of the Older Citizens' Days 180
Photograph 8: Leaflet advertising the Muza cinema as the Older Citizen's cinema 181
Photograph 9: Excerpts from the bulletin of the Poznan Local Tourist Organization, offering trips in and around Poznan for older people 181

Tables

Table 1:	The classification of aging policies in Polish literature and policy practice	31
Table 2:	Analysis of societal and individual levels, along with the factors that promote and restrict the social engagement of older adults in urban environments	47
Table 3:	Contexts of social activity for older people implemented on the city level	50
Table 4:	Moments of translation	75
Table 5:	Policy research with ANT application	78
Table 6:	The glocalization concept within management and political studies	87
Table 7:	Research objectives and their realization	94
Table 8:	Collected data	102
Table 9:	The applied codes and categories during data analysis	115
Table 10:	The names used in the empirical chapters	119
Table 11:	Moments of translation	121
Table 12:	Criteria within the framework of the open call for proposals for activities related to people of retirement age	130
Table 13:	The proposed results and their indicators	149
Table 14:	Ontologies of social activity for older people implementation	167
Table 15:	The list of additional materials	241
Table 16:	The list of interviews and event's observations	243
Table 17:	An example of coding process in Atlas.ti	252

Acknowledgements

This book is the outcome of my doctorate studies at Poznan University of Economics and Business. The research credits are attributed to my two supervisors: my primary supervisor, Professor Maciej Ławrynowicz from Poznan University of Economics and Business, and my assistant supervisor, PhD Michał Polakowski from the Economic and Social Research Institute. I am grateful for their openness and unwavering support during the analytical and writing phases. The ultimate outcome was made possible by the reviewers of my dissertation—Professor Piotr Błędowski (SGH Warsaw School of Economics), Professor Jolanta Perek-Białas (Jagiellonian University), and Professor Chris Phillipson (The University of Manchester)—and their insightful comments. I am also grateful to all research participants who chose to trust me, dedicate their valuable time, and also reach out additional interview opportunities.

Introduction

European societies are aging, which challenges the current socioeconomic order. The increase of the projected economic dependency ratio will lead to the prevalence of nonworking people (under 16 and older than 64 years) to people in productive age, by 2070 in the European Countries (European Commission, 2018). Hence, the principle of intergenerational solidarity will be shaken; meaning, the equilibrium between members of society paying contributions to the social security system and those receiving benefits from it will be altered. This imbalance, in turn, can lead to problems with the solvency of state systems responsible, among others, for the pension system, long-term care, and healthcare system (Andreotti & Mingione, 2016a; Buffel & Phillipson, 2018; European Commission, 2018). The weakening of social security systems has also been exacerbated by the 2008 financial crisis, which forced governments to reduce social spending, and by the ongoing pandemic, which in turn requires significant state resources in the area of health care and social support (Blyth, 2018; Kutsar & Kuronen, 2015a).

The repertory of these factors constitutes an introduction to research on aging and policies designed to cope with it (Boudiny, 2013; Buffel et al., 2020; Buffel & Phillipson, 2018; Foster & Walker, 2015; Katz, 2000a). The prognosis of unwieldy social systems drives policymakers at all administration levels to establish ideas and, based on these actions, to tackle this issue (Mehta, 2011; Pal, 2005; Wincott, 2011). Ideas, hence, along with discourses, pose core elements of policy formation, right in the moment of problem definition and later on during policy implementation (Guy, 2019; Hall & Taylor, 1996; Pal, 2005). The role of ideas and discourses in policymaking has been scrutinized with discursive institutionalism (DI), which has emerged as a strand within new intuitional economics (Hall, 1997; Lieberman, 2002; Schmidt, 2008). The perspective of ideational analysis in the policy analysis provides a framework which helps to analyze ideas' influence on policy definition and policy formation. Ideas can be understood as values or norms shared by policymakers (Béland & Cox, 2011; Hall, 1997; Mehta, 2011). By and large, ideas embody particular interpretations of an issue and, in the next stage, its solutions (Mehta, 2011). For instance, the idea of active aging or successful aging frames the problem of aging and proposes actions that should be taken by policymakers. These concepts, in turn, consist of other smaller ideas, such as the social activity of the older people, which, in turn, imply particular actions that should be implemented (Council of the European Union, 2012; World Health Organization, 2002).

The idea of social activity is being implemented by different levels of governance and by different policies. The implementation process complexity involves multiple actors. Furthermore, it is contextual, meaning it is formed by environment, such as institutional context, available resources, attitudes of bureaucrats, and heterogeneous recipients of policy (Mehta, 2011; Pressman & Wildavsky, 1974).

In the Polish context, researchers (Błędowski, 2016b; Theiss, 2007; Urbaniak, 2018) underline the important role of local government and the local community in the implementation of aging policies. Accordingly, public entities at this level most accurately perceive problems of older people and can act in the environment of people, using local resources (2016, p. 83). It is also in line with one of the last trends in policy implementation research, which emphasizes a bottom-up direction on policy implementation (Kutsar & Kuronen, 2015a; Matland, 1995). The upward policy implementation is also connected with the process of decentralization in public policies. This means the transfer of responsibility for the implementation of policies to lower levels of local government. We can see twofold reasoning in that trend:

1. Economic crisis and cuts in social policy expenditures.
2. Provision of services in the closest environment to the citizens and promotion of social participation (Andreotti & Mingione, 2016a; Caldarice, 2018).

In research, local welfare governance and the policies implemented by such governance is receiving increasing attention. The crucial factor is the relationship between national or regional governance, which, accordingly, to Dagmar Kutsar and Marjo Kuronen (2015a), seek further inquiries. In the Polish context, non-governmental organizations (NGOs) are key actors in local policy implementation, as they support the public sector and provide a wide range of activities for the community (Błędowski, 2016b; Urbaniak, 2018). In particular, cities, due to their diversity of resources, knowledge of the inhabitants, and better accuracy in diagnosing problems, become responsible for taking measures related to an aging society (Buffel et al., 2020; Klimczuk & Tomczyk, 2016; Phillipson & Scharf, 2005; Rémillard-Boilard et al., 2020). The city became noticed by urban studies scholars, who focus on relations between the metropolis and its inhabitants. In more contemporary urban studies, cities are presented as a scene of grassroots initiatives and different communities (Domaradzka, 2018). The power of globalization makes the city a very powerful entity; however, also much diversified (Jayne & Ward, 2017). The cities are seen more as a place of huge income inequalities. Its space is a matter of dispute between citizens, city authorities, entrepreneurs, and other social groups.

If the city is to consider the specificity of its inhabitants and to create the most suitable policy, taking into account top-down ideas, the question arises what influences urban policymakers, their interpretations of the problem in question, choices of actions, and ways they are implemented on the urban policy level. Hence, the research problem studied within this book: *the implementation of social activity for older people by the urban aging policy in Poznan*. Based on that, I have posed two questions:

1. What is the idea of social activity for older people implemented in Poznan?
   1.1. Who and what is involved in this process?
   1.2. How do the actors network to each other?
2. How is the idea of social activity implemented by urban policies?
   2.1. What are the practices of implementing social activity idea?
   2.2. What is the urban aging policy in Poznan?

The answers to these questions will broaden the knowledge of urban aging and urban policy implementation, which is relevant due to the aging of societies.

International organizations such as the European Union and the United Nations design aging policies' blueprints, providing a framework for national local authorities to act (Buffel & Phillipson, 2018; Sun et al., 2017; van Hoof et al., 2018). In turn, policies embody ideas which presuppose particular views on how aging should look like. For instance, an active aging idea, which in order to preserve better well-being and independence among the older people, promotes their longer labor activity as well as active social and cultural life (Council of the European Union, 2012; Foster & Walker, 2015; Walker, 2002, 2008). However, as mentioned, the actual implementation of ideas and policy depends on local authorities, for example, cities (Błędowski, 2016b; Buffel & Phillipson, 2018; Perek-Białas et al., 2006; van Hoof et al., 2018). Hence, within my study I will also explore local understanding of social activity idea and hence aging, which is reflected in the studied reality (Wildavsky, 2018).

Therefore, in this study, the aim is to understand the *implementation of social activity for older people by the urban aging policy in Poznan*. For this purpose, I traced social participation activities for the older people and further reconstruct the network of activities, the ideas that frame them, and actants[1] who organize them. As a result, the study will fill the research gap linking ideas, such as social activity of older people, and their practical implementation. Thus, the research aims are to:

1. Explore what the social activity for the older people that takes place in Poznan is.
   1.1. Recognize who and what organizes these activities and why they do it.
   1.2. Establish relations between actors.
2. Understand the implementation of the idea of social activity for older people at the city level.
   2.1. Identify practices of implementation.
   2.2. Trace ontologies and scales which form the urban aging policy in Poznan.

[1] This is term which comes from actor-network theory, refers to actors who take part in the process of policy formation, but it is broader as it includes human and nonhuman objects (Latour, 2005b; Law, 2019). I explain this term more deeply in section 2.1—Actor-network theory.

The proposed research problem stems from deliberations within a few fields, namely gerontology and social policy, and is conceptually considered from the perspective of DIs at the urban policy level.

To execute this research, I applied two theoretical frameworks, namely the actor-network theory (ANT) and the glocalization concept (Cox, 2009; Swyngedouw, 1996, 2004). Both frameworks allowed for exploring different ideas and discourses present in urban policy formation, and furthermore trace relations between them, elucidating the power relation and possible cooperation within, the *glocal* field (Swyngedouw, 1997; Wathen, 2020).

The analytical approach applied within policy research in the field of DI is an inductive approach. It means that the researcher establishes theories concerning the research phenomenon, based on only a few assertions about social reality as he rather stays open for what emerges from the data (Pieliński, 2013; Silverman, 2007; Sławecki, 2012). Within this approach, to understand the implementation of social activity of older people idea, I will apply the ANT, as a guideline for empirical inquiry as well as the analytical framework (Callon & Latour, 1981; Latour, 2005a). Within this approach, scholars ask how researched phenomena emerge and strive to study the process of its weaving. This includes translation analysis, which is a process of negotiations, conflicts, even wars between engaged actors over preferred interests, values, and planned actions. To study such a process is not easy as its network is hidden; researchers have to follow actants—human and nonhuman objects, that together create the network and thus the phenomenon (Latour, 2005a). The use of ANT is aimed at supporting the process of data collection, following important actants (human and nonhuman objects), but also it will drive the process of analysis and discovering a network of the social activity among older people enactment (Galis, 2011; Hardy & Williams, 2008; Iskandarova, 2017; Ranerup, 2008).

Furthermore, I deploy the concept of glocalization, which provides an analytical framework, both in the formulation of the research gap as well as data collection and analysis. The glocalization was introduced by Robert Robertson (1995), as a mix of the global and the local, two mutually constitutive powers. When the global idea is a set of local practices, the local in turn is constructed by global forces (Drori et al., 2014). The term glocalization, within urban and local policy studies, is strongly related to globalization which led to the decentralization and rescaling of political systems, diminishing power of states in favor of the international organization, but also local levels of administration (Swyngedouw, 1996, 1997; Wathen, 2020). Within this process, regional actors, such as cities, are much more powerful (Roudometof, 2015). The application of glocalization allow studying how urban aging policy is scaled, whereas the global and local forces are interacting, which results in new policy scales emergence (Swyngedouw, 1997). These scales are not only a way of measuring space in geographical terms, but also the realities between actors, the balance of power, and the agreements in place between them (1997).

To know how social activity is implemented in the city of Poznan, I decided to follow and observe such events happening in the city from February until December 2019. The event was understood as any activity happening for older people announced in newsletters, social media, or advertised on the outdoor posters, as long as it entailed a gathering of older people. Simultaneously to the period of participatory observations, I conducted interviews, which were held from April 2019 to June 2020, with people engaged in organizations of social activity events. Another group of data, consisting of additional materials, was collected along with the observations and interviews, and once more during the process of analysis (for the full list of collected data, see Appendix 1. The list of data sources). The sheer process of data collection was aimed at following the social activity events directed to older people. To gather a diversified group of observations, the inclusion criteria for the research was pretty open. However, I decided not include events concentrated on health promotion or physical activity into the analysis, as their superb aim was to influence the older people's health. The focus of this research was to examine activities intended for social activation of the older people.

Data analysis was based on the coding process, an analytic tool, applied within a qualitative study. It consists in naming a particular part of the data with two- or three-word labels, which synthesize it within a chosen by the researcher theoretical framework, which in my case was ANT and glocalization (Silverman, 2007). The established codes were analyzed in the phases of theorization to extract their saturation and translate them into the form of results. The process of analysis was conducted in the Atlas.ti, software, designed for qualitative data analysis. The presented data here are only a representation of a huge amount of interviews, documents, and additional materials collected in the analytical process, which together provided

229 pages of transcripts, field notes, and documents and 30 hours of observations. I present only a part of them, just to explain my emerging categories and the relation between them. However, I did not strive to prove the high frequency of category occurrence, but rather to explain their role in the social activity implementation, and for that, I used some fragments of data.

The structure of my book consists of four chapters. In Chapter 1, I explain my conceptual framework. Thus, I refer to the different conceptualization of aging and next I present various aging policies within Polish literature and policy discourse. In the second section of this chapter, I introduce the results of literature review on social activity for older people implemented on the city level. The third section is devoted to review of research perspective in social policy research and explanation of DI as applied in my study. Chapter 2—Theoretical framework, in turn, introduces my theoretical framework as well as my strategies for data collection and analysis. In the first section, I explain the ANT assumptions and show how this approach was used within research on local policy implementation as well as within urban studies. Subsequently, I present the glocalization concept and its contribution in analysis of decentralization in policy formation. The third chapter (Chapter 3—Research design) is devoted to my research strategy, namely case study, the process of data collection, and an explanation of my analytical process. Chapter 4—Results and conclusions—is an empirical one. In the first section I present data on what is social activity for older people, implemented in Poznan. In turn, in the next ones I explain identified by me ontologies and scales of urban aging policy. In the final section I am summing up my findings in reference to established research aim and research questions. Furthermore, I explain my contribution to understanding of aging by local policy actors as well as to knowledge on urban aging policy. The book's appendices provide the research dataset, encompassing a compilation of collected data, interview scenarios, field notes, the analytical technique, and an excerpt of the coded research material.

The context of social activity for older people at the local level

The notion of aging was reinvented by industrial society along with changes in family structures, modernization of work, and urban migration, which revealed the problem of fragile older people without care and livelihood (Marshall & Clarke, 2010). This institutionalization of the older age created a new social group, that is, retirees. Currently, the problem of aging gained another meaning in light of an increase in the number of older people compared to the rest of society, meaning the working age group. It is described as a social and economic phenomenon of population aging and posed a challenge for future societies and their economies (Achenbaum, 2010). Since then, the notion of aging has grown into the multidisciplinary field of gerontology and geriatrics, which discusses it from biological, medical, but also from economic, sociological, psychological, and policy perspectives (Joy, 2018).

In the research on aging, there are three main fields: experimental gerontology, gerontology, and geriatrics. The first one is devoted to the studies of aging from a biological perspective, focusing not only on humans, but also on other organisms (Szatur-Jaworska et al., 2006). Gerontology, in turn, problematizes aging in the context of economics, sociology, psychology, demography, and political science. Within more current threads it is extended to techno gerontology, environmental gerontology, and critical gerontology. Within the last one research presented in this book can be placed. (Dannefer & Phillipson, 2010; Szatur-Jaworska et al., 2006). Gerontology is multidisciplinary field of research and emerged on the cusps of the nineteenth and twentieth centuries (Gilleard & Higgs, 2016; Phillips et al., 2010). Its paradigms shaped the way scientists and practitioners perceived old age and designed policies. Over decades, the attitude toward aging evolved. According to Victor W. Marshall (1999), we can speak of three generations of gerontological paradigms (see Scheme x), rooted first in functionalism, then in interactive symbolism, and further in critical theory (Klimczuk, 2017). Other gerontological sources also mention an environmental paradigm, which emerged simultaneously with the critical one (Sánchez-González & Rodriguez-Rodriguez, 2016; Wahl & Gitlin, 2007).

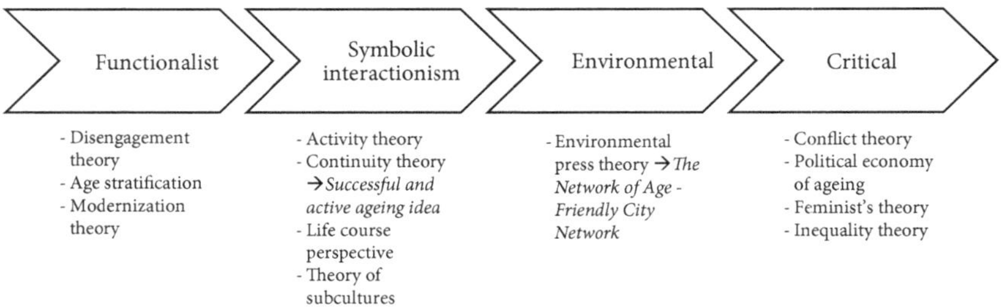

Figure 1: The development of paradigms and theories within gerontology.
Source: Own elaboration based on Achenbaum (2010), Gilleard and Higgs (2016), and Klimczuk (2015).

The first paradigm, functionalism, took place in the 1960s, when researchers focused on the broader picture of aging, capturing it from the macro and meso levels. Within this paradigm, society is perceived as one body with its elements dependent on each other (Klimczuk, 2017). The aging of the population is seen as a result of technical development and modernization, which caused longer life expectancy and thus changed the proportion of older people in society (Marshall & Clarke, 2010). The increase in older individuals compared to the rest of the age groups can upset the social equilibrium. So, the problems of older people will be sufferable for the rest of society, for example, with higher expenditures on healthcare due to extending needs of older people. In line with functionalism, social services are focused on problem solving. Furthermore, because the aging issue is perceived as an effect of modernization, older people are seen as supine victims, weave into social structure with little or no agency to stir their lives (2010). It, in turn, refers to the disengagement theory, established by E. Cumming and W. E. Henry (1961), which perceives the old age as a time to rest. Another functionalist gerontological theory is age stratification, in turn which looks at the society as a cluster of different cohorts. They use the chronological age to group individuals and according to this design proper policies, which support the group differentiation (Dannefer & Settersten, 2010; Klimczuk, 2017). Finally, the third, modernization theory, introduced by Burgess, Cowgill, and Holmes, underlines the change caused by industrialization, urbanization, and the deterioration of the traditional family, which caused individualization (Klimczuk, 2017). As writes E. W. Burgess (1960), older people are given a *roleless role*, which means that devoid of work, they have no other tasks to perform and involuntarily became a burden for the rest of society.

The second gerontological paradigm, symbolic interactionism, started in the 1970s and objected to the functionalistic theories on aging (Marshall, 1999). Oppose to the functionalistic paradigm theories within symbolic interactionism emphasize the interaction between individuals, groups, or institutions, and ways in which they communicate with each other and form common meanings (Blumer, 1969). Within this paradigm, getting older is just a process of entering into another set of meanings (Hooyman & Kiyak, 2017; Marshall & Clarke, 2010). Promoted within this paradigm *activity theory* proposed prolonged social, cultural, or labor activity of older people, which can have a positive influence on their well-being and self-development (Bengtson & DeLiema, 2016; Marshall & Clarke, 2010). Another gerontological theory within the symbolic interactionism paradigm is the continuity theory by R. C. Atchley (1989), which assumes that older individuals should not exit social life but rather change their roles along with the various life stages. Individuals aim to preserve their inner personality and remain engaged in external structures (Klimczuk 2016). Both activity and continuity theory can be also linked with another theoretical concept, namely the life-course perspective (Phillips et al., 2010). According to it, aging is considered a life process, which concerns not only older adults, but also those in their 40s and younger people, who are all aging. Thus, one's condition changes across various stages of life, and each subsequent state depends on the previous ones (Dannefer & Settersten, 2010). Another theory from this paradigm is the theory of subculture by A. M. Rose. In this theory, older people are seen as a distinct group, with discrete norms and lifestyles. They create a community of individuals of the same age and decrease contact with different age groups (Rose, 1962).

Aging theories based on symbolic interactionism provided the basis for two policy ideas: successful aging and active aging. Those two ideas differ according to the place of origin, time, and issues they tackle. Successful aging is an American idea launched in the 1980s, rooted in the continuity theory (Foster & Walker, 2015). The implementation of this idea was in opposition to the previously known image of aging, as a stage of illnesses and decrease. Within this idea, old age can be a joyful and healthy time, when individuals will attempt to remain engaged in their environment by maintaining their old roles and values (Foster & Walker, 2015; Havighurst, 1961). The emergence of successful aging allowed one to divide older people "from those doing poorly to those doing well" (Strawbridge et al., 2002).

In turn, an active aging idea was established in Europe and proliferated by the European Union (Foster & Walker, 2015). Its objectives were similar to successful aging, but more focused on encouraging labor activity and social participation of older people. As a result of continuous activities, older people are supposed to maintain good health longer and independence from social services (Foster & Walker, 2015; Walker, 2008). It also aimed to present aging as not the time of decline and poverty, but rather an activity and participation. In combination with healthy aging, social participation and the retained activity of older people were claimed to be beneficial for their health (Foster & Walker, 2015; Walker, 2008). Therefore, older people will be independent longer, not only on the economic base but also in their daily life. Both ideas—successful and active aging—were criticized (Estes & Grossman, 2007; Katz, 2000a; Martinson & Berridge, 2015). First, upon a persistent image of an active aging adult as working full or part time, which is claimed to be an embodiment of purely neoliberal ideas of efficiency and productivity (Katz, 2000a; Walker, 2008). Second, these ideas are seen as oppression for older people, who must age actively and healthy, thereby excluding the fragile and limited older people. Furthermore, the presented ideas seem to ignore issues such as economic or educational differences among older people and thus distinct needs. Such frameworks also do not consider national minorities and gender differences, which can influence experience aging (M. B. Holstein & Minkler, 2003; Walker, 2008).

In the cups of the 1970s, in turn, environmental paradigms emerged within gerontological studies, exploring the spatial background of aging (Sánchez-González & Rodriguez-Rodriguez, 2016). Within this paradigm, the center of the consideration is placed on the relation between the older individual and his or her environment. The aim of this paradigm is to explore and explain what factors of the socio-physical environment, such as security, accessibility, or independence, influence the quality of aging and how they affect older people and their behaviors (Wahl & Gitlin, 2007). The assumption within this paradigm is that both older individuals and their environment must take some adaptive actions.[2]

Subsequently, the 1980s brought the emergence of the critical paradigm and underlined the power of institutional actors in the construction of the aging. From their perspective, the process of aging is a socially constructed phenomenon. Critical theory combines studies of structures and individuals, in contrast to the macro-perspective of the functionalist and an individual approach within symbolic interactionism (Bengtson & DeLiema, 2016; Hooyman & Kiyak, 2017; Phillipson & Estes, 2007). The critical paradigm, also called cultural and humanistic gerontology or moral economy, applies interpretative studies to find values and norms that construct the phenomenon of aging and understand its subjective view (Klimczuk, 2017, p. 44). It started the development of participatory research (Buffel & Phillipson, 2018), which strives to create an emancipatory knowledge based on the experiences of academics, practitioners, and older people. Within the fourth paradigm of gerontology researchers distinguish conflict theory, political economy of aging theory, feminist theory, the theory of institutional racism and inequality

In conflict theory, researchers perceive society as a structure of competing groups. As a result of struggle, some groups are more powerful and resourceful with influences, social support, or money than others. In consequence, the first group has better access to education, healthcare, and well-paid jobs

---

[2] One of the attempts to influence the relation between older people and their environment is the Global Network of Age-Friendly Cities and Communities (Rémillard-Boilard et al., 2020), launched in 2010 by the World Health Organization. Within this network the WHO introduced a guide, which identified the eight domains of action to ensure the age-friendliness of cities (Buffel & Remillard-Boilard, 2019; Krzeczkowskiego, 2014; Rémillard-Boilard et al., 2020). The idea behind this network is to influence the relationship between older individuals and their closest environment, namely the local community and the neighborhood. This framework was also established as an answer to the cities' problems in tackling the aging issue, facing the budget limitation on social services due to economic austerity (Buffel et al., 2020). This concept will be discussed more in Section 1.2—Urban aging.

(Dannefer & Settersten, 2010; Klimczuk, 2017). The emergence of welfare, in turn, which is also an effect of struggles between those groups, reflects the interests of the most powerful groups (Phillips et al., 2010). In line with conflict theory, the formation of policy is an effect of resources allocation and their control. Therefore, social analysis aims to observe the relation between actions, which lead to changes in the field of social inequalities (Estes & Grossman, 2007). The political economy of aging, in turn, emerged in the 1970s and was elaborated by Caroll Estes (the United States), Peter Townsend and Alan Walker (the United Kingdom), John Myles (Canada), and Anne Marie Guillemard (France). Within this framework, the process of aging is placed in the context of social forces, politics, and institutional influences. The way individuals age and aging policy is designed is socially constructed by multiple actors. The state policy emerges as the result of struggles between different actors and then shape an individual's life (Bengtson & DeLiema, 2016; Estes & Portacolone, 2009). Aging policies are claimed to reflect intertwined interests of different stakeholders, such as the state, policymakers, international institutions and corporations, NGOs, social initiatives, and finally the older people. All those actors represent a particular layer of analysis, which with their power, values, and roles construct latter life (Bengtson & DeLiema, 2016; Klimczuk, 2012). For the researchers, it is necessary to study the output of struggles between those levels, both on the macro and meso levels—and explore their influence on the micro-level (Estes & Portacolone, 2009).

From the perspective of feminist theory, aging is perceived as a socially constructed phenomenon. The central point of their consideration scholars put on women's situations in the discourses on the aging process (Hooyman & Kiyak, 2017). Within this theory it is believed that gender differences play a significant role in the aging process and in result cause different experiences of old age among men and women. The more privileged positions of men in society and taking the men as a point of reference in the formulation of various policies results in the exclusion of women and their problems associated with the aging process, for example. Using men as a benchmark for various policy design results in the exclusion of women and their problems associated with the aging process (Estes & Grossman, 2007). Within a critical approach, researchers also focus on ethnic and racial inequalities that affect the experience of aging for both the individual and social groups, resulting in poorer access to health care or financial disadvantage in old age (2007).

The four paradigms and the theories of aging presented within them show the transformations in the perception of old age and older people. These oldest theories are responsible for creating aging as a phase of withdrawal from social life and giving way to younger generations (Marshall & Clarke, 2010). A reversal in thinking about old age occurs with concepts associated with interactional symbolism, at which time concepts are developed that promote the longest possible activity of older members of society. The research approach used in this book is related to the critical paradigm. Consequently, I perceived the idea of social activity as an actor, influencing the old age and thus policies to respond to its challenges. Researchers emphasize the strong influence of interests, dominant values and social groups on the way aging policies are shaped (Estes & Grossman, 2007). Adopting a critical paradigm allows you to look at the policy under study as the resultant of the actions of many actors, with different influences and interests. This means recognizing the influence that social, political, and institutional forces have on the aging process.

1.1. Social activity of older people within aging policy

The aim of this chapter is to present the conceptualization of aging policies in discourse of Polish literature and policymaking. This level of analysis is related to the location of the research problem addressed in the city of Poznan. This level of analysis is dictated by the decentralization of social policy, including the policy of aging, which is discussed in Section 1.2. As it was demonstrated in the introduction to this chapter aging can be framed differently by gerontological researchers. Their vision of an older person and their role in the society has been changing over the years, producing new ideas, which in turn can become influential actors in the process of policy formation (Blyth, 2010). When it comes to policies, aging can be also approached variously not only in regard of values embraced in them, but also the way it is conceptualized, meaning as a process, as group of people, or phase of life (Szatur-Jaworska, 2016). These, in turn, influence aims, and measures taken within aging policies, thus for each of them social activity of older people can be perceived diversely and be directed toward different individuals. This issue I will explain in the first section—Aging policies in the Polish literature and discourse, whereas in the second section—Locality of aging policies—I go down to the lower level of aging policy and bring its decentralization forward, which means the handover of tasks to the lower levels of administration. This fact is important as it guides my research to the lower levels of policy implementation.

Aging policies in the Polish literature and discourse

In this section, I present how aging is framed by policies and what is the place of social activity there. The policies presented here (see Table 1) are part of larger sets, namely social policy, which in turn belongs to public policy (Szatur-Jaworska, 2016; Urbaniak, 2018). Social policy can be understood as a complex of measures, targeted to fulfill social and individual needs and it is established by various public and social entities (Szarfenberg, 2008; Szatur-Jaworska, 2016). Public policy, in turn, can be defined as measures systematically taken by state institutions as well as by citizens to address collective problems (Zybała, 2012). This means that the set of public policies, apart from social policy, includes housing policy, health policy, education policy, etc. It is important to note that presented here aging policies can also engage different specific policies, which means that they go beyond social policy only.

The policies presented refer to the issue of aging from three perspectives: cohort, old age, and demographic process. The first draws attention to the group of older adults, who currently face this phase of life and its challenges. Whereas the next one frames actions at the old age, which can concern not only the current group of older people, but also the future generations. The latter, in turn, provides measures aimed at societies aging process, its causes, and possible effects. Therefore, it can refer to other social groups than just older people (Klimczuk, 2018; MacManus, 2010; Szatur-Jaworska, 2016). Although each perspective concerns the issue of aging, they all have different aims and strive to the realization of slightly different interests, namely older individuals, future generations, or a society as a whole. In addition, the three perspectives can all intersect within one policy. This means that action carried out with one policy can have threefold aims and meet different interests.

Table 1: The classification of aging policies in Polish literature and policy practice

Policy	Tackled problems	Role of social activity	Policy perspective
Life cycle policy	Problems of different age groups perceived as continuum of social investments.	Social investment, beneficial to individuals and society.	Demographic process, old age, and cohort perspective.
Life-course perspective	Focus on the older people throughout previous life phases and transitions.	The way to find new roles and activities in the new stage of life.	Older people perspective.
Policy of active aging	Enhancing the old age and increasing older people's productivity.	- Adjustment for the latter stage of life. - The increase in productivity among older people.	Old age perspective.
Policy on population aging	Facing the issue of aging societies on individual and social levels.	- The need of older individuals. - Preventive measures to prolong independency of older people and their well-being.	Demographic process, old age, and perspectives of older people.
Policy of the old age	Addressing problem of this particular age group, in the present, but also in future perception.	- The need of older people. - Promotion of the old age.	Old-age perspective
Policy for older people	Responding to the need for a current cohort of older people.	- The need of older people. - A response to older people's marginalization. - Enhancement of older people's independency.	Older people's perspective

(Continued)

Table 1: (*Continued*)

Policy	Tackled problems	Role of social activity	Policy perspective
Older citizen policy	Adapting to the process of aging societies. Responding to need of current cohort of older people.	– Improvement of well-being among older people. – The increase of productivity among older people.	Demographic process, old age, and older people's perspectives.

Source: Own elaboration based on Golinowska (2015), Szatur-Jaworska (2016), Szatur-Jaworska et al. (2021), and Urbaniak (2018).

The first policy perspective—the life cycle policy—poses a broad concept, as it concerns all members of society. This policy considers the impact of successive phases of life on those that follow. It is related to the concept of social investment popular in social policy. It suggests that measures of social policy should be orientated toward the future and equip individuals with capabilities useful in the future. The aim is to rather prepare for possible future problems than respond to them when they occur. The cost of such investment is believed to be lower-than-later interim consumption (Golinowska, 2015, p. 17). The application of this perspective to the latter phase of life is especially justified due to older people's heterogeneity. The group of older people can be divided into three subgroups. First, there are people aged 50 to 65. Their need is to ensure their labor activity and help them cope with the first symptoms of chronic diseases. Investments in this life phase will help to improve the health issues of the next one, which falls between 65 and 75 years old. It is focused on providing older adults with income that would guarantee stability after work. Moreover, at this stage, similarly to the previous stage, older people may have increased health needs. Finally, the needs alter for the group of individuals older than 80 years, who can suffer from a more severe health condition, and thus dependency on others in everyday life activities, which is being provided within long-term care policies (Golinowska, 2015; Szatur-Jaworska, 2016). Measures taken in each of the mentioned subgroups can influence problems in sequential phases, decreasing outlays for healthcare or long-term care systems. From the perspective of life cycle policy, the social activity of older people can be perceived as a social investment, which can influence individual well-being and limit expenditures for healthcare.

When talking about the life cycle approach within aging policies, it is also necessary to mention the life-course perspective (Dannefer & Settersten, 2010; Foster & Walker, 2015). While the first one refers more to the cycle of generations, focusing on the financial resources needed for later phases of life within the life of a family or society, the second one—life-course perspective—refers to social, economic, and health issues across individuals' lives (Alwin et al., 2016). Thus, how we experience our old age is conditioned by experiences from our earlier adulthood but also childhood (Golinowska, 2015; Szatur-Jaworska et al., 2021). It considers one's life transitions from one stage to another, namely the changes of roles within each phase and possible influences of each stage on another. The policy within the life-course approach is more orientated on helping individuals to age well across their whole lives. In order to do so, policymakers engage various policies, such as education policy, health care, or family policy, to ease individuals' transition from one life phase to another (Hagestad & Dykstra, 2016). Older people are encouraged to actively participate in social life and gain new roles to shape their daily life.

The policy on aging population, in turn, is directed at the demographic process (Szatur-Jaworska, 2016), which means that this policy strives to influence the process, and minimize its negative causes. Thus, it can be considered not only as an element of social policy, but also economic policy, as well as spatial or migration policy. It strives to meet individual and social needs stemming from the aging process, namely health, housing, social activity, endurance of consumption in later life, education, long-term care for dependent adults, and work activity (Błędowski, 2016a; Klimczuk, 2018; Szatur-Jaworska, 2016). Actions taken within policy on aging populations can also be divided into two types: preventive and adaptive. The first type refers to measures aimed to limit negative causes of aging process, whereas the second one concerns policies, which help older people to adjust to the effects of this process, such as loneliness and dependency of older people or insufficiency of the pension system (Szatur-Jaworska, 2016). This aging policy is a very broad one and approaches not only current older individuals but also the future cohorts. Moreover, it also responds to the social effects of the aging. Social activity, in turn, can be perceived as a need of older people, but also as a preventive measure, which can help maintain the independence of individuals and their well-being.

As for the policy toward the old age, it focuses on the aging issue from the perspective of a life stage. It strives to address the needs of current older people while also prepare the future older people generation. Additionally, the objective of this policy is to promote older age within the rest of the social groups and reduce age discrimination by supporting intergenerational actions (Klimczuk, 2018; Szatur-Jaworska, 2016). By and large, policy toward old age is a part of presented earlier life cycle policy, but it can be narrowed, meaning this policy does not consider earlier stages, but rather takes into account current social, economic, and cultural circumstances, influencing the old age (2016). Social activity is considered a need of older people, but also a way to promote this stage of life and its positive image.

The particular cohort of individuals is taken into account in the policy for older people. This policy aims to address the need of older individuals, prevent their marginalization, and enhance their independence (Błędowski & Szweda-Lewandowska, 2016; Klimczuk, 2018). Furthermore, it is specified to the needs of a particular group of older people, living within the designated environment and timeframe. Policy for older people can be realized at different policy levels. At the international level policies toward older people regulate pension entitlements, at the national level, they shape the basis of health care for older people, and at the local level, they seek to increase the social activity of older people (Szatur-Jaworska 2016a, p. 85). Thus, social activity would be aimed at addressing the needs of the current group of older people, preventing their marginalization, and improving their independence.

Older citizen policy, in turn, is a term introduced along with the governmental program and thus entered the scene of political terminology, and perhaps more importantly, public discourse (Szatur-Jaworska, 2016). Older citizen policy is understood as "all the activities of public administration and other organizations and institutions that are focused on implementing tasks and initiatives that shape the conditions for dignified and healthy aging" (Older Persons Act 2015, Article 4, point 2) (Urbaniak, 2018). Whereas in the Long-term Older Citizenship Policy in Poland 2014–2020, older citizen policy is defined as "[...] the set of activities throughout life, leading to ensure the extension of activity, both occupational and social, and self-reliant, healthy, safe and independent living for older people." In its assumptions, older citizen policy also refers to active aging policies by promoting social and labor activity of older people. Similarly to policy on aging societies, this one also extends its action to spatial policy or economic policy (Szatur-Jaworska, 2016). According to the literature, older citizen policy has more adaptive character, meaning it takes actions aimed rather at improving current issues than preventive measures (Szatur-Jaworska, 2015).

The presented policies, in terms of their aims and actions, refer to older people, old age, or the process of aging in the social and individual dimensions. On the one hand, it implies wide-ranging measures, which address aging issues. On the other hand, however, this variety of policies also provide distinct aims concerning desired effects. Within this section, I wanted to demonstrate how different conceptualizations of aging in policies were visible in their various values and interests regarding aging. However, these different conceptualizations intersect, rival each other, or cooperate within the process of policy formation (Schmidt, 2010). For example, the life cycle policy refers to older people's social activity as a social investment, which can be beneficial for an individual's well-being in later life and social expenditure. In turn, in terms of aging policy or older citizen citizenship policy, social activity is a tool for maintaining the productivity of older population groups. A yet different approach to social activity will be taken by aging or older citizenship policies, seeing in social activity opportunities to combat the marginalization of older people and increase their independence. By outlining these differences, I want to show in this study how complex the reality of implementing a given idea in policy is.

The perspectives described earlier represent the numerous approaches of aging policy that policymakers may take. It means that such a policy, for example, seeks to address concerns related to older persons as well as old age. They can be applied concurrently within a single national or regional policy. The decision is based on the goals of the ministry and government in charge of drafting such legislative documents. Currently, Poland has "Social Policy for Older Persons 2030: Safety-Participation-Support,"[3] a relatively recent policy document that follows "The Long-Term Objectives of

[3] The original title: "Polityka społeczna wobec osób starszych 2030. Bezpieczeństwo-Uczestnictwo-Wsparcie."

Older Citizens' Policy in Poland for 2014–2020."[4] However, according to a report prepared by experts at the Polish Ombudsman (Komisja Ekspertów ds. Osób Starszych przy Rzeczniku Praw Obywatelskich, 2018), the new policy paper is inconsistent. When constructing the existing policy framework, policymakers failed to take into account earlier policy judgments and suggestions. Furthermore, the information is ambiguous and lacks explicit activities. The policy statement appears to be primarily concerned with policies impacting older people and does not address old-age policy, which might deal with preconceptions and promote a positive picture of old age. The report's authors also highlight the lack of measures aimed at promoting older people's social and labor participation. These two factors are required for effective intergenerational solidarity and the creation of a better future. Another flaw in the strategy is the failure to consider older people as policy co-creators, which goes against current trends in policies aimed at this group. In terms of policy implementation structure, the authors consider local governments and nonprofit groups to be only policy contractors, while state governments are policy creators. This policy appears to be a relatively broad framework, with a lack of recognition of intersectional challenges, the need for additional financing, and support for local policy implementation. The objectives of this policy framework are being addressed by programs such as Active+, Senior+, and Care 75+ (formerly known as the Social Activity of Older People[5]). The schemes provide financial incentives to NGOs for them to carry out policy tasks. However, its implementation and evaluation are based on the intensity of the activities, which is just a quantitative measure. It is also worth noting that the present policy does not explicitly allude to the so-called Senior Policy. The concept present in polish policy discourse since 2013, when introduced by the ministry's. It is characterized as a broad range of policies that affect the lives of older people but are implemented by numerous policy agencies, including healthcare, housing, and transportation. Its creation highlights the importance of intersectionality in aging policy establishment and implementation.

---

4 The orginal title: "Założenia Długofalowej Polityki Senioralenej w Polsce na lata 2014–2020."

5 The original title: „Aktywność Społeczna Osób Starszych."

Locality of aging policies

This chapter presents a taxonomy of aging policies, explaining their varied orientations and goals. Thus, while studying data, policymakers and researchers can select whether they are interested in the long term, that is, future generations, or the current group of older people. This, in turn, determines the appropriate measures and policy tools. When planning and scrutinizing aging policies, it is equally crucial to consider their spatial dimension. According to researchers (Błędowski, 2002; Szatur-Jaworska, 2016), the aging process is heterogeneous due to both individual traits (Heaven et al., 2016; Nadobnik et al., 2021) and environmental factors (Błędowski, 2002; Buffel & Phillipson, 2023; Szatur-Jaworska, 2016; Van Hoof et al., 2018). The territorial component is equally important from a policy standpoint. At the national level, policy takes the shape of documents and frameworks, while at the local level, specific actions are used. In recent years, aging academics have highlighted the significance of the last one (Buffel & Phillipson, 2023; van Hoof & Kazak, 2018), which is also a study focus in this book.

The significance of local aging policy has twofold reasoning. First, the character of this policy (Theiss, 2017), and second, the decentralization of social policy in general (Evans et al., 2018; Kutsar & Kuronen, 2015b). The first reason, a specific character of this policy according to M. Theiss (2012), has three main groups of causes. First, it is concerned with varied local circumstances, such as social infrastructure, institutional environment, or space adjustments (Błędowski, 2016b; Błędowski & Kubicki, 2014). Second, the differences in the experience of aging by older people, who can have various needs and problems. Third, local aging policy is believed to possess the widest knowledge of local issues and available resources; thus, policymakers can establish the most suitable measures (Theiss, 2012). However, this third assertion about local policy is claimed to be too idealistic by some researchers. Local policymakers actually establish measures that are influenced by external experts and higher administration officials, which means these measures poorly reflect the unique characteristics of local problems and potential solutions (Krzyszkowski & Przywojska, 2010). Moreover, at the more theoretical level of policy analysis, scholars assert that local policy is shaped without consideration of the specificity of the local environment and is rather accidental (Theiss, 2012). Furthermore, the problem with the efficiency and accuracy of local policy can also be concerned with the decentralization of tasks to local levels of government without sufficient financial support (Theiss, 2012, 2017).

This local character of aging policy can also be connected with a more global issue of decentralization in the realization of social policies. This trend, called by E. Swyngedouw (2004) "the rolling of state," started in the 1980s, and is claimed to be connected with globalization and internationalization. These two important phenomena have shifted the scale of powers, ordering the economic and political course of events. It is called "jumping of the scale," since previously effective relations and influences' directions have been accompanied with newer points of reference. They are made up of actors from both the regional, local, and international level, sometimes representing competing interests and promoting compatible actions (Cox, 2009; Swyngedouw, 1997). More recently, decentralization became even more pronounced. First, it is connected with the economic crisis of 2008 and the tendency to reduce social policy expenditures. Therefore, the provision of services was passed on to the regional and local levels, without providing adequate resources from the central budget (Theiss, 2017), but also was based on the promotion of social participation among citizens to improve the satisfaction of needs in their closest environment (Andreotti & Mingione, 2016b; Caldarice, 2018). In the research, there is an increasing attention to local welfare systems[6] and policies implemented by them. However, a rather narrow view of it is emphasized, which is mainly concerned with the activities of official local policy actors and ignores issues of local networks between actors (Swianiewicz, 2016). What is meant here is the range of informal activities and practices on the part of policymakers but also other actors on the local political scene referred to as street-level bureaucracy (Sztandar-Sztanderska, 2016; Theiss, 2017).

In the Polish context, such a missing element in analysis of local aging policy, are NGOs, claimed to be key actors in local policy implementation. NGOs support the public sector with human resources and know-how and in the result provide a wide range of activities for the community as subcontractors

[6] The local welfare system is understood as: *as specific configurations of population needs and welfare providers and resources emerging at the local levels* (Andreotti et al., 2012).

(Błędowski, 2016b; Urbaniak, 2018). Furthermore, the locality of aging policy is specific in cities, due to their diversity of resources, knowledge of the inhabitants, and better accuracy in diagnosing problems. Cities become responsible for taking measures related to aging society (Buffel et al., 2020; Klimczuk & Tomczyk, 2016; Phillipson & Scharf, 2005). Scholars underline the need for research into local social policy regimes, which are developed in the cities (Andreotti & Mingione, 2016a).

The presented in this book research addresses the issue of localism in the field of aging policy and shows it's the relevance. As the literature shows, it is an area little explored in Polish research, and one of particular importance in the context of policy decentralization (Andreotti & Mingione, 2016a; Błędowski, 2016b; Swianiewicz, 2016; Theiss, 2012) and promoted participation of local government and citizens (Andreotti & Mingione, 2016a; Kutsar & Kuronen, 2015a). In the following chapter, I introduce the specificity of this level of analysis, that is, the city, through a brief characterization of urban studies and a review of research focusing precisely on the idea of social activeness of older people implemented in the city.

1.2. Urban ageing

Cities as entities of social and economic significance are becoming increasingly important in the national and international arena. They are home to about 60 % of the population, produce almost 50 % of waste worldwide and use 75 % of natural resources (Caldarice, 2018). It is much easier for us to feel and notice certain changes at this level of the city and it has become a tangible mechanism for us, setting in motion healthcare institutions, kindergartens, as well as supporting specific industries, organizing cultural events, and subsidizing our bus tickets. As city researchers and sociologists write, contemporary metropolises have evolved and become a place to solve global problems. According to Z. Bauman and M. Kostera (Bauman et al., 2017), we are now in the era of interregnum. A period in which new global problems do not yet have concrete solutions in the global dimension. M. Kostera (2017) writes that these are times when dealing with these problems is beyond the reach of international or national institutions. It is the city that takes over the responsibility for coping and creating solutions

(Bauman et al., 2017; Błędowski & Szweda-Lewandowska, 2016; Gawron, 2017). According to L. Mumford, the city is a "geographical interweaving, economic organization, and institutional process" (Mumford, 2016, p. 139). Within this book, the city is important as a local level of aging policy formation. The decentralization of aging policy, mentioned in the previous subsection, results in realization of the tasks by local levels of administration. According to the researchers (Błędowski, 2016b; Buffel & Phillipson, 2018; Rémillard-Boilard et al., 2020; Theiss, 2012, 2017), there is the need to examine the ways in which such local policies are implemented and in consequence form local aging. In this section, I examine aging on the city level. In the beginning I describe how the city became noticed by urban studies scholars. I will present the initial perspectives of urban studies scholars toward the city as well as more recent perspectives, that focus on relations between cities and their inhabitants (Domaradzka, 2018; Harding & Blockland, 2014; Rémillard-Boilard et al., 2020; Yung et al., 2016). Subsequently, I present aging at the city level, introducing research on the social activity of older citizens carried out on the city level. This literature review illustrates what social activity for older people can mean for scientists and its role in urban aging policies. In addition, the presented research indicates which areas of city functioning may be problematic for older people, that is, infrastructure, lack of social networks, and difficult access to city institutions or health centers.

Urban studies

Urban studies can be described as a multidisciplinary field, constituted by anthropologists, architectures, economists, environmentalists, geographers, planners, or sociologists (Jayne & Ward, 2017). The emergence of urban studies was evoked in the nineteenth century by industrializations and thus an immense migration of people into the city. From then until now urban researchers have tried to understand the phenomenon of the city as an administrative and geographical entity, a symbol of culture (*flaneur*), structural masterpieces, or a medium of capitalistic ideologies. The complexity of the urban life, as Simon Parker (2015) writes, can be described within four categories: culture, consumption, conflict, and community, later extended with a fifth category—commodification. These categories designate perspectives of various thinkers applied to the city for the past 150 years, which will be briefly described later.

To understand the multidimensionality of city, Max Weber in his essay *Die Stadt* goes back to ancient times through feudalism up to capitalism (Parker, 2015). M. Weber considers the city as *a market settlement* (M. Weber, 1958). In his analysis, he traced features of cities across different geographical placements. What seems to be important for the city is the economic power, meaning merchants, as well as political strength, expressed with city autonomy and defense capabilities. Furthermore, urban development was based on the feudalistic relation, which gave structures to simple settlement centers, introducing the power struggle and economic dependency between citizens (1958). In opposition to Max Webber's historical approach was George Simmel's (1950) research on the urban mentality, which was referring to the city as a more contemporary construct. The researcher was fascinated by the modern city, which caused the emergence of a new society, along with new social and economic relations. G. Simmel perceived the city as a chance for individual emancipation, where hitherto socially distant persons could *meet* in one endeavor, business, connected by money (Simmel, 1950).

The era of modernity involved great changes in cities, which made them an exciting metropolis. For Walter Benjamin, a modern city was the imagery of what ancient societies had dreamed about the city (Benjamin, 1999). He was fascinated by the streets and the window shops, which blurred the private and public spaces of the city, transforming it into *a masquerade of space* (Parker, 2015). Another thinker of the modern city was Henri Lefebvre, an author of essays about city space, its commodification and labor division (Parker, 2015). According to H. Lefebvre, a capitalist revolution, introduced the production mode into the city, changing its space into *heritage of industry* and its community to *consumer society*. He saw the city as fragmented, encompassing a few realities, which assemble interchangeably (Lefebvre, 2004).

Each of the authors mentioned earlier opened a thread of discussion in more contemporary urban studies, highlighting the political rules governing and constituting the city, noticing its class diversifications and commodification. They were observers of the emergence of the city, within its complexity.

They attempted to find out the essence of what the city is in the social, historical, and political meaning.

Over time, two disciplines, namely sociology and geography, took a leading place in urban studies and the creation of urban theories (Jayne & Ward, 2017; Parker, 2015). Within the first one, the Chicago School had its beginnings, started by R. E. Park and E. Burgess in 1892. Their interest was focused on the influence of the market economy on the structure of the city, both in societal and spatial dimensions. They developed diagrammatic illustrations of the city, which later on, however, were perceived as an oversimplification. Another view on the city was held by Frankfurt School, rooted in thoughts of Karl Marx. They perceived what is happening in the city—fashion, music, or literature—a culture industry, which replaced a folk culture with more standardized products consumed by the urban working class. Walter Benjamin went further and came with a concept of *commodity fetishism* which aimed to distract the working class from socially unjust working conditions. The next thread, also related to the legacy of urban managerialists, developed in the 1970s. They were rooted in the work of Karl Marx and Max Weber. In their perspective, the city was governed by some agents who control assets and act for their gain. However, their approach was considered to not contribute anything significant to the development of the modern city (Jayne & Ward, 2017, p. 8).

The development of urban geography took place simultaneously with the advance in urban sociology; however, they adopted a diverse perspective on urban theory. In their beginnings, they perceived the city as an object that could be measured and modeled (Jayne & Ward, 2017). Such studies were seen as an *objective* representation of the city used in planning and policy formation. The positivistic turn in urban geography has introduced the unpredictability of citizen behavior. It in turn induced scientists to extend the modeling and improve the planning process (Harding & Blockland, 2014). However, a more significant change has taken place in the 1970s, when geographers have turned to a critical approach, which linked urbanity with art, sociology, and humanities. In those times, geographers perceived city also in line with Marx and Weber heritage. This means that city was a spatial product of the capitalistic economy, as a result of which some actors possessed particular urban assets, whereas others, none (2014).

At this moment, the two perspectives on urbanity, namely sociology and geography, come together. Urban scientists speak of urban injustice, segregation, gentrification, and many more, which were considered from more sociological or geographical angles. Such scientists as David Harvey, Manuel Castells, or Peter Saunders represented separate in urban theory geography and sociology (Jayne & Ward, 2017). Their focus was to observe the influence of capitalism on the city, perceived as a spatial entity, but primarily as a social structure, having in mind its class structure (Castells, 1977; Harvey, 1989; Saunders, 1986). The urban theories of the 1970s and 1980s were also powered by the crises and common unemployment, as well as the decline of the city. The crises were succeeded by the era of globalization and the pursuit of governments to support markets regardless of the social injustices. Such a revival of the city resulted in the gentrification of the entrepreneurial part of the city and an even stronger division between poor and rich urban areas. Whereas some urban theorists perceived those times as a time of further capitalistic development, others believed in the power of modernity, with its rationality and planning helping citizens (Harding & Blockland, 2014; Jayne & Ward, 2017).

The 1990s brought the concept of "postmodernity" which was identified with the culture of consumption and "aestheticization," described by Jean Baudrillard as *Disneyfication*, which meant the transformation of cities into a kind of hyperreal places, such as Las Vegas (Jayne & Ward, 2017). Such voices started a discussion on postmodernity lasting until the beginning of the next century. Scientists were discussing whether we experience an era of postmodernity or just another stage of modern capitalism.

In more contemporary urban studies, cities are presented as a *scene* of grassroots initiatives and communities of different origins (Domaradzka, 2018). The power of globalization makes the city a very powerful entity, but also very diversified (Jayne & Ward, 2017). The cities are seen more as a place of huge income inequalities. Its space is a matter of dispute between citizens, city authorities, entrepreneurs, and other social groups. This is a fertile ground for *the right to the city* movements fighting for a sustainable environment and social justice (Domaradzka, 2014, 2018). Within such a city, aging individuals also try to participate and demand their needs to be respected.

CITY'S PERCEPTION

Max Weber	"market settlement"
George Simmel	"new society, a chance for emancipation"
Walter Benjamin	"place where public and private space intertwined
Henri Lefebvre	city as "heritage of industry" and citizens as "consumer society"

Urban studies within sociology	Urban studies within geography
Chicago School → focus on market economy influence on the city structure	City as an object which can be modelled and measured
Frankfurter School → city as a "culture industry", place of working-class exploitation	Positivistic turn → subsuming unpredictability of human behaviours in modelling
Urban managerialisms → city managed by agents, who control assets and act in their interests	Critical approach → geographer build on the legacy of sociology, art, anthropology

Urban studies formed by combined disciplines of sociology and geography

1970–1980
- a city as a spatial entity, social structure, under a strong influence of modernization
- cities as a place of inequalities as the result of globalisation and gentrification
- development of city planning

1990
- cities as a culture of consumption
- escetization

2000
- emergence of grassroots activities
- city as a place where the interests of different actors and social groups intermingle
- city as a network of relation

Figure 2: The changing perception of city in urban studies.
Source: Own elaboration.

This introduction of urban studies, synthesized in Figure 2, demonstrates the emergence of the city, which within current research becomes a very complex phenomenon, formed by relational networks of human and nonhuman networks looming from city, perceived rather as object than network ("Urban Assemblages. How Actor-Network Theory Changes Urban Studies," 2010). Considering city complexity, it is framed as an *urban assemblage*, which reflects the multiplicity of realities that intermingle there. Researchers focus on the process in which different actors enter the urban scene and interrelate with each other (Betancur & Arciniegas, 2018). By and large, it can be seen that aiming at exploring social activity among older people at the city level, there is a need to consider the city as an assemblage of urban networks, which driven by their own values and norm form what scholars regard as a city ("Urban Assemblages. How Actor-Network Theory Changes Urban Studies," 2010). This approach to the city, in turn, is related to applied in my research ANT, which serves as analytical tool and allows to explore emergence of city as an assemblage of network between human and nonhuman actors (Latour, 2005a) (see Section 2.1—Actor-network theory).

Ageing in cities—Social activity of older people in city

The concept of social activity for older persons has evolved as a crucial component of successful and active aging theories, alongside activity theory and continuity theory. Over time, these ideas have established the broad goals for aging policies adopted by international and national bodies. However, researchers linked with the critical strands of gerontology have critiqued this approach to aging (Achenbaum, 2010; O'Rand et al., 2010). Within this thread, academics accused successful and active aging concepts of commodifying older people, which is viewing them as socially and commercially valuable things (O'Rand et al., 2010). According to Stephen Katz's (2000b) research, introducing a drive for higher activity among older people is not always the solution to their difficulties, because older individuals are more concerned with making sense of these activities. Despite some academics' critical attitudes toward the concept of social activity among older persons, it remains a part of plans and programs. The transfer of responsibilities to local governance levels (Błędowski, 2016b; Evans et al., 2018; Kutsar & Kuronen, 2015b; Van Hoof et al., 2018) has led to the development of local aging strategies predominantly in urban areas. These strategies are shaped by both bottom-up and top-down relationships, highlighting the interdependence of authorities across different levels (Kutsar & Kuronen, 2015b). Thus, the question arises: how do urban policymakers understand the concept of social activity? Many research and systematic literature reviews have focused on social activity for older people (de Oliveira et al., 2019; Douglas et al., 2017; Wanchai & Phrompayak, 2019). However, their primary focus is on the relationship between social participation and health (2019), highlighting the former's favorable impact on human well-being. Scholars elaborate on the many sorts of social activity (Wanchai & Phrompayak, 2019), rather than its understanding by policymakers. As a result, it appears vital to investigate how the concept of social activity among older people, as a tool of public policy, is interpreted in micro- and meso-level research (DeLeon & DeLeon, 2002; Linder & Peters, 1989). The purpose of this subsection, then, is to present a literature review with the goal of determining what the concept of social activity entails for academics and urban aging policymakers. The literature review for this book puts the concept of social engagement within its local context and examines its interpretations.

Aging vs. population aging—*twofold influence of social activity*

The dominant aspect presents in the analyzed articles was the prevalent information on aging societies, which served as an introduction and a starting point for further consideration. The presented data warned about the increasing number of people in the postproduction age to those still economically active (Afacan, 2013; Asadollahi et al., 2013; A. C. M. Chan & Cao, 2015; Chen & Chen, 2012; Dawidowicz et al., 2020; Fu et al., 2018; Tong et al., 2019). As a result, the rising cost of care for older people and the problem of maintaining them by those who work have been predicted. One of the answers to the presented challenges, namely aging societies, was precisely the social activity of older people, which according to researchers has the potential to improve the living conditions of the individual and at the same time relieve the burden on society. This is noticeable in the ways in which social activity has been studied, either as a factor, or a desired effect, which both can be influenced by social or individual conditions, which is presented in the following table.

Table 2: Analysis of societal and individual levels, along with the factors that promote and restrict the social engagement of older adults in urban environments

	Society	Individual
What does social activity give older people?	- Financial independency (Suzuki et al., 2021) - A low-cost support for older people (Novak & Vute, 2013; Suzuki et al., 2021) - Productive society (Carr et al., 2015) - Decrease in the morbidity of older people (Carr et al., 2015; Granbom et al., 2017) - Addressing social marginalization (Carr et al., 2015; Ho, 2017; Rezaeipandari et al., 2020) - Unpaid work—volunteerism (Pei et al., 2014)	- A prevention of dementia (Yung et al., 2016) - Influence on self-satisfaction and stress reduction (Ahmad & Hafeez, 2011; Fu et al., 2018; Ho, 2017) - Provides mental stability, satisfaction with life (Ho, 2017) - Gives sense of utility and development (Ho, 2017; Rezaeipandari et al., 2020) - Facilitates coping with problems (Pei et al., 2014) - Maintenance of good health and physical performance (Bilotta et al., 2012; Fu et al., 2018; Granbom et al., 2017; Pei et al., 2014; Tong et al., 2019)
What fosters social activity of older people?	- Community support (Beard & Montawi, 2015) - Availability of social and health services (Tong et al., 2019)	- Confidence, sense of community (Asadollahi et al., 2013; Pei et al., 2014; Yung et al., 2016) - Good self-esteem (Yung et al., 2016) - Religiousness (Pei et al., 2014) - Public spaces, e.g., libraries, places to spend time, rest (Yung et al., 2016)

(Continued)

Table 2: *(Continued)*

	Society	Individual
What limits the social activity of older people?	– Globalization, consumerism, emergence of metropolises (Barrett & McGoldrick, 2013) – Patriarchy, marginalization of women in conservative societies (Ahmad & Hafeez, 2011) – The role of men as breadwinners (Rezaeipandari et al., 2020) – Stereotype of older people, age discrimination (Pasquallie, 2018; Rezaeipandari et al., 2020) – Inadequate, unsafe environment, lack of adapted transport (Afacan, 2013; Ahmad & Hafeez, 2011; Barrett & McGoldrick, 2013; Beard & Montawi, 2015; Rezaeipandari et al., 2020; Xiong et al., 2020)	– Poor health, disability (Ahmad & Hafeez, 2011; Barrett & McGoldrick, 2013; Rezaeipandari et al., 2020; Tong et al., 2019) – A lack of self-confidence (Rezaeipandari et al., 2020) – Family obligation (Rezaeipandari et al., 2020) – Poverty, lower social status (Ahmad & Hafeez, 2011; Barrett & McGoldrick, 2013) – Bad life experiences and health habits (Ahmad & Hafeez, 2011)

Source: Own elaboration.

In terms of society, activity provides a means of solving older people's problems without much financial investment. This, in turn, is desirable due to the lower expenditure on social services (Novak & Vute, 2013a; Suzuki et al., 2021). For older adults, then, being active helps maintain mental (Ho, 2017a; Pei et al., 2014) and physical well-being (Bilotta et al., 2012; Fu et al., 2018; Granbom et al., 2017; Pei et al., 2014; Tong et al., 2019), as well as gives a chance to thrive and live with a sense of purpose (Ho, 2017a; Rezaeipandari et al., 2020). Turning to what stops an individual from being socially active, researchers point to limitations related to health and mobility (Ahmad & Hafeez, 2011; Barrett & McGoldrick, 2013; Rezaeipandari et al., 2020; Tong et al., 2019), as well as poverty (Ahmad & Hafeez, 2011; Barrett & McGoldrick, 2013). These characteristics, in addition to poverty, are somehow inherent in old age and therefore inevitable. Moreover, this part of the table reveals the marginalization of older people who are unable to be active (Afacan, 2013; Carr et al., 2015). Furthermore, from a perspective of society, activity of older people must fight against stereotypes toward older people in general (Pasquallie, 2018; Rezaeipandari et al., 2020) as well as separately in relation to women (Ahmad & Hafeez, 2011) and men (Rezaeipandari et al., 2020). Public spaces that do not provide safety (high curbs, unsuitable urban transport) and opportunities to relax in their space can also be unhelpful and hinder older citizens from social participation (Afacan, 2013; Barrett & McGoldrick, 2013; Beard & Montawi, 2015; Rezaeipandari et al., 2020; Xiong et al., 2020). Although the research does not indicate what the community can do, in terms of specific actions, it does emphasize that its support is important (Beard & Montawi, 2015), for example, the local religious community, which can serve as a support network for the older person (Chen & Chen, 2012; Pei et al., 2014).

Research indicates that social activity serves as a means to mitigate social isolation among older adults, improve health outcomes, and foster opportunities for self-development. Simultaneously, it alleviates the financial burden on state and local authorities by decreasing future treatment and care costs for older people. This raises the question of the type of community in which older individuals ought to be involved actively. The analyzed articles reveal the absence of community, focusing solely on the public space itself.

Dimensions of older people's social activity

The social participation of older people can be categorized within seven types, coming from literature (see Table 3). From the very basic activity of moving around in public spaces (Xiong et al., 2020) to diverse social, political, and cultural activities (Granbom et al., 2017; Novak & Vute, 2013a). Moreover, some researchers considered social activity of older people as an individual's right to exist in society, which is denied to them due to age (Chiribuca & Teodorescu, 2020), income or mobility limitations (Afacan, 2013; Barrett & McGoldrick, 2013). While for others social activity is a responsibility of older people, their way of contributing to the community in which they live (Barrett & McGoldrick, 2013; A. C. M. Chan & Cao, 2015; Ho, 2017a).

Table 3: Contexts of social activity for older people implemented on the city level

Context	Articles	Social activity definition	Related concepts	Notes
Public space	(Xiong et al., 2020)	Understood as moving through the streets of a city (the street as a space for social activity).	- Spatial planning - Mobility - Social inclusion	
	(Yung et al., 2016)	It determines active aging and is one of the social needs of older people. Also understood as being in the urban space.	- Active aging - Spatial planning - Urban planning	Space is seen as a catalyst for active aging, as a key element of social activity for older people in the city.
	(Dawidowicz et al., 2020)	Following the World Health Organization, they see social activity as part of active aging and therefore living as long a healthy life as possible.	- Age-friendly city - Active aging	
	(Beard & Montawi, 2015)	Living in the local community and actively participating in its activities.	- Age-friendly city	
Social exclusion, inequality	(Afacan, 2013)	Being able to enjoy urban spaces despite age-related limitations.	- Social exclusion - Urban planning - Active aging	The problem of poverty in the context of social activity. They draw attention to inequalities in access to social activity, due to a worse financial situation, origin, or education.

(Barrett & McGoldrick, 2013)	Part of active and healthy aging. Understood as active participation in social, cultural, economic, spiritual, and urban life, also as activity in the family.	- Active and healthy aging - Racism, inequality - Public space	The problem of poverty in the context of social activity. They draw attention to inequalities in access to social activity, due to a worse financial situation, origin, or education.
(Carr et al., 2015)	Acting for the community in the form of volunteering.	- Economic inequalities	They draw attention to inequalities in access to volunteering among older people, due to education or low income, which limit the possibility of receiving the benefits of such activity.
(Chiribuca & Teodorescu, 2020)	Participating in social media, using its possibilities for your own needs.	- Social media - Empowerment	
(Ahmad & Hafeez, 2011)	Opportunities to participate in political, local community, and religious life.	- Inequalities - Well-being	They draw attention to the problem with the social activity of women and people of lower socioeconomic status.

(Continued)

Table 3: (*Continued*)

Context	Articles	Social activity definition	Related concepts	Notes
Loneliness	(Suzuki et al., 2021)	Understood as existing in social consciousness, having a social network.	– Loneliness	Creating a local support network (co-production) outside the institutions of the state.
	(Coll-Planas et al., 2017)	Seen as a structural element of human social capital, necessary for human well-being. More specifically described as interaction with others.	– Social capital	
	(Granbom et al., 2017)	Engaging in activities that individuals perceive as valuable.		
	(Rezaeipandari et al., 2020)	Definition adopted from the Canadian Association for Community Health, where social activity involves taking part in communal religious events, team sports, educational and cultural activities, and social or charitable events.	– Successful aging – Loneliness	
Productivity	(Carr et al., 2015)	Acting for the community in the form of volunteering.	– Volunteering – Productivity	Volunteering as a socially beneficial, rewarding activity of older people for society as a whole.

	(Tong et al., 2019)	They divide it into formal and informal social activities. The latter refers to individual interactions with friends and family, while formal means participation in events organized by others.		The activities of older people in formal social activities are beneficial to society, such as volunteering. In turn, for older people, doing activities for others has health benefits.
	(Suzuki et al., 2021)	As existing in social consciousness, having a social network.	- Co-production	Aging generates costs that can be minimized by creating local communities that provide opportunities for social activity and a sense of security.
	(Novak & Vute, 2013)	Leisure and relaxation activities (climbing, walking, etc.) to keep older people in shape and able to participate in social, cultural, and economic life.	- Well-being - Self	The good physical condition of older people encourages them to remain active in the labor market for longer or to carry out voluntary activities, which benefit society as well as older people. In addition, they reduce the costs of caring for dependent older people.
	(A. C. M. Chan & Cao, 2015)	Involvement in the local community and participation in community events.	- Productive aging - Active aging	

(Continued)

Table 3: (*Continued*)

Context	Articles	Social activity definition	Related concepts	Notes
Independence and self	(Ho, 2017)	Perceived as an activity that allows rebuilding, re-forming the self after retirement.	– Active aging – Volunteering – self	
	(Pe et al., 2014)	Religious activities, leisure activities, political activities related to education.	– Quality of Life	
	(Fu et al., 2018)	Understood as interaction with other people that has a positive impact on the well-being and health of older people.	– Activity theory – Well-being	
	(Novak & Vute, 2013)	Recreational and relaxation activities (climbing, walking, etc.) to keep older people in shape and able to participate in social, cultural, and economic life.	– Independence	Fitness gives a sense of empowerment and independence.
Quality of life, health	(Coll-Planas et al., 2017)	Understood as a structural element of human social capital, necessary for human well-being. More specifically described as interaction with others.	– Quality of life – Social capital	Social capital plays an important role in older people's quality of life, which is, however, threatened by aging

	(Granbom et al., 2017)	Activities within some formal group—educational classes, or visits to places such as the cinema or theater, or within informal groups such as family or friends.		
	(Bilotta et al., 2012)	Seen as part of Quality of Life (QOL), meaning being among people.	- Quality of life	Social activity in the context of people undergoing outpatient treatment
Sense of community	(Pasquallie, 2018), (Tong et al., 2019) (A. C. M. Chan & Cao, 2015)	The kind of activities that give a sense of community and togetherness.	- Community - Practices	An alternative image of older people bonding the local community through their activity.

Source: Own elaboration.

Within the first type related to public space, researchers have addressed the interaction between urban space and older people (Beard & Montawi, 2015; Dawidowicz et al., 2020; Xiong et al., 2020; Yung et al., 2016). They emphasized the large role of social activity in maintaining the health of older people. According to researchers, the streets of the city or the appearance of the neighborhood are catalysts for the activity of the oldest citizens. Well-designed recreational zones, pedestrian crossings, bus stops (Afacan, 2013; Xiong et al., 2020), but also places of entertainment, cinemas, theaters, give a chance for people with reduced mobility or not used to crowds to stay there (Dawidowicz et al., 2020).

Inequalities is another type of research on older people's social activity. Because social activity's impact is so beneficial to an individual, researchers highlight that it is not equally available to all older people (Afacan, 2013; Ahmad & Hafeez, 2011; Barrett & McGoldrick, 2013; Beard & Montawi, 2015; Carr et al., 2015; Chiribuca & Teodorescu, 2020). Reasons include poorer socioeconomic status, financial problems (Barrett & McGoldrick, 2013; Carr et al., 2015; Tong et al., 2019), and consequently poorer health (Ahmad & Hafeez, 2011). In the articles, researchers imply the positive impact of, for example, volunteering as a form of social activity, but at the same time emphasize its elitism. Researchers present social activity as an individual's right to function in society.

The social activity of older people is also a means of counteracting their solitude by within their local community. The role of activity is to create some sort of support network that provides older people with a community, which will over watch their daily functioning (Suzuki et al., 2021). For example, as in Japan, where the co-production of local businesses and organizations was established to monitor the lives of lonely older residents. There is no denying that creating such a support network shifts the burden and cost of care from the state to the local community (Chiribuca & Teodorescu, 2020).

Researchers also perceive the activity of older people as an extension of their preretirement activities. This ensures their physical and mental health as well as benefits society, for example, through volunteering or helping with grandchildren or older ailing parents. This kind of study resonates with the problem of aging and the associated costs—healthcare expenditure, financial assistance, and long-term care (Carr et al., 2015; A. C. M. Chan & Cao, 2015). The challenge is to keep societies productive despite their aging (Carr et al., 2015).

There is also a body of research that portrays social activity as a route to independence and reconstruction of one's own identity after retirement (see Independence and self) (Gao et al., 2020; Ho, 2017b; Novak & Vute, 2013b; Pe et al., 2014). According to this research, the retirement process itself challenges the perception of self and the identity one has (Nadobnik et al., 2021). From the analyzed articles, it appears that participation in social life provides the opportunity to find oneself in retirement, to regain agency and self-esteem through appreciation from other community or family members. Here, the emphasis is on interactions with other people that allow one to feel at ease and provide opportunities to enjoy cultural life, physical activity, or further education (Fu et al., 2018).

An individual perspective on aging was also applied in studies that focused on the impact of social participation on the health and QOL of older people. According to the researchers, it is difficult for an individual to have a good standard of living in the absence of social activities and social relationships (Bilotta et al., 2012). In a way, complementary to these studies are those that point to the role of participation in the formation of a sense of community, not only for older people, but also for other social groups (Pasquallie, 2018). Older people, by sharing their knowledge and experience, become leaders of such communities (2018), with their time (Chen & Chen, 2012) and regular financial resources (Pasquallie, 2018).

There is no doubt about social participation having a positive impact on older people. Furthermore, presented here literature review reveals its multidisciplinary nature and ability to influence on different levels (social and individual). For some actors it can appear as a lucrative factor and for others desired effect. Therefore, there is a need to explore the idea, to take a closer look at networks that enable its enactments at the urban level. This review is a starting point for research presented in this book, which aims to unravel the idea of social activity among older people from a policymaking perspective. The results will introduce this idea from the opposite perspective of urban policy and add to the literature the understanding of its role on the local level of aging policy.

The subsequent sections 1.1—Social activity of older people within aging policies and 1.2—Urban aging—aim to elucidate local aging policy and the concept of social involvement among older adults. The aging policy can be viewed through the lens of the aging process, an older population, or old age as a stage of life. These three viewpoints overlap within the framework of the tasks performed (Szatur-Jaworska, 2016). Nevertheless, the key matter pertains to the localization of aging strategies. It arises from the decentralization of public policies and the belief that solutions to contemporary issues of aging may be most effectively articulated at the local level (Błędowski, 2016b; Błędowski, 2002; Rémillard-Boilard et al., 2020; Theiss, 2012; Urbaniak, 2018). Researchers specifically underscore the significance of urban areas in policy formulation. Their expanding authority and reach, position them as a hub for the development of local social policy regimes (Theiss, 2017). Thus, local public policy and urban studies scientists point to the necessity to take into consideration the complexity of actor relationships and collecting concepts that impact policy formation and subsequently concrete implementation. Furthermore, the literature review presented earlier, a dearth of in-depth research into what constitutes social engagement at the municipal level and how it is implemented by urban policies.

1.3. The idea and the process of policy implementation

The discussions in the preceding sections highlight the necessity of comprehending the enactment of local aging policy and the framing of its specific assumptions, such as the social activity of older individuals, within local policies and actors.

In social policy research, academics categorize numerous study typologies according to distinct studied characteristics (O'Connor & Netting, 2011b; Szarfenberg, 2013; Zybała, 2013). For example, scholars of comparative public policy delineate four distinct schools of public policy research: the Cultural School, the Economic School, the Political School, and the Institutional School (Adolino & Blake, 2010, pp. 31–45). The initial school emphasizes the impact of tradition and history on the development of public policies and the potential augmentation of the state's involvement in their implementation (Zybała, 2013). Within the Economic School, policy analysis considers the resources available in a country as factors that impact certain policies and the aspirations of individuals. Consequently, the Political School emphasizes research, strategy, and political parties, with the interests of certain groups, such as employees against employers, frequently influencing state actions. The final category of research, known as the Institutional School, primarily examines state institutions and the regulations they establish that affect the policymaking process. Nonetheless, the rise of new institutionalism has led to the inclusion of informal institutions, such as espoused values, in analytical frameworks. Furthermore, entities beyond governmental institutions are incorporated into the investigation. This school studies how different levels of public administration and other decision-making players impact policies. The Institutional School of Public Policy Research is most pertinent to the issue I am presenting, as it broadly encompasses factors influencing policy formation and considers the interactions among actors from various levels and domains in this process. This is significant as it addresses the municipal level and takes into account many groups of stakeholders, not solely those representing public institutions.

However, the study presented in this book is limited to local-level policy, providing an extra analytical perspective to broader social policy research. For example, M. Theiss (2017) offered a taxonomy of local social policy research. She mentions research that focuses on economic issues, such as how a municipality's budget affects local policies. Another category of research focuses on structural factors. Academics regard characteristics such as the municipality type (rural or urban), its spatial configuration, geographic location, and demographic composition as essential to local policy development. M. Theiss also specifies governance research, in which academics highlight competent resource management and task distribution among local players. This strategy is based on actor networking and flexibility in managing available resources. The subsequent group of studies focuses on political characteristics. The approach regards the political affiliation of local administrations as essential in policy formulation. Academics regard the social capital of the local community as significant. It may arise from the significant involvement of local elites in policy formulation or a wide array of grassroots efforts. Lastly, the final category pertains to study centered on cultural attributes. Academics assert that local customs, esteemed ideals, perceptions of policy, and the tenure of the present President can influence local policy. These strands of study within local social policy may develop concurrently (Swianiewicz, 2016).

To capture the understanding of social activity from the perspective of local policymakers (Szarfenberg, 2013), I intend to conduct my research in the Institutional School (Adolino & Blake, 2010), but with an emphasis on an integrated approach (Theiss, 2017) to the study of local social policies. Thus, in the following sections, I will provide a detailed study of the institutional approach to policy analysis, with a focus on DI and ideational analysis. Both concepts represent an extension of prior institutional forms (Schmidt, 2008), introducing ideas and discourses into the formation process, as well as dynamicity in relations that shape policy realities (Hall & Taylor, 1996).

Institutional origins of idea analysis in social policy

The emergence of an institutional approach was linked with observed shortcomings of orthodox economics, which omitted the social aspect in analysis of economic relations (G. Hodgson, 2018; Lambooy & Moulaert, 1996). The assumptions of institutional economics differ from mainstream economics, meaning neoclassical, in the perception of individuals. The latter asserts that individuals in their decision-making are governed by rational and well-calculated decisions, which help them choose the most lucrative option. Whereas institutional thinkers, such as T. Veblen or later D. North underlined, that individuals are limited in their decisions and their agency is influenced by institutions, such as norms, customs, or policies (G. Hodgson, 2018). This is also applicable to policy formulations by various actors, which can be influenced by institutions, which in turn consist of normative systems, or sheer institutions can actively design policy (G. Hodgson, 2018; North, 1990). They are vehicles that can form policy from their mutual interaction (Pieliński, 2013). Furthermore, they stand behind individual behaviors and beliefs, but mutually they are also formed by them (G. Hodgson, 2004). With their norms, institutions form rationalities, which with mutual relations influence the decision process of actors (Lambooy & Moulaert, 1996).

To cite the classic of institutional economics, the institutions are agents of human interactions:

> Institutions are the rules of the game in a society or, more formally, are the humanly devised constraints that shape human interaction. In consequence, they structure incentives in human exchange, whether political, social, or economic. (North, 1990, p. 3)

Over the twentieth century, paths of institutional economists have crossed with events such as The Great Crisis in the late 30s or the emergence of newer theoretical constructs in economics such as behavioral science. These incidents caused the emergence of new institutionalism, which still deriving from classic institutionalism, formed a wide range of approaches, within economics, political science, or sociology, explaining human behaviors and interactions (Pieliński, 2013). I will introduce the threads of new institutional economics' application in research concerning political science.

There are few ways to classify the threads emerging within new institutionalism. First, some researchers within the new institutionalism perceive institutions as constraints of individual actions, others analyze them as vehicles which help form social reality (Scott, 2014, pp. 31–34). Second, there is a dissonance between scientists on what kind of carrier *transport* institutions. Whereas it is culture, with a set of meanings and norms regulating how reality is interpreted, or routines and customs. Finally, threads within new institutionalism differ accordingly to the level of analysis they carry out, from global systems, throughout organizations to smaller entities (2014). However, the mainstream divisions of new institutionalism resist in three prominent types, such as *rational theory*, *sociological institutionalism*, and *historical institutionalism* (Guy, 2019; Hall & Taylor, 1996; Pieliński, 2013; Schmidt, 2008).

Within the rational theory scholars focus on individuals' perspectives, and their actions, as they claim that what we observe within economic and political life are just aggregates of human practices. Furthermore, individuals are treated as rational beings, who strive to elevate their utility as much as possible within available resources. Regarding the institution, individuals are perceived as regulations that coordinate individuals' interactions (Pieliński, 2013).

In turn, the sociological institutionalism, also called by researchers as the theory of organization (Hall & Taylor, 1996; Immergut, 1998), argued that contemporary organizations embody some kind of intuitional forms, but they are not adopted to maximize their performance. Researchers within this tread of institutionalism claimed that those are more cultural practices, established within society the organization is functioning in (Hall & Taylor, 1996). Institutions are then understood as symbols, moral values, or cognitive texts, which influence individuals' behaviors. In research scholars focus on reasons why organizations choose some institutional setting and how different customs, beliefs, or cognitive maps can alter organizations across country or within one political system (1996).

Finally, there is the third strand, called historical institutionalism. At the bottom of this thread of new institutionalism underlies the premise that economic and political processes are formed by different groups, which compete over limited resources. The result of this struggle is dictated by the advantage of some groups over the others, stemming from institutional settings, consequential political decisions and difficult-to-predict coincidences (Hall & Taylor, 1996; Pieliński, 2013). In historical institutionalism, institutions are defined rather broadly in comparison to other approaches. They range from political structures, by formal institutions, to less formally designated social groups (Guy, 2019). What is also at the central point of this new institutional economics strand are the interactions between actors and their influence on political and economic systems. The definition of institutions within historical institutionalism is so broad that by some scholars their definition can be extended to ideas which are treated as institutions in the policy analysis (Guy, 2019; Immergut, 1998). They contain an array of solutions to a problem that emerged within a policy domain. This approach is further developed by DI, which takes actually ideas a central institution and the unit of analysis (Schmidt, 2008, 2010).

Before I turn to this particular strand of new institutionalism, which is a part of the conceptual framework in my research, I want to mention that an institutional approach has also been applied in the analysis of urban economics (Lambooy & Moulaert, 1996). The institutional city is portrayed as combinations of sometimes opposing groups of interests and attitudes which results in a variety of categories in urban economy categories, such as innovations, knowledge, relations, or information. Such diversity within the mentioned categories is caused by a diverse institutional context, such as market production, political, sociological, and cultural life (1996). These interact with each other, forming city economics.

Discursive institutionalism and the role of ideas

There are two crucial elements within this approach that serve as vehicles of political science analysis, namely an idea and discourse. These two elements are central for DI, they derive from the role of institutions in policy analysis, and hence the importance of previously described rational institutionalism (RI), sociological institutionalism (SI), and historical institutionalism (HI) (Carstensen & Schmidt, 2016; Schmidt, 2008, 2010). What, however, differs DI from older threads of institutionalism is its dynamic approach toward political processes, and active participation of institutions in their formation.

It is in contrast to a very static view of institutions as guards of rational preferences (RI), path-depending circumstances (HI) or culturally constructed norms (SI) (Schmidt, 2008). In this section, I will explain the role ideas and discourses can play in the policy analysis.

First, I want to elaborate on ideas which have been perceived by political science scholars as signposts, ways of expressing interests, strategies, narrations, or reference point (Blyth, 2002; Goldstein & Keohane, 1993; Polakowski, 2012; Roe, 1994). These varieties of ideas can be clarified with their division to three levels of abstraction, namely, *policy solutions, policy definitions or programs, and public philosophies*. In the first case, an idea presents a solution to previously given objectives. This level is restricted to the moment when a problem has been established, for example, low retirement benefits caused by too brief labor activity. In this phase, possible solutions can come with the most suitable idea (Mehta, 2011). The second level of idea abstraction concerns programs, frames that consist of essential premises for a policy. They provide a perspective, which frames a problem, designating possible choices and solutions to tackle an issue (2011). The problem definition phase is understood as a realization of a particular paradigm, which is a way political reality is understood by some group or institutions; it provides a repertoire of choices, but also determines their nature (Hall, 1993). The process of defining a problem is complex and involves those who make a claim and their opponents (Mehta, 2011). In the example of my study, a major problem I refer to is the aging of societies, causing a shortage in the state's budgets. However, in this case, the problem was defined even earlier, when aging was determined as a cause of state problems.

The third level of ideational analysis in policy research is public philosophy that is even broader than problem definition. Public philosophy determines policies and the programs which stand behind them, providing society and economy with values, for example, older people are a burden for the economy. In opposition to policy solutions and programs, which are topics of public debate, the philosophy is something hidden in the background, sometimes it can even be unknown to the public, but also policymakers (Schmidt, 2008).

Furthermore, there is another way of idea division, for cognitive ideas and normative ideas. The first one is guiding scripts, which indicate what the problem is and what can be done with it. Whereas normative ideas imply judgments on what is supposed to happen. They serve as a legitimization of programs carried out by policies (2008).

What becomes an interest in researchers within ideational analysis of social policy is why some ideas develop into policy solutions, programs, or philosophies, when other ideas disappear. For that, various scholars focus on different levels of idea abstraction in policy, mentioned earlier (Hall, 1993; Kingdon, 2014). Besides the question why some ideas are failures and others succeed or are the good ideas those that last, or maybe actually bad ideas endure, there are also doubts concerning how ideas move, who does it, why and how. These imply the question about their agency, which in turn is linked with the second element of DI, *discourse.*

It is a broader and more functional concept than ideas. Discourse encompasses ideas in different forms and reciprocal processes throughout which ideas are conveyed, so in the way discourse is responsible for idea *promotion* and thus their failure or success (Schmidt, 2008). Discourse itself can be defined as "institutionalized structures of meaning that channel political thought and actions in certain directions" (Connolly, 1983). What is also important to underline is that discourses are multiple and can dominate or diminish with ideas and arguments behind them (Schmidt, 2008). The information which can be found in discourse concerns the process of policy development and communication, namely what is in it, to whom it is directed, where it takes place, and in what manner (Habermas, 1996). We can distinguish two types of discourses within policy: *coordinative* and *communicative.* The first one consists in the coordination of negotiations settled between actors, referring to chosen and applied ideas. Coordinative discourse can be enacted by various coalitions, networks of actors, who share a common interest in functioning and endurance of particular discourse. The second type, a communicative discourse in turn, refers to the process of propagation and legitimization of ideas to people. The role of such a promoter of a specific political program can be played by the government, political parties, activists, NGOs, the media, and other actors (Schmidt, 2008, 2010). However, the direction of discourse can also be from the bottom to the top, which means citizen engagement in discourse, grassroots initiatives, or demonstrations.

In the end, I want to come back to the way the institution is understood in DI, as it is a prominent element of the other three institutionalisms. In contrast to rational, sociological, and historical institutionalism, with DI, actors are neither embodied in structures (institutions), nor impersonated in maximization of one utility (RI), nor cultural custom (SI) nor path-dependent circumstances (HI). Instead, actors are driven by agency, expressed in DI by the understanding of institutions (Schmidt, 2008). First, institutions are both constitutive toward actors, and simultaneously they can be constituted by actors. Hence, institutions can be external factors that drive actors to act, but in the same time institutions are understood as result of actions taken by actors (2008).

The assumptions I have outlined for DI show its two main elements, namely the ideas and discourse with which researchers undertake describing the actions of individuals in economics, politics, and other areas of social life. As already mentioned, ideas play an important role at every level of policy-making: defining the problem, choosing the best solutions, and the values adopted by the policy. It is difficult to identify a single moment of influence of ideas in the process of implementing social active aging in Poznan as these stages are interrelated. The ideas chosen in defining the problem may permeate subsequent stages of policy formation. It is worth noting, however, that in the research presented by me, the effects of the policy are analyzed, and the aim will be to understand what ideas led to this.

Implementation process and Ideational analysis

As indicated earlier researchers within DI, in contrast to other strands of new institutional economics (such as rational theory, sociological institutionalism, or historical institutionalism), assert that ideas provide policymakers with concrete values and agreements on how to frame a problem and what can be done about it. Furthermore, ideas assemble objects and actors. However, they, in turn, can change the idea responding to the environment in which it is implemented (Béland & Cox, 2011). The ideational analysis, rooted in DI, is currently applied in the field of policymaking, comparative policy analysis, the political economy, or social movements (Blyth, 2018; Domaradzka, 2018; Katz, 2000a; Wincott, 2011). However, in the past, it concurred with more-materialistic concepts of institutions and interests, perceived as a better explanation of policy outcomes, related to other threads of new institutionalism. As was presented by Peter Hall (1997), the tension between idea, institution, and interest comes from a diverse perspective toward policy analysis each concept present itself. He described the interest-based approach as strongly determined with economic narration driven by the *producer-group*. Their lobbying powers shape the policy. Alternatively, according to P. Hall (1993), deterministic interests can be also dictated by the *electoral group*, which then establish policies, which will lead to their re-election. Peter Hall (1997) presented the interest-based approach as still scarcely developed in comparison to the two mentioned before. In more recent literature (Béland & Cox, 2011), we can observe a great development in the ideational perspective, incorporating a more cultural perspective into policy formation. Within ideational analysis, researchers can grasp human interactions, missing in the institutional and interest-based approaches, in the process of policy formulation (1997). Furthermore, ideas, incorporated into strategies or good practices, shape policies that dictate appropriate values and actions. However, to have an impact the idea has to be embedded by the important actor, a kind of gatekeeper who has the decision in the process of policymaking (1997).

In the more recent literature, ideas are not placed instead of institutions and interests, but rather in relations to them. It means that researchers attempt to combine them as a complementary element in policy analysis. (Béland & Cox, 2011; Campbell, 2002; Schmidt, 2008). Institutions can be perceived as operators of an idea, who for some reasons decide to implement the idea (Lieberman, 2002; Orloff & Palier, 2009). Interests, in turn, are seen as one of ideas components, among others, such as thoughts, desires, and emotions (Béland & Cox, 2011).

As ideational analysis has taken a significant place in the research agenda on the policy (Berman, 2001), scientists have started to explore how exactly ideas influence policy formulation. In the literature concerning the role of an idea in policy analysis, we owe naming two prominent figures, namely Peter Hall and John W. Kingdon, who both created a theoretical proposition to ideational analysis in the field (Wincott, 2011). The first one subordinates the idea implementation to its viability on the political, administrative, and policy level. The latter, in turn, claims that the idea is embedded when it fits *the political window*, meaning it has its proponents and necessary resources (Mehta, 2011).

By and large, ideas are important in policy analysis; however, they are hard to study within only quantitative methods, as they do not translate easily into testable variables (Guy, 2018). Nevertheless, a constructivist approach comes with the help to see how ideas and policies are established via interactions of actors. A. Wildavsky indicated the need to reject the objective perspective in the policy research in favor of inductive methods. He stated that an idea and then the policy are reflections of political struggles and social processes, and it resembles some conception about reality (2018).

To *work*, the idea has to be implemented that means its goals are being achieved with sequential political actions (Pressman & Wildavsky, 1974).

Ideas form a casual chain of mutually dependent actions involving various actors. The seminal work on the policy implementation was presented by J. L. Pressman and A. Wildavsky in their study on the entitlement programs implemented in Oakland by the federal institution, which ended with failure (DeLeon & DeLeon, 2002; Linder & Peters, 1989; Pressman & Wildavsky, 1974). However, their extended analysis has illustrated the complexity and unpredictability of policy implementation. Although all the money was invested and administrative decisions were obtained, the project, to reduce unemployment and improve the life of the city's minorities, did not meet its goals. It appeared that what seemed simple and beneficial for all got lost in between the untranslated interests of actors, binding regulations, and levels of government (Pressman & Wildavsky, 1974; Wildavsky, 2018).

Starting from the 1970s researchers have begun to trace the bumpy road between policy definition and its implementation (DeLeon & DeLeon, 2002; Goggin et al., 1990). In the decades following, researchers have been disputing the proper orientation of policy implementation. On the one hand, a group of top-down perspective proponents claimed that implementation has to be controlled and authorized by a relevant level of governance (DeLeon & DeLeon, 2002). On the other hand, an alternative opinion to hierarchic control was a bottom-up perspective—a successful implementation needs to account for street-level officials (2002). By the end of the previous century, implementation researchers thereinafter explored the local perspective, underlining, however, the importance of context in policy implementations. While embedding particular policy solutions, the bureaucrats, activists, or policymakers should observe how these solutions react with their surroundings (DeLeon & DeLeon, 2002).

The understanding of policy implementation is broad as it is simply: "what happens between policy expectations and (perceived) policy results" (DeLeon & DeLeon, 2002, p. 472). In this gap, previously made objectives are pursued, but along with different stages, they can evolve to meet the needs or interests of diverse actors. To more precisely describe an implementation, we present the scheme, established by Richard E. Matland (1995), which describes the implementation from two perspectives. First, its ambiguity, meaning whether it is a clear-cut issue or raising much controversy taboo. The second dimensions define how confrontational the problem is between different interest groups.

	CONFLICT	
AMBIGUITY	**Low**	**High**
Low	Administrative Implementation	Political Implementation
High	Experimental Implementation	Symbolic Implementation

Figure 3: Ambiguity-conflict matrix: policy implementation processes.
Source: Matland (1995, p. 160).

The low ambiguity and conflict are the *administrative implementation*, which encompasses significant procedures for the functioning of the government. In turn, *political implementation* indicates a high probability of disagreement between interest groups along with the approval of problem definitions. In this case, the power of the most influential actor is decided, and previously designed actions can be revised to obtain assumed aims. Less confrontational is *experimental implementation*, when there is an overall agreement that some action must be taken, but it is not clear and agreed on how to achieve it. This includes bottom-up implementation as the most suitable for finding acceptable solutions for everyone. Finally, there is the most difficult one, namely *symbolic implementation*. In this matter, it is hard to agree on the definition of the problem and to achieve one direction of actions. It concerns problems from an ethical sphere of life, such as faith or abortion (DeLeon & DeLeon, 2002; Matland, 1995).

Presented in this chapter theoretical aspects of policy analysis were aimed to provide a framework for analyzed in the book research problem, namely implementation of social activity idea for older people by urban aging policy in Poznan. Given the complexity of the problem under investigation I decided to set in the approach of DI. One of its central elements is idea, which represent particular values and agreements (Schmidt, 2008). Ideational analysis is widely used in the analysis of policy implementation as it provides an opportunity to explore its complexity, including various actors and influences they have on the policy solutions (Hall, 1997).

Theoretical framework

In this chapter, I will present the theoretical assumptions applied. Above all, the researchers emphasize the complexity of urban aging policy, which is a multidisciplinary area involving both social policy and urban studies. Equally complex is the subject of analysis, that is, the process of implementing the idea of social activity of older people. The intricacy of the research problem requires a method that allows us to grasp the overlapping relations and interactions of individuals, institutions, concepts, and documents with each other to then unite these fragmented networks. This is what the ANT and the concept of glocalization presented in this chapter provide.

2.1. Actor-network theory

Before describing ANT analytical constructs, I will discuss ethnomethodology, science and technology studies, and socio-material approach, which define this study framework. Ethnomethodology, which originated in sociology, has expanded to include social science, anthropology, science, and communication studies (Lynch, 1993). Focus is also a starting point for ANT research (Law, 2008).

Ethnomethodology is defined as an area of research that focuses on interactions that occur in everyday settings such as the streets, stores, or during socializing—essentially micro-level phenomena (Lynch, 1993). Harold Garfinkel created it in the 1950s while investigating jury deliberations (Francis & Hester, 2004; Lynch, 1993). He was influenced by Talcott Parsons' thoughts on social order and Alfred Schutz's phenomenological approach to society. H. Garfinkel studied jury discussions to find out how members reach consensus (Francis & Hester, 2004) and was interested in their interactions. People and groups create all social activities through their interactions and communications based on observations (Francis & Hester, 2004). Ethnomethodology, then, explains why and how social phenomena are observed (2004), such studies focus on a specific group engaging and producing social activity.

Science and technology studies, created by Bruno Latour, Steve Woolgar, and Micheala Lynch, is another following foundation of ANT, related to a way of experiencing reality. This interdisciplinary field emerged from the abandonment of modernist time divisions (premodern, modern, and post-modern) as well as society-nature divisions. Bruno Latour's *We Have Never Been Modern* addresses modernity's divide of social and natural realms. He argued that these modern worlds impact each other and use scientists and politicians as examples of people who are assumed to belong to two worlds, each guided by its own ontology. However, as B. Latour (Latour & Woolgar, 1986) explains, this is not the case, because what occurs in the laboratory is influenced by politics, and vice versa (Latour, 1993). B. Latour believes that modernists' cleansing of our reality deprives us of hybrids, networks of translation between nature and culture in which we function (1993). He defines non-modern reality as a dynamic relationship between the technological and social worlds and a dialectical representation of local and global or natural and cultural (Callon & Latour, 1981).

Material-semiotic approach, the third component of ANT, studies this nature-culture dialectic. A combination of instruments or methods that allows empirical and theoretical concerns to cross. It sees the apparent void as filled with networks of relations, which have mutual influence (Law, 2019). Diverse materials, including animals, architecture, people, and technology, can form such a network. The variability of bits in the network is indicative of the material-semiotic approach. This method emphasizes threads rather than features (2019). Networks are not meant to explain social order or simplify social practices. It's not what material semiotics seeks; it gives rather a patchwork network reality. First, it is because networks are not a stable state of affairs, the role of particular elements can change, and further actants, within their characteristics, influence the web relations. Thus, the networks are performative, they influence each other and the weaves, but also in the result, on what will come from such process (Law, 2008). As indicated, material-semiotic tools cannot explain practices because they do not describe one social order. Instead, it reveals numerous orders that thread the examined world (Law, 2008). Multiple realities, with diverse practices and values, materialize the phenomenon under study in different ways. Material semiotic aims to understand the differences in weaves of realities and how they occur, and then how the ontological politics emerges (Law, 2008). Power connections between network actors help researchers identify the dominant and, more significantly, periphery threads.

In those three mentioned approaches, ANT takes its origins, or better to say, its philosophical stances. It traces the network of relations between actants, who translate their interests to achieve some desirable set of effects. Actants within ANT are both human and nonhuman objects. They do not necessarily weave together due to common characteristics, but rather relations in which they influence each other (Latour, 2005a). As ethnomethodology focuses on the way groups communicate with each other to perform something together, it is the same for ANT. ANT strives to reveal networks of actants, which performs some practices (Law, 2008). Both, communication within ethnomethodology, and networking within ANT, lead to the emergence of reality.

Since its inception in the 1960s and 1970s, ANT has been reborn through the efforts of academics such as Andreas Blok, Ignacio Farias, and Cecilia Roberts, who allude to previously known ANT while simultaneously designating its new companion. After years of its first application, ANT has remained an open book, disassembling reality and leaving researchers with sensitivities for reassembling it. Its advantage is the ability to monitor who and how develops the research reality (2019, p. 2). Scholars view ANT as an intellectual practice that challenges the social order (2019, p. xxiii).

Actor-network theory framework

Bruno Latour, in his book *Re-assembling the Social: An Introduction to Actor-Network Theory* (2005a), laid out uncertainties concerning social sciences and simultaneously expounded core assumptions on ANT, which form a solution to diagnosed uncertainties. To understand how ANT perceives researched reality I will shortly explain them.

At first, ANT reframes scientists' understanding of social and brings back its primary meaning *someone following someone else* (Latour, 2005a, p. 108). In ANT, social does not refer to the *material* from which actants come, meaning social reality, but the movement in which actants are grouping. There are no fixed social groups (2005a, p. 28), which are the subject of research and whose existence is pre-established by scholars. Instead of it, the analysis consists in tracing how actants weave with each other and what makes these weaves durable, so one establishes social groups. The formed webs are visible to the naked eye in the practice they perform (Latour, 2005a; Law, 2008). This shift in the unit of analysis, in Latour's opinion, allows tracing how the association between observed objects is formed and thus how reality is constructed (Latour, 2005a, p. 42).

Within the change in the way *social* is understood by actor-network scientists, the social world is being expanded to much more than society itself: its ties, forces, and groups being causes of whatever is happening and what interests' scholars. Social aggregates are not made only of human entities, but also from nonhuman objects. Hence ANT introduces the term *actant*, which serves as an extension of actor and embraces not only *anthropomorphism*, but also ideomorphism, technomorphism, or biomorphism. In the simpler way of saying that an actant in ANT is "*anything* that does modify a state of affairs by making a difference" (Latour, 2005a, p. 71). So far social science accepted only entities that could be described as humans, who acted intentionally, whereas, in ANT, there are no such criteria. Thereby a hammer driving nail is an actant too. Although objects do not provoke the action, they can permit, stop, alter, or reverse it (Latour, 2005a, p. 71; Latour & Woolgar, 1986).

Within another of his uncertainties, Bruno Latour revealed the confusion which emerges when we want to understand why something is happening. What he claims is that scientists should reframe this question and ask who made it happen. Among entities forming networks, there are ones called intermediaries, and the others called mediators. The infinitesimal difference between those two types provides a divide among ANT scholars and social scientists so far. Within intermediaries, we look for a cause and we know its effect. Whereas with mediators, we deal with a concatenation of factors, which made someone, or something act, but it is not defined how it will end. Mediators are linked with the previous idea of social aggregates that are constantly evoking and evolving, influencing each other actions. To put it much simpler and more colloquially, B. Latour asks: "how come I never do what I want?" (Latour, 2005a, p. 43) This very day-to-day experience illustrates how action can be overtaken, meaning influenced by someone or something. For ANT scholars, the researched reality is complex as all forming it entities might be a mediator, who transforms and translates another object into something unsuspected, changing the existing state of affair. As B. Latour emphasized, a distinction between intermediaries and mediators is merely infinitesimal and responsible for uncertainty which a scientist needs to follow and decide what influenced one's action. Is there a simple cause of it or is it threaded from the *concatenation of mediators*?

In line with this, an action is not a deliberative and fully independent process but is constructed by an array of agencies that weave the action. Within ANT, agency consists of its figuration and a theory of action. Furthermore, it embraces some transformation of affairs. A figuration of agency can be expressed with concrete individual figuration as well as with an abstract one, both equally powerful, prompt actions of actants. For example, an abstract figuration will be: "common sense dictates to not spend more money than you have"; whereas an example of an individual is: "my mother wants me to have children before 30" (2005a). Moreover, figurations are engaged by an earlier-mentioned theory of action, which responses to the question of how one actant made another actant do something. We can have two different ideas on how this happens: the first is more limited as it treats agencies as a cause that transport an action to some expected effects (intermediaries). Whereas the second idea is that agencies trigger other ones, and it can lead to unexpected and sort of unfinished traces. ANT stays with the latter one, as it prefers to see the world as *a concatenation of mediators* (agencies). Mediators can act and thus evoke other actions (Latour, 2005a; Sayes, 2014).

The next uncertainty observed in social science by B. Latour is its objective to find the truth, as truth forms a frame of reference to whatever is happening. This kind of epistemological study searches for a source of knowledge in "outside reality" (Latour, 2005a; Mol, 2002). Whereas for actor-network scholars, knowledge is not an external source, about which objects are researched, but is constructed in various practices, the same as law or fashion (Latour, 2005a). The focus on actions and the concatenations of mediators, which prompt others to act, illustrates the interlacement of networks that form those practices and enact knowledge (Mol, 2002).

The next premise of ANT is flat land of researched reality. For B. Latour (2005a), a division between local and global or micro and macro limits our understanding of what is happening and how it is enacted. All that seems to be a context for the local interaction, namely scale, place, or size, are all products of actions between various objects. There is no micro and macro, they are both equal and we can see it if we track associations that form micro- and macro-objects, actants. They render some actants seemingly global, but it is only a relative scale assembled by complex social aggregates.

Bruno Latour and Michel Callon (1981) in their essay entitled *Unscrewing the big Leviathan: how macro actors structure reality and how sociologists help them to do so* introduce the notion of the *black box,* which scales the flat landscape and forms this micro-macro reality, apparently so far from each other. Those black boxes contain: "modes of thoughts, habits, forces, and objects" (1981, p. 285) which enact scales and make one actant more dominant over another. So, for a researcher to develop a map of associations and understand scales, it is important to unfold the reality packed in black boxes.

In some way, when we assume that local and global are equal sites, the actants are equal too and the researcher focuses on the interactions between them. We remain with local face-to-face interactions between actants. However, B. Latour warns, that local is much more complicated than pure interactions (Latour, 2005a). For ANT scholars, local is visible when we notice a change, a displacement of actants and their actions. During the process of such change arise webs of actants and relations between them. These webs, in turn, produce practices and enact realities (Mol, 2002). The plural noun is deliberately used because in ANT one reality is limited to its ontology, as it was mentioned earlier, and there is more than one ontology in the social world. For this reason, we can say that there are more realities and they are multiple, as they are not cloistered beings, but related sites, influencing each other (2002).

The process that helps describe what happens between actants is translation (Callon, 1984; Outila & Kiuru, 2021; Po-An Hsieh et al., 2012). With ANT, translation describes the process in which actants negotiate and delimit their identities, possible interactions, and plans (Callon, 1984). As writes S. Star, "translate is to exercise power: some elements are endowed with the capacity to delegate, coordinate, and translate other elements into specific programs of action, while others are translated, coordinated, and become delegates of others instead" (Star, 1991, p. 29). Furthermore, we can distinguish four stages in the translation process, namely: *problematization, interessement, enrollment,* and *mobilization.* Those are moments that are not visible to the naked eye but are crucial for actants whose *lots* become tied together (Callon, 1984).

Table 4: Moments of translation

PROBLEMATIZATION	In this stage actants of the network are identified and their interests are being formed.
INTERESSEMENT	Actants are locked in the network of social activity, within declared identities and goals and become indispensable for each other.
ENROLLMENT	The ways in which actants are assigned to previously declared roles.
MOBILIZATION	The emergence of new elements from the network.

Source: Callon (1984).

In the first step, each actant in some way *voices* their problems. As within this approach, we do not exclude nonhuman objects, thus the expression of their issues can be less direct than claimed. For example, policies produce documents expressing their assumptions. Doing this, actants express their goal and interests and find a common problem important for all of them. Furthermore, actants cannot achieve what they desire only by themselves, they need the whole network of actants. Thus, they are prone to make alliances and plans to fulfill what they want (Callon, 1984). Relations between the actants, members of a particular project, are strengthened by *the interessement*. By this, we understand the construction of particular dependencies between actants, making their relations more exclusive and their aims more available (Hardy & Williams, 2008; Ranerup, 2008). So far, actants' interests are combined by a common aim, which makes them related to each other. In the next moment, actants become *enrolled* into "a set of interrelated roles" (Callon, 1984, p. 211; Ranerup, 2008), which will ensure the achievement of earlier accepted aims. In the final stage, the interests of actants are *mobilized* by a spokesman, who is responsible for achieving the mutual goals of the other actants (Callon, 1984). If the network is working, meaning the needs of particular actants are met, then mobilization will succeed, and the network will gain its performative function of establishing something new (Po-An Hsieh et al., 2012). The translation process will serve as an important construct in the process of analysis to understand enactment of social activity for older people and its implementation by various local actants.

Another concept used by actor-network research to describe results of networks is ontology. It was used by A. Mol (2002) to describe various enactments of disease she was researching, namely atherosclerosis. Ontology is considered by researchers associated with ANT as one of the possible embodiments of the phenomenon under study. Hence, A. Mol in her study, established a few of ontologies of atherosclerosis, but not to imply that there are few realities of the disease. The identified ontologies refer to the different practices that constitute a given phenomenon. In addition, they may conceive of the phenomenon under study differently; in the case of A. Mol's research, atherosclerosis was, on the one hand, a swollen leg that makes walking difficult, and on the other, a narrowed vein that prevents the free flow of blood. The different ontologies interact with each other to constitute the totality of a given reality. Within ontologies scholars can observe the multiplicity of studied reality (Law, 2008; Mol, 2002). Researchers apply ontologies to understand a phenomenon studied and observe different discourses influencing it. In the next section, I present how ANT constructs were applied within the research on policy implementation and urban studies, also drawing attention to the role ontology plays in understanding different realities of policy formation, for example, the disabled and policymakers (Galis, 2011).

Application of actor-network theory

In this section, I would like to demonstrate the employment of ANT in research on policy implementation and next within urban studies. In my study, I combine those two disciplines by analyzing urban aging policy, represented by its element, namely social activity of older people. In the first part, I draw attention to the application of ANT within research on the policy implementation process. The review of policy research with ANT indicates that this theoretical framework is unique for this type of research (see Table 6). Second, I present ANT as an important concept in current urban studies (Blok, A., Farias, I., & Roberts, 2019; "Urban Assemblages. How Actor-Network Theory Changes Urban Studies," 2010). Its application resulted in the establishment of the special term—*urban assemblage*—which refers to the reassembling of relations between actants at the urban policy scene. Within this section I aim to present ANT as a more concrete scientific tool, showing its analytical capacity in my research.

The application of ANT in policy research is strongly linked with researchers' aim to trace the process of policymaking, with particular emphasis on policy implementation (Galis, 2011; Kaljonen, 2006; Po-An Hsieh et al., 2012; Ranerup, 2008; Sanders et al., 2017). Moreover, scholars were drawn to employ this theoretical framework as it allowed us to explore the context of the studied problem as well as its local characteristics (Galis, 2011; Outila & Kiuru, 2021; Po-An Hsieh et al., 2012). Table 5 contains all information and illustrate applied by scholars' research aims and justification of ANT application.

As for policy implementation process, scholars underlined the advantage of ANT to capture it as a networking activity between different actants, which could be human or nonhuman objects. Within such a tool, meaning network of actants, scientists strived to grasp the complexity of the implementation process, from its formulation, usually at the global level, to its practical implementation. Furthermore, the emphasis on the assembling of the network, which reflects multiplicity of policy implementation, is another important ANT's concept (Galis, 2011). Within ontologies, scholars are able to see how different realities, constructed from assemblages of relations, are allowed to speak in the implementation process, and values and interests stand behind their actions. Ontologies also enabled the analysis of phenomena formation, such as disability. It works on recreation of vocabulary used in daily experiences of body impairment and its problem definition with the policymaking process.

Another aspect of ANT weighing in favor of it applying to policy implementation research is scholars' interests in contextualizing this process (Kaljonen, 2006; Outila & Kiuru, 2021; Po-An Hsieh et al., 2012). Meaning, taking into consideration social, economic, political factors as well as technological developments. Furthermore, the context that scientists are looking for in this kind of research is the local one. Tracing the implementation from a top-down direction, they strive to understand how indigenousness influences globally formed ideas (Sanders et al., 2017).

The actor-network openness for human and nonhuman aggregates, multiplying researched reality, gives space to the analytical process. Namely, it allows the researcher to look for additional and new aspects of policy formation and to expand existing knowledge on the subject.

ANT was used by researchers to explore the process of policy implementation or the relation between various public policies and other concepts. What is worth noticing is that scholars take and adjust elements from ANT to suit their research needs. Whereas some researchers strive to detect ontologies of political reality, intermediaries and mediaries of network formations, specific actants and their role, such as assistive technology, others focus more on translation process, tracing its four moments: *problematization*, *interessement*, *enrollment*, and *mobilization*.

Table 5: Policy research with ANT application[7]

Article	Aim of research	ANT concept used	ANT justification (What/why does it contribute to this research?)	Accompanying concepts	Data
Hsieh et al. (2012)	– Investigation of broadband Internet initiative launched by municipal of La Grange. – Attempt to understand why such initiatives fail. – To grasp different context engaged in this implementation within its actors and interests	– Translation process—how interests are translated and influence the initiative enactment – Focus on the four moments of translation	– Complex interplay between stakeholders, interested in implementation of initiative – The need to consider a wide set of contextual triggers (sociological, economical, and political) in the analysis.	– Digital inclusion – Information and communication technology (ICT) – Implementation process	– 3-year case study

[7] This document contains literature sourced from the Web of Science database. The search utilized keywords including: "policy implementation" AND "actor-network theory"; "implementation" AND "actor-network theory." I obtained 384 articles, which were analyzed and refined based on the research topic.

Galis (2011)	– Exploration of disability construction, through body limitations, surroundings, and policy – Propose alternative framing of disability in literature	– Politics as a compromise between human and nonhuman actors. – Ontology as a political reality – Network of actants	– Allow combining dichotomy in disability construction between the body and socio-material practices, present in the literature.	– Social constructivism – Policymaking	– Literature review – Analysis of scientific fora
Outila and Kiuru (2021)	– Effects' analysis of assistive technology influence on older people's network—*picture phone*	– Actants – Intermediators, mediators – Translation process – Network	– Current conclusions on older people's technological preferences are recognized to be unified, lacking social context and individual preferences	– Foucauldian discourse analysis (FDA)	– Interviews with eight older adults from Finland
Carson and Koch (2013)	– See if taking into consideration scale and mobility can enhance understanding of local economic planning within rural areas	– Actor-network – Association	– ANT allows to set aside applied predesigned scale, such as social, spatial, and temporal	– Scale – Fragmented development	– Comparative case study

(Continued)

Table 5: (*Continued*)

Article	Aim of research	ANT concept used	ANT justification (What/why does it contribute to this research?)	Accompanying concepts	Data
Ranerup (2008)	– Analysis of implementation process—pension system reform accompanied by decision support system	– Translation process	– It is assumed to be a good tool for researching interrelation in between public policy implementation and technology	– Public policy implementation	– Case study—elements of ethnography – Interviews, observation, document analysis
Hardy and Williams (2007)	– How e-procurement policies are translated into practice	– Translation process – Obligatory passage point – Inscription	– ANT includes socio-material reality – Underline role of power and politics in the analysis	– Social construction of policy – Implementation process	– Three case studies

Sanders et al. (2017)	- Explore implementation process of global initiative (Reducing Emissions from Deforestation and Forest Degradation) to the local level	- Translation process - Intermediaries and mediators	- Help to understand problems in top-down implementation process, tracing matters of local irregularity	- Implementation process - Multi-level governance	- Case study with elements of ethnography - Field observation
Kaljonen (2006)	- Strive to trace how European agri-environmental policy goals were implemented in Finland.	- Agency performed with network - Network of relations between actants	- ANT is used to help understand the process of implementation global goals of agri-environmental policy in local settings—how the agency of this policy is con-constructed by global aims and local settings. - Allow to combine a hybrid character of environmental policy	- Implementation process - Local knowledge - Co-construction of agency	- 31 interviews with farmers

(Continued)

Table 5: (*Continued*)

Article	Aim of research	ANT concept used	ANT justification (What/why does it contribute to this research?)	Accompanying concepts	Data
Iskandrova (2016)	– Explore development of policy within emerging industry of wave energy	– Network – Actants as human and nonhuman objects	– Provide a chance for observation of policy perceived as a network and actant	– Policy as an actant	– Case study

Source: Own elaboration.

ANT in the city

In turn, the urban research to which I refer when studying urban policy in Poznan argues that ANT is applicable because it helps us understand the muddled nature of urban processes (McFarlane, 2011a, 2011b; Swanton, 2011). *Assemblage*, the term commonly used by scholars, is perceived as valuable by introducing socio-material practices which form urban reality. Moreover, it involves the issue of agency, which is a driver of assemblage forming and allowing tracing the dynamicity of urban processes (McFarlane, 2011a, 2011b). Within the broad discussion on ANT application in urban research, which was published in the journal *City* vol. 15, its supporters drew attention to additional possibilities that ANT offers in comparison to critical urban studies. Namely, it shifts attention from a critical analysis of capitalism domination to the inquiry of urban assemblage (Swanton, 2011, p. 245).

Furthermore, the analysis of agency distribution within the city allows for better understanding of its multiplicity and incidental character (Farber, 2020). It challenges the well-known perception of the city as an object of study and instead proposes urban assemblage as a new way of seeing the city ("Urban Assemblages. How Actor-Network Theory Changes Urban Studies," 2010). As a result of ANT's relational, flat, but symmetrical attitude, scholars are able to see more unexpected phenomena than with settled concepts of critical urbanity, such as capitalism, war of power or inequalities (Swanton, 2011; "Urban Assemblages. How Actor-Network Theory Changes Urban Studies," 2010). It is not that they are not important and unnecessary in city analysis, but they can bring limitation to the study by narrowing it to issues related with analyzed concepts (McFarlane, 2011a).

The issue of relativity refers to common pursuits of different actants, such as humans, objects, devices, documents, and many others, which instead of being perceived as distinct entities, are seen as collectives forming each other (Latour, 2005a; Law, 2008). Symmetry, in turn, brings equality between human and nonhuman worlds, and changes the understanding of society. It does not refer to the matter of study but rather describes it. The social world is being enhanced with *non-social* elements and associations, which has a performative role in the assembling of reality ("Urban Assemblages. How Actor-Network Theory Changes Urban Studies," 2010). Furthermore, the mentioned earlier flatness of reality within ANT (see p. 77), does not indicate the lack of hierarchy or domination in the city reality, but it rejects taking them for granted. The role of the researcher is to trace socio-material practices and based on that reconstruct possible relations of power (2010).

The actor-network inquiry into urban assemblage also brings plurality of urban reality, framing it with ontologies. Thanks to this, the previously mentioned messiness of the city can be framed with networks of actants. These webs, in turn, form multiple realities (Blok, A., Farias, I., & Roberts, 2019). These multiple ways of city's being enacted are introduced by A. Mol (2002) in her book *The Body Multiple*, where she also presented the notion of ontology. She demonstrated that it is not that the object, here the city, is being enacted differently, in the matter of epistemology, but rather in the matter of ontology. It means that an urban scholar can encounter more than one reality behind the studied process or phenomenon ("Urban Assemblages. How Actor-Network Theory Changes Urban Studies," 2010). Thus, the term urban assemblages reflects multiplicity of enactments and underline that there is no one single object, but a variety of them. The aim is to trace how they are produced and later how they become visible.

The ANT, then, is claimed to bring to urban research the possibility to scrutinize *the context of context*. The diversity of actants and plurality of network in which they enter enhance observation of city, which simultaneously can be a historical heritage, transporting system, age-friendly community, or space for graffiti and street art fulfillment. Furthermore, within ANT distinction, present also in the urban studies, between local and global, or endogenous and indigenous, disappears. The ANT scholars claim that this gap between mentioned pairs of object classification can be explanatory for city process and practices (Blok, A., Farias, I., & Roberts, 2019). By and large, urban assemblages are perceived as a valuable set of sensibilities, accompanying the exploration of complexity and contingency of city's reality (2019).

2.2. Glocalization

In this chapter, I introduce the concept of glocalization, aimed at supporting the analytical process. It was introduced as a result of globalization, which changed the distribution of power within economies, societies, and politics (Robertson, 1995). The researchers observed new constitutive forces, namely global and local, which both formed *glocal spaces*. It is also of great significance in the field of public policy, as based on the concept of glocalization scholars draw attention to *the politics of scale* that are aimed to understand new and floating relations between actors (Swyngedouw, 1997, 2004, 2005). Glocalization, thus, strives to unveil the system of allies that govern local public policy and explore characteristics of glocal spaces (Wathen, 2020). It corresponds with a decentralization of aging policy and social policy in general, which is altering the old order of vertical policy implementation and causing the emergence of multiply policies managed horizontally or with other more specific scales, for example, networking (DeLeon & DeLeon, 2002).

From global to glocal

The term globalization was introduced into social theory in the 1980s (Robertson, 1995). The globalization perspective does not see society as a unified force, but it rather draws attention to trans-societal flows. The concept of globalization is considered mostly in terms of global and local and the interaction between them. The relation between them has been perceived by some researchers as dialectical, which comes from tension between universalism and particularism. Globalization is evoked by market forces—reorganization of production, differentiation of capital locations, and its flaws across boundaries. It, in turn, influences political, social systems, which have to deal with a new set of actors, meaning new entrepreneurs, their workers, social system payers, and beneficiaries (Hong & Song, 2010). The universalistic power of globalization leads to the emergence of social problems that increasingly concern most of the population. However, they can vary when it comes to a more particular set of circumstances of the local environment (2010). The International Federation of Social Workers defines globalization as a common experience of global populations in the matter of social, economic, and cultural conditions. Globalization changed the rules of the game, knocking off the influential position of the nation-state (Poole & Negi, 2008). Paradoxically, this has empowered local levels of government, contributing to strengthening their political identity, shaped by networks of various international and local actors (Robertson, 2013).

The global and local forces of globalization can be seen also within the aging problem, which concerns a great part of societies. Moreover, the aging issue is addressed by the global civil community (Hong & Song, 2010; Poole & Negi, 2008), as members of international or national organizations (European Union, World Health Organization) strive to tackle the issue with such ideas as active aging, within Decade of Healthy Aging [8] or The Global Network of Age-Friendly Communities (Buffel et al., 2020; World Health Organization, 2002). These ideas, in turn, arrive at local levels of governance, and are implemented by local social movements, policymakers or civil society initiatives, often bypassing the national levels of administration (Błędowski, 2016b; Kubiak, 2018; Michael et al., 2006; Rémillard-Boilard et al., 2020). It can be seen, then, that the phenomenon of globalization also frames the societies' aging issue, as it also is affected by its universalistic and particularistic powers.

To capture this polarity of globality, Robert Robertson (1995) proposed the term *glocalization*. In the chapter *Glocalization: Time-Space and Homogeneity-Heterogeneity*, he disputes the misleading understanding of globalization as a homogenization in the result of modernity. Instead, he introduced *glocalization* as a more adequate description of tension between the global idea, which is a collage of local practices, and the local idea, constructed within the elements provides by global forces (Drori et al. 2014).

Glocalization by some researchers is perceived as one of discourses of globalization and the positive one, in contrast to globalization. The first one focuses on the process of adaptation to the local levels, resulting both in homogenizing but also heterogenizing effects. The latter concept, constituted from words *growth* and globalization, refers to the devastating power of global forces within local levels, dominated by the standardization of consumer culture (Robertson, 2013; Roudometof, 2015).

The glocalization concept, although, introduced firstly in the management and organization studies (Czarniawska, 2000; Drori et al., 2014; Giulianotti & Robertson, 2007; Robertson, 2013) has disseminated also into other disciplines, such as geography, political economy (Cox, 2009; Swyngedouw, 1996, 2004, 2005), urban studies (Brenner, 1999; Roudometof, 2015; Tsukamoto,

---

8 <https://www.who.int/initiatives/decade-of-healthy-ageing>

2012), local policy studies (Sun et al., 2017; Wathen, 2020). The application of this term and its understanding varies (see Table 6).

Table 6: The glocalization concept within management and political studies

	Management and organizational studies	**Political studies**
Focus	Ideas, concepts translated within organizations (Drori et al., 2014).	Politics of scales—transformation of relation between social, political and economic actors from international and local levels (Roudometof, 2015; Swyngedouw, 1997a).
Accompanying concepts	Translation theory—ideas and concepts travel—they are re-embedded within time and space into new local context (Wæraas & Nielsen, 2016).	- Scales—describes temporal relations of power, binding compromises and strategies (Swyngedouw, 1997a). - Glocal—new sphere emerged in the result of globalization (Paganoni, 2012; Roudometof, 2015; Wathen, 2020)
Glocalization definition	Glocalization describes the specific types of translation of ideas between different entities, organizations. In regard to the different relations between those, three dimensions of glocalization can be listed: vertical, horizontal, and temporal (Drori et al., 2014).	Glocalization is understood as rolling of the state, upward to the international organization and downward to the local level of governance (Cox, 2009; Swyngedouw, 1997a).

Source: Own elaboration.

Glocalization used by organizational and management researchers (Czarniawska, 2000; Drori et al., 2014; Wæraas & Nielsen, 2016) brings multidimensionality of forces, causing cultural variance against globalization tendencies for homogenization. Glocalization introduced a new quality to division between global and local and seeks to find processes that interlace the global and local world. The implementation of some global concepts is compared to isomorphism, which can be a result of corrective regulations, an imitation of the best practices or the adjustment to norms of some group. Thus, the localization of certain global ideas (translations) is done in relation to the identity and alterity of the entity in question. Translation is an attempt to achieve similarity and at the same time preserve the character of the entity in question (Czarniawska, 2002, p. 35).

Glocalization describes the specific types of idea translation between different entities. Regarding the different relations between those, three dimensions of glocalization can be listed: vertical, horizontal, and temporal. The first one refers to a hierarchical order or nested entities; horizontal represents the transfer of ideas between equal entities, such as companies from the one industry. The last one provides for the translation of ideas in time, meaning from the past up to now (Drori et al., 2014, p. 91). All of them refer to one direction of glocalization; however, they rarely occur individually but rather intersect with each other. What is more, the four different phases of glocalization can be distinguished. Each of them allows the researcher to identify what an object of glocalization is, who the subject is and how it is performed.

Glocal and the politics of scale

Glocalization is a process of interaction between two forces engaged in globalization, namely global and local. According to M. Watchen, this is a kind of narration that opens up the marginalized, in some globalization discourses, actors such as: “local professional organizations, governments, policymakers, educators, and social work practitioners” (Wathen, 2020, p. 150). The term glocalization, within urban and local policy studies, is strongly related to globalization that led to the decentralization and rescaling of political systems, diminishing state power in favor of the international organization, but also local levels of administration (Swyngedouw, 1996, 1997; Wathen, 2020). Within this process regional actors, such as cities, become much more powerful (Roudometof, 2015).

Furthermore, glocalization’s combining global and local forces form a kind of new space, called *glocal*, which characterizes with great differentiation between localities as well as relative and unforeseen processes within society. Individuals are not dominated by leading forces and discourses, but instead are able to accommodate, operate, and evolve within the glocal space (Ritzer, 2004).

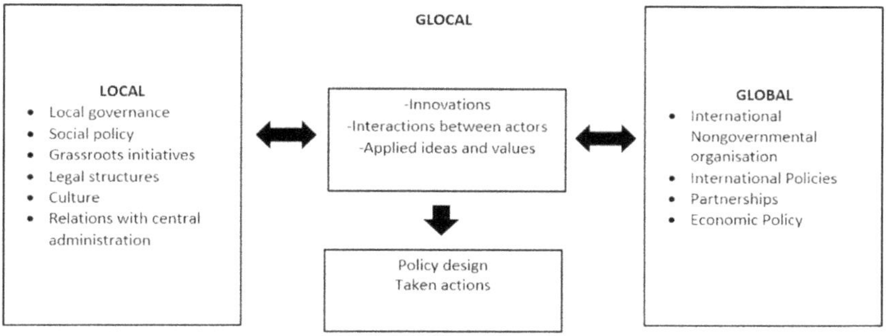

Figure 4: Glocal space.
Source: Ritzer (2004) and Wathen (2020).

As presented in Figure 4 the glocal space captures a unique set of interactions between actors and their values, influenced by global and local contexts, which contributes to measures taken by policymakers or community workers (Wathen, 2020). Of course, the scheme presents an idealistic even distributions of influences from both sides. However, their impact is in constant flux and their force of impact can vary, depending on the areas of action taken (2020). Thus, local policy and urban studies researchers refer to glocalization as an "ongoing conversation" (Szulecki 2011, Swyngedouw 2004). The glocal as *place of this conversation* gives ground to the interchange of ideas and values between actors, to give it back in the next step (indicated by two-way arrows in Figure 4).

Glocal space can be understood as a state of limbo, in relation to both locally and globally applicable scales. They are one more element of glocalization, taken into consideration within policy and urban studies. The processes that glocalization describes are referred to by researchers as politics of scale (Latham & McCormack, 2010; Sun et al., 2017; Swyngedouw, 1996). Scale traditionally has been associated with geographical division of territories, within politic of scale is perceived as representation of binding strategies, relations between actors and compromises. Scale articulates socio-spatial and political order of the analyzed reality (Swyngedouw, 1996, 1997). Furthermore, they are subjected to constant influences and dynamic relations of the glocal. Scales, then, are not given a way of structuring the socio-spatial reality, but they express a metaphorical representation of local relations. They cannot be taken for granted, but rather as discourse, capturing the fluidity of the world and expressing processual character of relations between political actors (Swyngedouw, 1997, p. 140). The fluid character of scales is linked with the globalization, which resulted in "stretching and deepening of social relationships and institutions across time and space" (in Dickens 2004: 9). Scalar researchers thus strive to explore how applied scales transform, what social relations and actors they embrace and which they omit (Latham & McCormack, 2010).

Taking into account the actor-network attitude toward hierarchical order and scales and its encouragement to flat ontology, I must explain how those two seemingly contradictory assumptions are complemented within my research. As it was mentioned, scales within glocalization in the policy and urban study (Latham & McCormack, 2010; Mehta, 2011; Sun et al., 2017; Swyngedouw, 1996, 2005; "Urban Assemblages. How Actor-Network Theory Changes Urban Studies," 2010; Wathen, 2020) reflects narratives of ruling strategies and relations between actors. They nest actions of actors within a socio-spatial context, linking it to the local, national or international levels. ANT, in turn, proposes to see studied reality as flat ontology. This means abrogating top-down scales, or prevailing hierarchies, and equating local and global actors. However, ANT scholars do not recognize that micro and macro actors are equal, but in doing so they seek to abrogate the arrangements that stand behind the superiority of one actor over another (Callon & Latour, 1981; Latour, 2005a). In turn, these assumptions, formed as a result of the translation between actors, are what create scales, in glocal space, and influence the possibilities and actions taken by local policy makers (Latham & McCormack, 2010; "Urban Assemblages. How Actor-Network Theory Changes Urban Studies," 2010).

The aim of the study, then, is to unveil existing hierarchies between actors and the reasons for it, black boxes, which cloak agreements between actants, translated into networks. Within glocalization, this framework is being extended by the *glocal* space and its reference to globalization (Latham & McCormack, 2010). It is important for the research context of my study, namely handling the global crises of aging societies, which is being passed to local policies. Glocalization and the politics of scale allow people to go a step further in the analysis, and apart from tracing the networks of actants' enacting social activity of older people, see within what scales these policies work.

Glocalization is therefore a framework for the phenomenon that is occurring within public policy and aging policy in particular, namely its decentralization and this locality (Błędowski, 2016b; Buffel et al., 2020; Theiss, 2012, 2017). This concept allows us to describe this process within politics of scale and seeks to unveil what scales can describe the implementation of urban aging policy.

Research design

The framework of my research, as stated in the previous chapter, attempted to illustrate the foundation of the topic under study, namely the implementation of social activity ideas for older people by urban aging policy in Poznan. Within the framework of gerontology, we can see how diverse the phenomenon of aging is and how experts interpret it differently. In my research, I use one of the most recent paradigms, the critical paradigm, which views aging as the consequence of a battle between many actors, their interests, and influences (Phillipson and Estes, 2007). Aging is also a significant issue in social policy since it influences changes in demographic structures and, as a result, can disrupt the functioning of social security systems. However, many measures for older people are established at the local level of governance. It is believed to be the most suited and efficient because it is employed there (Andreotti & Mingione, 2016; Błędowski, 2016b; Theiss, 2012). As a result, cities are playing an increasingly essential role in the creation of aging strategies (Buffel & Remillard-Boilard, 2019; Remillard-Boilard et al., 2020). These offer justification for the study issue I have selected to investigate in this book. This chapter presents the research design intended to address the following research objectives.

To achieve the aforementioned research objectives, I employed certain research approaches. I performed the research with the framework of a case study. The initial section (3.1—Case study approach) will delineate its objectives and rationale. In the subsequent section (3.2—Data collection), I will elucidate the whole data collection process. It involved conducting interviews, observing, and collecting promotional brochures or pertinent

Table 7: Research objectives and their realization

Research objectives	Its realization
1. Explore what the social activity for older people that takes place in Poznan is. 1.1. Recognize who and what (actants) organizes these activities and why they do it. 1.2. Establish relations between actants.	Data collection level: - Observing of social activity events. - Interviewing organizers of social activity. - Collecting additional materials, such as promotional brochures or the city hall relevant documentation. Data analysis level: - What are the actants? (Anything or anyone with influence and the ability to change the situation) - Why are they (actants) engaged in the enactment of social activity for older people? - The analysis of the translation process by following actants. - What are their (actants) aims, and how do they depend on one another?
2. Understand the implementation of the idea of social participation for older people at the city level. 2.1. Identify practices of implementation. Describe ontologies and scales which form the urban aging policy in Poznan.	Data collection level: - Observing of social activity events. - Interviewing organizers of social activity. - Collecting additional materials, such as promotional brochures or city hall documentation. Data analysis level: - How is something being done?—Searching for practices. - What are powers and influences forming the social activity for older people in Poznań? - The analysis of values, norms, definitions, forming powers and its classification into ontologies and scales.

Source: Own elaboration based on Callon and Latour (1981a), Iskandarova (2017), Latour (2005b), Law (2008, 2019), Mol (2002), and Swyngedouw (1996, 1997b).

municipal documents, including proposals for social activity initiatives. In the subsequent section (3.3—Data analysis), I will demonstrate the use of content analysis utilizing ANT categories and the notion of glocalization.

3.1. Case study

The research topic and problems identified in my study indicate a necessity for investigation, facilitating an in-depth examination of urban aging policy. Policy researchers employ the qualitative case study method to examine the intricate process of policy formulation at local governance levels (Flyvbjerg, 2006; Pal, 2005). The purpose of employing this qualitative method is to acquire in-depth information of the phenomenon under investigation, rather than to formulate a generalized theory applicable to the entire population (Strumińska-Kutra & Koładkiewicz, 2012). Moreover, qualitative case study facilitates a more intersectional examination of urban aging strategies. According to the researchers, previous analyses of urban strategies have been too narrow, focusing on a single area, such as culture or finance. Conversely, the case study I employed offers a chance to examine the urban policy creation process comprehensively and to pinpoint significant aspects pertinent to its execution (Theiss, 2017). The utilization of case study as a research design for my investigation was determined by the objectives and prevalence of the approach in policy analysis, particularly in studies of policy implementation (Pal, 2005; Pressman & Wildavsky, 1974).

The case study is one of the methods of the qualitative approach, which is characterized by a desire to understand why certain phenomenon occur and how it becomes real. The emphasis in this type of research is on process, interaction, and dynamics of the phenomena. The researcher seeks to capture the problem in its environment to understand its impact, taking into account how it is perceived from the perspective of the subjects (Denzin & Lincoln, 2005; Strumińska-Kutra & Koładkiewicz, 2012). The use of the case study method is very widespread among researchers who, however, represent different paradigms, reflecting different ontological and epistemological assumptions about the reality under study. As a result, the method itself may serve them to achieve different goals. For example, in the positivist paradigm, researchers aim to make generalizations about the theory on the basis of the case study, whereas in the relativist approach the aim is to describe and understand the phenomenon and its local context (Strumińska-Kutra & Koładkiewicz, 2012, p. 2). Consequently, individual researchers, specialists in this methodology such as R. Yin (1989), B. Flyvbjerg (2006) or R. Stake (2008) specify different types of case studies. However, before

I refer to them, I will try to broadly define how this research strategy can be understood. Following J. W. Creswell (2007), a case study can be defined as a study method in which the researcher analyses a limited system, a case, and as a result obtains a comprehensive description of the case together with its relevant themes. The study is conducted through the use of in-depth data collection strategies such as observations, interviews, documents or audio-visual materials (2007, p. 73). As far as the types of case studies are concerned, I will start with the division made by R. Yin (1989), which takes into account questions of the purpose of the type:

- Exploratory case—can be treated as a prelude to further research, allows questions or hypotheses to be raised for future analysis.
- Descriptive case—a comprehensive description of a case, taking into account its context, features and possible structure.
- Exponential case—the aim is to examine the causes and effects within the case under study, e.g., the introduction of healthcare reform.

The aforementioned three types of case study are related to the research possibilities that the study may have, and what goals it may therefore achieve. A slightly different classification is presented by H. Eckstein:

- Disciplined-configurative case studies—in this type of case study, the researcher focuses on some unique problem, and by describing it, aims to create some laws that define it. This type of study, in the analytical procedure applies a theory, on the basis of which interpretations are created (Eckstein, 2000).
- Heuristic case studies—in this case study, the researcher aims to clarify a theoretical problem, so the selection of the case and the research design itself are designed to do so. This type overlaps with exploratory case study detailed by R. Y. in (Eckstein, 2000; Pal, 2005).
- Plausibility probes—this type serves to confirm or refute a certain hypothesis or theory. Thus, this type of case study can give support for further research already on a larger scale (Eckstein, 2000).
- Crucial-case study—a kind of case study which, by its very nature, can help to verify a given theory. The choice of case is then strictly dictated by the theory to be disproved or confirmed (2000). This kind of case

study is also called by other scholars as *critical case study* (Flyvbjerg, 2006; Strumińska-Kutra & Koładkiewicz, 2012).

Classifying a study into a specific type of case study is difficult, as researchers specializing in this method stress that the boundaries between specific types are fluid (Flyvbjerg, 2006; Pal, 2005; Strumińska-Kutra & Koładkiewicz, 2012; Yin, 1989). However, referring to the classifications presented, the study presented in this book is a comprehensive description of a local policy on aging, which aims to provide knowledge in the field of implementing local policies and to propose concrete theoretical implications. Therefore, it is classified as a kind of descriptive study, or considering H. Eckstein's classification *disciplined-configurative case study*. At the same time, the study responds to a research gap concerning the local policy on aging and, more specifically, the processes that comprise it. Therefore, the case study presented in the next section can be partly called an *explanatory or heuristic case study* as it seeks to explain a certain phenomenon.

Another important issue in the case study is the place of theory. Namely, whether it is the basis for the selection of the case and the design of the study itself, or rather whether it emerges at subsequent stages as a tool for interpretation and the creation of theoretical implications (Strumińska-Kutra & Koładkiewicz, 2012). The former approach will involve a positivist paradigm in research, that is, focusing on the discovery of general facts that can explain the causes of a given phenomenon. The second approach, on the other hand, is more characteristic of the interpretative paradigm, which is directed more toward understanding the reality under study, taking into account the individual's understanding (Sławecki, 2012). In the case of the research presented in this thesis, theory was not a criterion for case selection but was included as a conceptual framework for the study, which helped to clarify the research problem. In turn, in the analytical part, I apply a theoretical framework as a set of research tools (Strumińska-Kutra & Koładkiewicz, 2012). Thus, the collected data were analyzed using ANT (Callon, 1984; Callon & Latour, 1981; Latour, 1993), and then the concept of glocalization was applied in the next stage of theorization (Latham & McCormack, 2010; Swyngedouw, 1997).

Turning to the application of the case study to the field of social policy itself, it is important to note the considerations regarding the possibility of generalization based on this method (Pal, 2005). However, as emphasized by researchers using case studies also in the field of policy research, the role of this method is not to provide a sufficient sample for the verification of specific variables. The study, due to its nature, makes it possible to test the validity of some theory, then a researcher is guided by it in the choice of a particular study, or to provide the most complete description of the phenomenon under study (2005). For my study, the aim was not to produce some general knowledge on the level of policy theory, but to understand the process of the implementation of aging policy at the urban level. It was related with the decentralization of aging policy to local levels of governance, so the lowest layers are given the most responsibility for its implementation (Błędowski, 2016b; Buffel & Phillipson, 2018; Buffel & Remillard-Boilard, 2019; Perek-Białas et al., 2006; Theiss, 2012). As there is not much research on how such aging urban policy is implemented (Andreotti & Mingione, 2016a; Błędowski, 2016b; Theiss, 2012, 2017; Urbaniak, 2018), I strive to conduct research that will give a chance to understand it and be able to present a broad picture of the occurring process (Flyvbjerg, 2006).

The use of case studies in policy research is very popular (Pal, 2005). Especially if the focus is on the process of policymaking, and trying to understand its specific outcomes (Hall, 2013). In particular, the method is popular among public policy researchers associated with historical institutionalism, related to the DI I use in this book. Researchers believe that the case study method allows the complexity of the processes that constitute a given policy to be explored, providing the opportunity to capture the context that is so important in this approach. Furthermore, for researchers who recognize politics as an ongoing process that is defined through ideas, discourses and language, the case study is an opportunity to capture these elements, including their use by policy makers. Such an approach will be alien to policy researchers who focus on its effectiveness and the verifiability of expected outcomes, in which case methods such as surveys or structured interviews will be more appropriate (Eckstein, 2000; Pal, 2005; Yin, 1989).

The method presented was chosen for this study because of the possibilities it offers in the context of this research. Firstly, it allows us to explore what the idea of social activity of older people in urban policy is, and secondly, how the process of its implementation takes place, that is, through which ideas and discourses (Schmidt, 2008) it is carried out. The selection of the case study is related to the purpose of the study. In case selection, the researcher may aim to collect as standard a group of cases as possible, to generalize the findings. He or she may also make the selection based on the information needed, arising from the objectives of the study. Then it is not about generalization, but about exploration of the given phenomenon. In my study, the second principle applies. The selection of the case study was dictated precisely by its informative value for understanding the local level of urban aging policy. Besides, in case selection, the researcher may aim to look for the most extreme, diverse, or appropriate for the research area, that is, able to provide the information needed to explore a given research problem; such selection is called paradigmatic. In the research presented in this thesis, the case study selection was based precisely on the inclusion of the most canonical case possible to answer the research problem posed (Flyvbjerg, 2006).

This study on Poznań, Poland's fifth-largest city and the capital of the Wielkopolskie Voivodeship, examines local aging policies and presents theoretical conclusions to improve understanding of city-level governance. Multiple factors impacted the decision to use Poznań as a case study. Initially, it is a city that exemplifies a typical case study, functioning as a model for a medium-sized urban area. During the selection process, I excluded any city that was overly large or located near other major metropolises, as these variables could impact policymaking. Additionally, I discovered that Poznań has a detailed strategy for older persons. It formed the Municipal Council of Older Citizens and the Centre for Older Citizen Initiatives, as well as joined the Age-Friendly Cities Network. As a result, I could conclude that Poznan has the potential to deliver the information I sought. The membership in the Age-Friendly City (AFC) Network was also an essential international context, as I wanted to understand how local-level policy implementation interacts with global concepts. Furthermore, Poznań, as a capital of the Wielkopolskie Voivodeship, has a responsibility in providing policy for older citizens but also a certain level of autonomy in comparison to smaller cities. The study then includes observations, interviews, and supporting materials obtained during data collection and analysis. The following sections describe the various data collection methods, and I conclude with a list of data used in the analysis.

3.2. Data collection

The data used in my research come from the city of Poznań, which is the fifth-largest city in Poland, located in the west of Poland. The city has a surface area of over 260 square kilometers and over 500 thousand citizens. As the capital of the Wielkopolski Voivodeship, it is a place where all local public institutions are based. Poznań, with its old market, museums, monuments, and international fairs, has a broad cultural, educational and business offer. Furthermore, it has also a place for many initiatives toward older citizens. The City Older Citizens Council has been functioning in Poznań since 2007 and serves as an advisory entity to the mayor, intended to raise awareness among city officials on the needs and problems of older people. Every four years, nongovernmental groups nominate the candidates for council, and then select the members through voting. Another public entity is the Older Citizens Initiatives Centre, functioning in Poznań since 2010. It is a municipal organizational unit that, on behalf of the mayor, undertakes initiatives for the welfare of older citizens. Its establishment is linked to Poznań's implementation of the chosen plan for this aim and its inclusion in the network of age-friendly cities.

Alongside municipal institutions, numerous older citizens' clubs' function in Poznań, situated in various neighborhoods of the city. They are operated either by NGOs or by older individuals themselves; however, their legal status remains ambiguous; for instance, they are ineligible to seek funding for municipal projects. NGOs, foundations, and local community initiative centers also plan activities for older people, as one of their main target groups. Activities for older citizens are also organized by public institutions, like museums, universities, and libraries. Moreover, private sector organizations engage in initiatives aimed at older individuals too, usually through activities that are established by municipal units. For example, the Senior Gold Card, Senior-Friendly Places, and the Viva Senior! Fair.[9] As a part of these programs, private businesses such as movie theaters, cafes, swimming pools, retail stores, and travel agencies create special deals for older citizens.

---

9 I purposefully keep the original nomenclature, which includes the word "senior." It has been introduced from English into Polish policy discourse as a term used to refer to older people.

The collected data came from various organizations and institutions. In some of these organizations, I conducted observations during social activity events that were aimed at older adults. I followed and observed social activity events that were organized for older people in the city from February to December 2019. The event was understood as any form of gathering for older people published in newsletters, on social media, or advertised[10] on outdoor posters. The primary source of this information was the Internet, which I used to search for events. I was checking the agendas of major cultural institutions (such as museums, cinemas, and others); a comprehensive source was also in the material provided to older citizens by the Centre for Older Citizens. Simultaneously with this period of participatory observation, I conducted interviews with people engaged in organizations of social activity events, which were held from April 2019 to June 2020. Another group of data consists of materials and bodies of documents created by city halls, organizations, and other government-level institutions. This group of data was collected along with the observations and interview process, and once again during the analysis process, additional materials and documents emerged as important for the research. Different data sources are a common research technique called data triangulation.[11] It is aimed at capturing researched phenomena from as many different perspectives as possible (Flick, 2018). There are three reasons for that. First, it allows seeing the social activity of older people in Poznan from different angles, which could complement and allow obtaining realities of social activity. Second, mixing the data sources helps to better understand how these various realities intersect with each other and influence the enactment of the studied policy. Third, the aim of obtaining data from diversified sources is important to get comprehensive expert knowledge within a single case study (Pal, 2005).

---

10 The sources of information were Facebook profiles of nongovernmental organizations, the city's website (<https://www.poznan.pl>), The Centre for Older Citizens website (<https://centrumis.pl>).

11 Data triangulation is a methodological strategy designed to offer a more comprehensive research perspective. It is highly beneficial in qualitative research. Data triangulation refers to the collection of data through many procedures, including observation, interviews, visual materials, or alternative methods. This research methodology yields data from multiple viewpoints regarding the studied phenomenon (Flick, 2018).

I offer the collected data in the following table, illustrating its context. I acquired access to the data by reaching out to specific organizations, groups, or individuals. Typically, it involved email or telephone communication, accompanied by a request for an interview. During multiple interviews, I used the relationships of my interlocutors, who facilitated introductions to those engaged in aging services inside the city. The concluding phase of data collecting coincided with the onset of the COVID-19 epidemic, necessitating that certain interviews be completed remotely by telephone or online platforms. Additional materials were acquired during observations when I collected booklets or brochures targeted at older persons. Additionally, certain materials persisted in the analysis following the interview. Because the interviewees mentioned them, for instance: *Act of April 24, 2003 on public benefit activity and voluntary work* or *An offer for the realisation of a public task submitted by the Polish Association of the Blind—Wielkopolska Voivodship and its Older Citizens' Club Hillary*. The more extensive description of collected data can be found in Appendix 1. The gathered data comprised 229 pages of transcriptions, observational field notes, and documents, in addition to 82 pages of visual resources, including booklets, brochures, and images.

Table 8: Collected data

Entity \ *Data type*	**Interview**	**Observation**	**Additional materials**
National Government			Act on public benefit activity and voluntary work.
City Hall			· Declaration on cooperation of presidents in the field of older citizen policy · Older Citizens' Policy of the City of Poznan for 2017–2021
			· Announcement of the open competition · Report · An offer for the realization of a public task

Entity \ *Data type*	Interview	Observation	Additional materials
The Centre for Older Citizens' Initiatives (Public Institution)	2	Meeting "KAWKA"	· Organizational Regulations · Older citizen package · Program of Older Citizen Days
Porta Posnania ICHOT (museum)	1	Guided tours for older people	· Statutes
The Museum of Applied Arts	1	Guided tour for older people	
The Flandria Foundation (NGOs)	1		
The Green Group (NGOs and the Centre for Local Initiatives)	1		
The Mill of Support Foundation (NGOs)	1		
The Municipal Council of Older Citizens	1	The monthly meeting	
The Silver Years Foundation and Older Citizen Club (NGOs)	1		
The Municipal Centre for Family Support (Public Institutions)	1		
NGOs (anonymous)	1		
Older Citizens' Club	2	City forum of older citizens clubs	
The Polish Tourist and Sightseeing Society (association)		Excursion for older citizen citizens	

(Continued)

Table 8: *(Continued)*

Entity / *Data type*	Interview	Observation	Additional materials
VIVA Older citizen Fair (event)		One day participation	· Report of Older Citizens' Club Astra · Leaflets
Poznan Adam Mickiewicz University		The debate of generations	

Source: Own elaboration.

Observation

Before the data collection process a set up certain selection criteria for observations. The process of data collection was designed to follow events of social activity geared toward older people. To gather a diversified group of observations, the inclusion criteria of observed events for the research were open, meaning that I followed events organized by various types of organizations as long as they were directed to older citizens. However, I decided to exclude events focused on health promotion or physical activity from the analysis, as their overall aim was to influence the health of older people, whereas the focus of this research was to examine activities intended for social activities of older people. Furthermore, during observation and interviews, I aimed to collect data from various types of organizations and people. In the result my knowledge comes from municipal and cultural institutions, university, the third-sector organizations, older citizens clubs, local council, The Municipal Council of Older Citizens or city fairs.

Observation is a way of capturing the dynamics of interaction between specific actors in the study, and possibly noticing additional actors relevant to the phenomenon under study. By means of this method, researchers try to capture the space in which the observation takes place, its characteristics, which may possibly co-shape the studied phenomenon, but also its influence on people in it. It is also obvious to focus on the actors who take part in the observed situation, what actions they undertake and what objects accompany them. Within the framework of observation, the researcher may try to group activities which together form concrete measures and then events.

Other elements to be considered in the observation are the time, that is the sequence of the action, and the goals of the actors. Moreover, the researcher can take into account his or her own emotions and feelings related to the observed situation (Bratich, 2017; Ciesielska et al., 2012).

Within the different kinds of observation, we can distinguish several types due to the attitude of the observer to the situation under study:

- Direct participant observation—most characteristic of ethnographic research, where the researcher becomes totally involved in the given environment, e.g., being employed in the researched organization or living with convicted minors. It is a form of observation that requires great commitment and time from the researcher. However, it makes it possible to obtain very detailed information which is difficult to grasp by an ordinary observer. A special case of such observation is when the researcher does not reveal his or her identity, but becomes one of the subjects, in which case access to information is even more detailed.
- Direct non-participant observation—the researcher is an eyewitness but does not become involved in the situation being observed. The researcher can then take on the role of an observer who properly blends into the background and tries to be unnoticeable to those involved in the situation to capture as much of its ordinary course as possible. He or she may also interact with the people being observed, asking them questions about their actions and behavior while they are still being observed.
- Indirect observation—the researcher collects information about a given situation indirectly, using a hidden camera or dictaphone, or using available materials documenting the situation, for example, archive recordings or available databases of recordings from webcams (Ciesielska et al., 2012; Hammersley & Atkinson, 2000).

In practice it is difficult to distinguish those types of observation, as they often occur in combination. A mass observation can consist of two types, for example, when one researcher is actively participating in some event and conducting direct participant observation, while other researchers only observe the event and make direct non-participants observation. During my research I also came across two types of observations (the full list of observations and their descriptions are presented in the Appendix 1.). Namely, when I was attending events organized for older people, which were aimed at their social activity, it happened that I also was a participant in such an event, for example, during a museum tour or a tour of the old market. Another time, I was just observing older people sitting together and making paper decorations during a special event.

Observation is very particular method, in comparison to other qualitative ones, as a researcher has very little control over the studied situations, and he or she must be flexible to unexpected situations and be able to react if necessary (Bratich, 2017; Ciesielska et al., 2012). Within the observation, the researcher takes field notes that are later included into the data. Thus, they need to comprise as much information as possible regarding the situation, but also additional observation and reflection made by the researcher during and after the observation. Apart from the field notes, observation can bring also additional materials related to organized events or to the institution organizing it, such as leaflets or posters (2012).

Interview

Another data collection method used in case study strategies is the interview. It is a method used by researchers coming from both positivist and interpretivist approaches. However, the difference lies in what researchers expect. In the case of the former approach, the researcher is compared to a miner who digs out valuable stones and must separate them from the less valuable ones. This can be understood as the researcher's quest to discover objective facts. In the interpretative approach, the researcher, in contrast, is identified with a traveler who explores new territories and tries to learn about them from the perspective of the people who live there. In the same way, during the research, the person collecting the data is open to everything that happens and that he or she encounters, and pays particular attention to how the world is created by the world under study (Gudkova, 2012; Kvale, 2010). Thus, the purpose of the interview in qualitative research is to understand the perspective of the people we are studying, to understand the meanings they use, creating their reality. The researcher retains a certain sensitivity to emerging themes and is flexible about the themes explored, as new themes may emerge during the course of the research which the researcher had not previously assumed (Kvale, 2010).

Within this method of data collection there a several types of interviews. Firstly, a distinction is made between standardized and non-standardized interviews based on the order in which the questions are asked. In the latter case, the interview is loosely structured, there is a script of questions, but it is more of a support for the researcher, telling him what thematic areas he wants to cover in the research (Gudkova, 2012; Silverman, 2007). We then distinguish between structured and unstructured interviews, which differ in terms of the questions asked. The latter, otherwise known as free-form, refers to interviews that use open-ended questions with phrases such as "why" or "how." A structured interview, on the other hand, will consist of closed-ended questions, where the form of the answer is restricted, e.g., "How many times a year do you go to the cinema?" (Gudkova, 2012).

Unstructured and non-standardized interviews are often used in qualitative research, especially those of an exploratory nature, as they allow the researcher to explore the understanding of certain facts and actions from the perspective of the individual's experiences. The interview script may then be just an outline of the general topics the researcher will want to address, or the questions proposed. However, the aim will be to obtain information of interest in relation to the problem under investigation, so it will not be necessary for the interview to be in a strictly prescribed form, but rather to give the researcher the opportunity to explore the perspective of the person they are talking to (Silverman, 2007).

The interview used in this study can be described as unstructured and non-standardized. The interviews were usually combined with my observations, that is, during the observation process I also tried to talk to people who were involved in running the events I was following. To supplement the data, I also conducted follow-up interviews to gain as much knowledge as possible about the activities carried out in Poznan to promote social participation of older people. The choice of people to interview was linked to events I came across during my research. The purpose of the interviews was to talk to people involved in the organization of events related to social activity for older people. Some of my interlocutors were also organizers of the events I observed (museum employees, The Centre for Older Citizens' Initiatives employees, the founder of the Mill of Support Foundation), and the remaining group consisted of people involved in activities for older people within NGOs, the City Council for Older Citizens, or an informal group. I wanted to include in my group of interviewees people with the widest possible range of experience, that is, people working in public institutions, in the third sector, activists or activists of informal groups such as Older Citizens' Clubs. The interview schedule was based on pre-prepared questions related to a given person's activities for older people or concerned a specific event I had observed. The following are sample questions that formed the script for the interviews. However, their content was revised depending on the interviewee and what he or she told (Gudkova, 2012):

1. I wanted to talk about these events that you are organizing for older people, I understand that you are the person who does this. Could I ask who came up with the idea for these events or why do you organize them at all?
2. How does it work in general, the very process of organizing these events, coming up with this idea and so on?
3. And do I understand correctly that the fact that you are doing something for older people is due to the kind of organization you are?
4. Apart from the strategy and consultation, what else inspires you in your activities for older people?

The collected interviews in the form of transcriptions were included in the data, as were field notes from observations.

During the study's interviews, I engaged with persons possessing diverse levels of responsibility and roles. Consequently, the interview script varied among participants. In the interview with the director of Citizen Initiatives (CIS), the inquiries focused on the center's comprehensive programs for older people, older citizens' clubs, and collaboration with private companies and NGOs. In the instance of the employee from The Municipal Centre for Family Support, the inquiries pertained to her experiences collaborating with local older citizens clubs and their integration within the specified territory. Consequently, formulating the interview script necessitated the creation of multiple question sets tailored to the interviewee. In Appendix 2 I present the full range of questions.

Additional materials

The last group of data used in the research were documents and additional materials. In research, the introduction of such additional materials allows us to extend the scope of the study and include areas that are difficult to reach or concern events that have already taken place. Such data may include formal documents such as official regulations, laws, or agreements, but also informal documents such as sketches or diaries. The use of documents can have a variety of applications:

- it can be used to create a research problem,
- deeper exploration of the phenomenon under study, and
- explaining a phenomenon (Łuczewski & Bednarz-Łuczewska, 2012).

It is precisely in the analysis of policy and public action that documents are particularly relevant, as their content is precisely about policy regulation. The study of documents, for example, strategy documents (Rémillard-Boilard et al., 2020; van Hoof et al., 2018), policy documents (Sun et al., 2017), city hall documents (Kotus, 2013), is also popular in urban policy research on aging. As in other studies, formal and informal documents (see Appendix 1) were included in the study to deepen the understanding of the studied problem, but also according to the applied ANT, they were considered as actors who could take part in policymaking and thus their inclusion allows for a better explanation of the studied problem

3.3. Data analysis

In this section, I will show how the analytical framework presented previously was translated into the process of analysis. The detailed outlines the process of analysis, highlighting the use of specific analytical concepts within each stage, is in answering attached in the Appendix 3.

Data analysis was based on content analysis, which is a qualitative method for research analysis (Julien, 2008; R. P. Weber, 1990). It is an iterative process, consisting of multiple data readings and its reorganization with codes and categories established within the applied theoretical framework (Julien, 2008). This qualitative strategy allowed me to recognize content of my data. The aim of the conducted analysis was to approach collected data with a constructed analytical framework, namely ANT, and the concept of glocalization. (Adu, 2019). The content analysis is, in comparison to other strategies used within qualitative studies, not related to any specific theoretical framework. That is why its application is recommended if a researcher wants to use earlier established theoretical assumption toward the study, which is the case within this work (Hsieh & Shannon, 2005; Yin, 1989).

The qualitative approach to data analysis that I use in this thesis means that the research focuses on the search for meanings and perceptions of phenomena attributed by people. The qualitative approach undertakes interpretative practices to discover and understand the phenomenon under study, paying particular attention to the categories used by the respondents themselves (Denzin & Lincoln, 2017). This research approach derives from the tenets of phenomenology, developed by E. Husserl and further developed by A. Schutz, who found particular value in researching the process of constructing a given phenomenon by the individuals involved individuals. The idea was to avoid imposing assumptions on the observer (researcher) that may consequently not reflect the reality we are dealing with (J. A. Holstein & Gubrium, 2005). Such an approach toward data is in line with this book's research aims and literature recommendation. I strived to understand what older people's activities implemented in Poznan is and further how it is implemented within urban aging policy there. The answers for these questions fit the need for further research of urban aging policies, which accordingly to scholars, should be explored within its complexity and diversity of actors (Andreotti & Mingione, 2016a; Buffel & Remillard-Boilard, 2019; Kutsar & Kuronen, 2015a; Rémillard-Boilard et al., 2020; Theiss, 2012). Therefore, qualitative analysis application seems to respond to those requirements.

Content analysis is an analysis strategy that can be used with a wide range of data, for example, interview transcripts, observations, photographs, documents, etc. The main assumption of to reorganize data within established codes and later broader categories (Julien, 2008). The Final result, can be described as "aboutness" of text, meaning it gives the researcher information on data interpretation and meaning found there (2008). To achieve it I needed to establish codes and categories that helped me understand the data

Coding process and category building

The following figure illustrates the coding process in relation to analytical categories drawn from ANT and the concept of glocalization.

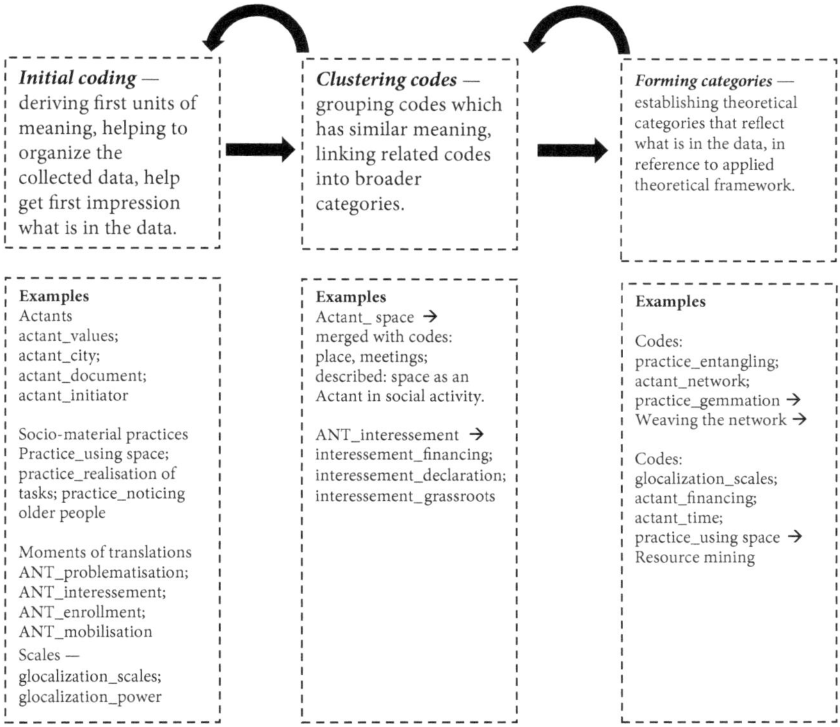

Figure 5: Coding process and applied codes.

The three stages of coding were applied, and it is important to reiterate that the coding process was an iterative one, which is marked with the black arrows over the coding stages on the scheme. It means that while coding a part of data with initial codes and moving to the next steps, namely clustering, I happened to go back again to the initial coding. This repeatability of coding process stemmed from the need for data saturation. This term describes the moment in the process of qualitative data analysis, when a researcher finds his/her categories, describing the studied phenomenon, comprehensive. This means that adding new data will not change the results, and the created category descriptions and recognized relationships between them allow the results to be presented (Creswell, 2007; Silverman, 2007). Hence, when the researcher finds some category incomplete, he or she goes backward to search for missing information or maybe an error in interpretations made earlier. To help with data saturation, qualitative scholars do data triangulations, which in the case of my study, consisted of collecting wide types of data, coming from diversified sources as well as deep and multiple data readings (Julien, 2008).

Within each stage of coding, I strived to understand the idea of social activity for older people, applying established theoretical framework. Thus, at the first stage I searched for actants, socio-material practices, and moments of translations (Callon & Latour, 1981; Latour, 2005a; Law, 2008). In reference to ANT I aimed to understand what human and nonhuman objects take part in enactment of the studied idea. The aim was to see what elements form the networks, which are a performative construct, weaving reality (Latour, 2005a). Apart from actants, networks are formed with translation processes, which consist of aggregation of actants striving to achieve a common goal. The engagement of actants in the translation process is divided into four moments: problematization, interessement, enrollment and mobilization (Callon & Latour, 1981). The first one refers to problem definition, which induces actants to enter the network. Within interessement, in turn, actants present their interests and check if they can be fulfilled with this network. The next step is the enrollment, which leads to achieving the common goal. Finally, within mobilization, if the assumed aims and actions became performed by actants, the network endures further and in the result form new elements of reality (Callon & Latour, 2015; Galis, 2011). As the result of network weaving, ANT's scholars speak about socio-material practices, which became a broader concept. Practice describes how things are done and hence how reality occurs. Practices are weaved with networks (Law, 2008, 2019). As it can be seen in the analytical process, I strive to find mentioned elements of ANT framework to understand and get an expertise knowledge of the social activity for older people, enacted in Poznan. In the final stage of coding process, I move one step further and attempted to trace the implementation process, thus I applied one more ANT term: ontology (Mol, 2002). This construction was introduced by A. Mol (2002) in her research of atherosclerosis, in which she strived to understand how the disease was enacted by medical practices. Within different ontologies, she demonstrated various realities of the disease. Each of them was separate, but at the same time all of them co-created the studied phenomenon. Ontology, thus, is the construction, which allows us to see how various realities, with distinct values and practices, can weave a single phenomenon. It was also used in other research on policymaking (Galis, 2011), when researchers aimed to see the influence of policy formulation on experience of disability. Seemingly in my study with ontologies, I strived to illustrate how different realities enacted the same idea, framing it with different values and practices. I also propose this construction as a counterpart to the term discourse, which is an element of DI (for full explanation of DI, see Section 1.3. The idea and the process of policy implementation). Discourse is, along with ideas, a mean of policy formation, encompasses ideas in various forms and reciprocal processes throughout which ideas are conveyed (Schmidt, 2008).

Simultaneously to coding within ANT framework, I also applied codes within the glocalization concept. As it can be seen in Figure 5, within initial coding I aimed to identify scales and the indication of power one actants over others. Scales are elements of the glocalization concept widespread in policy research (Swyngedouw, 2005; Szulecki, 2011; Wathen, 2020). Glocalization within my research is understood as the rolling of the state, upward to the international organization and downward to the local level of governance as a result of globalization (Cox, 2009; Swyngedouw, 1996, 2005). Scales, in turn, are elements which allow us to capture these shifting directions of policy formations on the local level, which become significant as an outcome of welfare decentralization (Andreotti & Mingione, 2016a; Kutsar & Kuronen, 2015a). They are represented in the data with dominant values and leading actants (Wathen, 2020). The searched scales were in the next steps divided accordingly to common values and dominant actants. In the final stage, I strove to retrace the politics of scale, which describe how studied policy implementation can be described in reference to international and local forces (Swyngedouw, 1997). This element of glocalization was an additional theoretical framework aimed at considering the decentralization process within aging policy, which pose a new set of relations, far from well-known vertical governance (Kutsar & Kuronen, 2015a). While establishing codes of glocalization concept, I also used codes from ANT framework, such as actant_values, actant_assumption or practices_using space, as they provided an additional explanation to emerging from data scales.

The data analysis comes to an end when created categories are saturated. It means that when the researcher goes through the data, he or she does not find any new relevant information regarding research phenomenon and established categories (saturation). To achieve it, and also the validity and reliability of the study, research can do data triangulations (Flick, 2017). It can be carried out in two ways—to pass the data to a second researcher for analysis, or to include data of a different nature in the analysis, such as interviews, documents, or photographs. In my study, the saturation of the categories created, as well as their reliability and validity, was ensured by triangulating the data, consisting of interviews, field notes of observations, and documents collected during the observations and included during the analysis. Moreover, during the process of data collection and analysis I consulted the collected material and the emerging codes and categories with other researchers in order to triangulate the data and confirm the validity of the categories I created (Flick, 2017).

The coding process in my study was enhanced with preformed concepts, which stemmed from ANT and the concept of glocalization. The following table describes their use at successive stages of coding. As it was written, the coding process was iterative, which means that I started coding with small number of codes that had broad description and later on I came back to data a few times to develop sequential codes, built categories and establish relations. This work was partially done within notebooks, which served as place for code descriptions and development of theoretical categories and patterns (Latour, 2005a, p. 134).

The code types presented in Table 9, on the left, and the specific activities performed in my data analysis, on the right, are a simplified representation of the analysis process. As part of the coding process itself, I went back to the data several times to verify the codes I had created and to describe the dependencies between them. I started my analysis with broad codes to help me group the data, which contained overlapping translation processes. Isolating practices, actants and scales allowed me to navigate through quite large fragments of data. However, only re-coding these areas with more detailed codes provided me with better information about the process of translation between actors (practices à practice_using space), the ways in which they engage in relationships, that is, practices, as well as first indications of how relationships between actors are perceived, what the local and global level is in a given urban aging policy. The codes and categories I obtained, in turn, allowed me to understand what the social activity of older people in Poznan is, that is, how it is constructed by acting people, institutions, binding documents or other objects. At a further stage I was able to see ontologies, that is, dominant narratives, as well as scales, understood as a reflection of dependencies between actors, involved in the implementation of the idea itself. The results of the analysis are presented in the next two empirical chapters.

Table 9: The applied codes and categories during data analysis

	Applied codes
Initial codes—first units of meaning, helping to organize the collected data. Those are *working* units of meaning, which help get first impression what is in the data.	Actor-network theory code: **Actants**—human and nonhuman objects, which together create the network and thus the phenomenon. actant_values; actant_city; actant_document; actant_initiator **Socio-material practice**—the way of doing something, engaging in specific action. Practice_using space; practice_realisation of tasks; practice_noticing older people **Moments of translations**—problematization, interessement, enrollment and mobilization. Glocalization codes **scales**—moments in the text which refers to relations between actants and their mutual interdependency glocalization_scales
Clustering codes—grouping codes which has similar meaning, linking related codes into broader categories.	ANT - Elimination of redundant codes, which had not appeared once. - Grouping codes into broader codes and describing it: Actant_space à merged with codes: place, meetings; described: space as an actor in social activity. - Iterative coding within moment of translations, to obtain more detailed and context dependent codes: ANT_interessement à interessement_financing; interessement_declaration; interessement_ grassroots - Describing codes and relation between them

(Continued)

Table 9: (*Continued*)

	Applied codes
	Glocalization – Iterative coding within scales to find categories describing their relations and elements Scales à values; assumptions, interests, network – Applying codes developed within ANT, which are significant for glocalization concept—actant_documents, practice_ taking over, etc. – Describing codes and relations between them
Categories—are ready-made theoretical categories that link the information found in the data with the theories applied by the researcher, through which the results themselves are presented.	– Combining codes into categories which describe enactment of older people's social activity, based on identified moments of translations and engaged in it actants, such as reason for problematization described interests (actant_ finincing, actant_programme), associations (interessement_membership; actant_document), coming ahead, or reasons comes by themselves. – Forming ontologies—which are sites of social activity and describe realities of its enactment and implementation – Weaving the network à practice_weaving; actant_network; practice_gemmation – Building scales of older people social activity implementation Resource mining à glocalization_scales; actant_ financing; actant_time; practice_using space

Source: Own elaboration.

Results and conclusions

The conceptual and theoretical framework presented earlier was intended to situate my study within academic fields such as gerontology, social policy, urban policy, and DI. Discovering each of them, I unveiled the complexity of the research problem and point to premises for theoretical framework. The latter, in turn, provided analytical guidance for answering the posed research questions, by conducting case study research and analyzing it with ANT and the glocalization concept. Therefore, in this chapter I will present the results of my study. In Section 4.1—Social activity enacted—how does social activity happen in Poznan?—I introduce the first part of my findings, answering the question what social activity for older people is in Poznan. How it is perceived and formed by actants[12] as well as what influences its enactment. The understanding of this phenomenon is an introduction to the next sections— 4.2 Ontologies of social activity implementation and 4.3. Scales of Social activity Implementation, where I describe urban aging policy implementation, within two constructs, namely ontology and scale; the first is an element of ANT and the latter refers to the glocalization concept.

I have included the following list of the documents cited in this chapter. Each cited document has the designations that identify them, that is, [Dx]. This is not a complete list of the sources I used. A list of all materials: interviews, field notes, photographs, and additional materials can be found in Appendix 1 or in Section 3.2—Data collection.

12 Actants is word I use to describe human and nonhuman actors identified in my data. The term comes from actor-network theory (Latour, 2005b, p. 71).

List of citied documents:

D1 — First interview with a worker of the Centre for Older Citizens' Initiatives

D2 — Interview with the Director of the Centre for Older Citizens Initiatives.

D3 — Interview with a museum worker at Porta Posnania ICHOT.

D4 — Interview with a museum worker at The Museum of Applied Arts.

D5 — Interview with the foundation worker (interview granted anonymously).

D6 — Second interview with a worker at the Centre for Older Citizens' Initiatives.

D7 — Interview with a worker at the Flandria Foundation.

D8 — Interview with the founder of the Green Group (NGOs and the leader of the Centre for Local Initiatives).

D9 — Interview with the founder of The Mill of Support Foundation.

D10 — Interview with a member of The Municipal Council of Older Citizens.

D11 — Interview with the founders of the Silver Years Foundation and Older Citizen Club.

D12 — Interview with a worker at the Municipal Centre for Family Support.

D13 — The interview with older citizen activists.

D14 — Older Citizens' Policy of the City of Poznan for 2017–2021.

D15 — Program of Older Citizen Days.

D16 — Declaration on cooperation of presidents in the field of older citizen policy.

D17 — Announcement of the open competition No. 45/2021 for assigning the tasks of the City of Poznan in the area of activity for people of retirement age.

D18 — Act of April 24, 2003 on public benefit activity and voluntary work.

D19 — Report on the implementation of the annual program of cooperation with NGOs in Poznan for the year 2020.

D20 — The report on the activities of the Older Citizens Club Astra in the local newspaper of the Kiekrz district.

D21 — An offer for the realization of a public task submitted by the Polish Association of the Blind—Wielkopolska Voivodship and its Older Citizens' Club Hillary.

Furthermore, I attach Table 10, which includes names of institutions, organizations, or events used in this chapter.

Table 10: The names used in the empirical chapters

Polish name	English name	Applied shortcut	Description
Centrum Inicjatyw Senioralnych	The Centre for Older Citizens' Initiatives	CIS	The municipal institutions, called by the president and city board, which is responsible for realization of policy for older citizens.
Centrum Inicjatyw Lokalnych	The Centre for Local Initiatives	CIL	The program formed by the city but carried out by nongovernmental organizations. The aim is to animate local communities within city districts.
Organizowanie Społeczności Lokalnych	Animation of Local Communities	OSL	The method is applied by CIL. It underlines the need for self-organization of local communities. The emphasis is put on available within community human, social, and material resources.
Targi Viva Senior!	VIVA Older Citizens Fairs!		Annual event organized by the city and voivodship in the space of city fairs. The exhibitors are organization from private and third sectors acting for older people.
Klub Seniora	Older Citizens Clubs		Those are formal (when established within some organization or company) or informal groups of older people, who meet regularly. Older Citizens Clubs are formed based on members' district, but not necessarily. They are also established by nongovernmental organization or parishes and then gather older citizens from various parts of the city.
Miejska Rada Seniorów	The Municipal Council of Older Citizens		The council called every four years in the by vote. The elected representatives represent both the city and NGOs working for older people. The Council is an advisory body.

(Continued)

Table 10: *(Continued)*

Polish name	English name	Applied shortcut	Description
Tytka Seniora	Older Citizens Package		A form of newsletter published by CIS, collecting information on all events in the city.
Miejsca Przyjazne Seniorom	Older Citizens-Friendly Spaces		A program created by CIS to identify age-friendly places—restaurants, cinemas, cultural institutions, shops. The program has a program board and describes criteria that must be met to obtain the title.
Senioralni	Older Citizens' month		An annual event inspired by the Students' Days. It includes a month-long series of events for older residents, usually in October.

4.1. Social activity enacted—how does social activity happen in Poznan?

In this section, I want to present four phases of social activity enactment, as stages of the translation process, applied from ANT (Callon & Latour, 2015). In the course of this research, it was impossible to distinguish one smooth translation process. Moreover, social activities were not enacted by a strictly delineated group of actants, but rather constantly reassembling networks of them (Latour, 2005a; Mol, 2002). Instead, I attempted to find moments in social activity enactment which could provide an understanding of older people social activity in Poznan and appeared to be an important point on a map of social activity implementation, serving as its explanation. Table 11 demonstrates moments of translation and the respective sections describing them.

In reference to an earlier described (see Section 1.3—The idea and the process of policy implementation) level of abstraction in policy formation, which are *policy solutions*, *policy definitions* and *public philosophies* (Mehta, 2011), in this section I tried to unveil public philosophies, maybe sometimes unconsciously hidden behind actant actions, which push them to implement social activity for older people.

Table 11: Moments of translation

Definition	The moment of translation	Section
In this stage actants of the network are identified and their interests are being formed	PROBLEMATIZATION	*III.1.1. Why do you care?* *Interests* *Obligations* *Measures* *Reasons comes by themselves*
Actants are *locked in* the network of social activity, within declared identities and goals and become indispensable for each other.	INTERESSEMENT	*III.1.2. Entering the network.* *Looking for the support* *In search of sites* *Positioning* *Casting the net*
The ways in which actants are assigned to previously declared roles.	ENROLLMENT	*III.1.3. Vehicles of social activity.* *Seduction* *Engaged social activity* *Commission to actants* *To kill two birds with one stone*
The emergence of new elements from the network.	MOBILISATION	*III.1.4. Desired product.* *Life full of events* *Acting for others* *Endurance of relations* *Proliferation of networks*

Source: Callon and Latour (1981b), Galis (2011), and Po-An Hsieh et al. (2012).

4.1.1. Why do you care?

During my research, I managed to observe and attend a quite differentiated group of events, carried out by various public entities, such as NGOs, older citizen clubs, private enterprises, or public institutions. Along this process, I tried to find a starting point for actants to join a network, the thread, which would lead me to other actants engaged in the network and further sequential moments of translations. So, the question in the section's title - *Why do you care?* - places actants enacting social activity on different endings of these threads, which together form a starting point for enactment of the social activity for older people. In the next four sections, I will therefore describe the reasons why the actants decided to join the network. I will start with *Interests*, which refer to the possibility that the actants see in the social activity of older people to realize their own benefits. Then I will refer to *Obligations*, which, contained in the documents, push the actants to act. In the next section—*Measures*—I will present the actants' involvement in creating social activity as a way to counteract the crisis of aging. In the last section, *Reasons come by themselves*, I will draw attention to the issue of grassroots activism initiated by older people themselves.

Interests

The emergence of social activity is related to the desire of the actants for alliances and their identity that trigger them to weave into the network. In some cases, the social activity of older people appears to be valuable from the perspective of their functioning. Taking part in social activity seems lucrative for them and they see it as an engagement that can bring profit.

Such perspective was mentioned by the director of the Centre for Older CIS who talked about cooperation with private companies, which have come forward to participate:

> Most companies that have an interest like this do a bit of CSR (Corporate Social Responsibility), a bit of promotion, and a bit of selling their services. I don't see anything wrong with that so that older peoples can benefit, but it must be clear, fair, and transparent. […] The business needs sales, some CSR, some promotion, some attention to the needs of older peoples to create a product tailored to them. [D2]

In saying so, the director explained the presence of private enterprises as their partners in organization of social activity for older people. The firms' interest is to reach their potential older customers, but also their friends and relatives and in exchange donate some money for actions, which could be a response to older people's needs. Yet, the idea of CSR is not purely promotional, as it is supposed to impose the social duty on large companies and give them a chance to redeem themselves if their actions contributed to some social inequalities or harm (Latapí Agudelo et al., 2019). However, it is also known that CSR serves as a good tool for promotion (Freitag, 2008; Mullerat, 2009). The firm, which supports social ventures, presents itself as sensible and responsible, builds a positive organizational image, and as a result, attracts more customers.

Furthermore, as it was mentioned by CIS director and was also visible during my observations at *VIVA Older Citizen Fairs!* the private entrepreneurs participate in the social activity of older citizens, as they make up most of their customers. In this sense, the social participation of older people is somehow used to establish a consumer-producer relation and as mentioned by the director, adjust the offer to specific needs of older customers.

Photograph 1: Halls of VIVA Older Citizens Fairs. Visitors marching from stall to stall, established by firms, travel agencies, public bodies or non-governmental organisations.

Source: Private collection.

Photograph 2: Leaflet from a company offering gas valves recommended for use in the homes of dependent people with memory impairments.

Source: Private collection.

The aforementioned leaflet shows a company specializing in products dedicated to older people, specifically to their caretakers. The product addresses the issue of memory problems among some older people. The company offers safe gas valves to be installed in homes of older people. The social activity at a trade fair for older people is therefore used by the company as an opportunity to meet potential customers.

The private sector is not the only one interested in the social activity of older people. During the fairs and while interviewing, I came across NGOs and public entities expressing a similar desire to ally themselves with older people, among. It seems that having activities for older people in their offer they also strive to attract an audience. When talking to museum staff and trying to see the moment when they engage in the network, I also observed that social activity is a chance for promotion for them.

The following is an excerpt from a conversation about the involvement of the Museum of Applied Arts in Poznan in the Older People month program organized by the city:

> **Interviewer:** They (representatives of the city) are encouraging you to take part in this event (Older Citizens month), yes?
>
> **Expert:** Yes. Each year, they collect a proposal from various institutions and organizations. They announce a deadline, and then they collect proposals. [...]
>
> **I:** And why do you decide to do it?
>
> **E:** Because, first of all, we are open to various initiatives and we know that we can also attract new viewers, who may not otherwise come to the museum, and then they come and experience something nice here, see the interiors, and they will want to come back and attend other meetings. [D4]

It was also true for the worker from another museum, with whom I talked:

> That is, we generally assumed that we wanted to create an offer for very different audiences, which is why we wanted to create an offer for older peoples. [D3]

The social activity of older people is a chance for these places to carry out their mission. It takes the form of museum tours, educational workshops, or thematic lectures. Older visitors through their activity ally with museums in realizing their aims, namely, to disseminate cultural heritage and knowledge of humankind development. It is worth mentioning that although museum workers use the word *offer*, their services are free of charge, funded by the city budget or appropriate ministry.

By and large, both private and public entities use social events for older people to develop their activities. For the private sector, social activity for older people provides an opportunity to attract a wider range of customers or to promote a positive image of themselves through their involvement in activities for older people. For cultural institutions, in turn, it is also a promotional tool, but one aimed at fulfilling the institution's mission. In both cases, we are dealing with the involvement of these actants in social activity because of the possible benefits. In the case of the private sector, these benefits include increased profits from new customers. For cultural institutions, on the other hand, it is the possibility to fulfill their mission and gain popularity among different groups of citizens.

Obligations

Another element, prompting an actant to be interested in the implementation of social activity for older people, is the idea's proximity to the actant's mission:

> **I:** So, it is a bit like these activities for older peoples are a part of the idea of the foundation itself?
>
> **E:** Yes, yes, absolutely, it has to be embedded in that, well that is the first thing that it has to be consistent. [D5]

From this statement, the social activity for older people to be enacted needs to be put somehow in regulatory documents of organization from the second and third sector as their actions are determined with organizations' statutes. Such a trigger for this man, a foundation leader, is the mission of his organization, which involves him into the sequential networks of actions. One more example comes from the Porta Posnania Museum:

> This also stems from the nature of the institution, because since we are in the field of interpreting heritage, bringing it closer, and helping people to experience it personally, we need to find ways of doing this. And education is a very good way to do it, because we can use various forms and methods of work and adapt them to particular groups, their needs and interests, and also adapt them so that learning about heritage is a pleasure and is also fun. So, education is very important here. [D3]

This quotation shows that the social activity of older people can emerge as an emanation of an entity's mission. For this museum worker, participation in social activity was a way to execute strategies present within the museum. Furthermore, there can be other documents than statues, which weave actants into the network of actions. The following two examples demonstrate threads involving the city of Poznan into social activity implementation.

> For example, there was a document entitled "Social Policy for the City of Poznan," in which older peoples were strongly emphasised. Then there was the strategy for solving social problems, then older peoples were included in the city development strategy, etc. But we needed a new, up-to-date document, and based on the fact that we are a network of Ageing Friendly Cities, based on their experience and recommendations, the city prepared a separate document. [...] Because the Ageing Friendly Cities programme defines a certain course of action and indicates certain things that we should do. It is divided just like the WHO guide. [D2]

Another extract, this time from policy documents:

> The Program 'Older Citizenship Policy of the City of Poznan' for 2017–2021 indicates actions, tasks, and initiatives that shape conditions for a healthy and dignified and healthy ageing. [D14]

Similar to museum statutes, these documents direct action that should be taken, in this example, by local public entities. The obligations embraced in the documents link them with the idea of social activity as one of the ways to execute the city's policy. In addition to their missions and other documents, the actants also refer to the term of a public task, which comes from *the Act of April 24, 2003 on public benefit activity and voluntary work.*[13] It determines the activity of third-sector organizations and names public tasks commissioned to them. An excerpt from the Older Citizens' Club's newsletter reports on events aimed at the social involvement of its members. The activities were carried out by the club as part of a public task delegated to the club for implementation in a tender conducted by the town hall:

> In this year, the club activities were co-financed from the funds of the City of Poznan—two public task projects were delivered, which received support in the competitions of the Department of Health and Social Affairs of the Poznan City Hall. [D20]

---

[13] pl. *Ustawa z dnia 24 kwietnia 2003 r. o działalności pożytku publicznego i o wolontariacie.*

As can be seen in this section, sometimes the reason for getting involved in older people's social activity is an obligation that creates a link between an organization or institution and social activity. Such an obligation may arise from the statutes adopted by the organization, documents created, such as the Older Citizen policy of the City of Poznan. It may also refer to acts regulating e.g., the activity of the third sector, which imposes on them a certain range of tasks, among them the activity for people at the retirement age. As in the previous section, I have pointed out the interests and benefits that drive actants to engage in social activity, I introduce another element, namely obligations that weave organizations and institutions into the network of social activity implementations.

Measures

The sequential elements which bring about the reality of social activity are diagnosis and observations. The city authorities are triggered to take some actions toward older people as the response to worrying prediction of aging societies:

> The city authorities, aware of the challenges that result from the ageing of society, meet the changing needs of older residents and their families by taking various measures aimed at ensuring dignified ageing by improving the quality of life and creating conditions for the professional and social activity of older people. [D16]

The fact that actions of authorities on the state level come from implications and recommendations based on research and expertise concerning society or the economy is not surprising. However, what I want to indicate in this section is that local policymakers see actions toward older people, among them social activity, as a response to the aging problem. If they did not think so, they would not consider undertaking social participation activities. It serves as a justification for designed and planned policy actions:

> Poznan's current demographic situation and projections indicate a need to continue the current plan and take further measures, in particular, to introduce increasingly effective instruments to ensure the best possible living conditions for Poznan's older people citizens. [D14]

These two examples show that at the city level and in emerging documents shaping the city's activities, social activism for older people is emerging as a way of counteracting the effects of an aging society. As a measure it is supposed to foster the creation of a better environment for older people, precisely by creating opportunities for their social activity. Social activity of older people is also used as a response to the aging problem on the lower city levels, namely by foundation, which regularly carries out events for them:

> In another project that we had, I noticed that very often older citizens in older citizens' clubs are not fully integrated, they form groups, subgroups, that if older citizens' clubs have some funding for activities, that is great, but very often they don't, and they don't necessarily know how to make use of the time they have when they meet. [D9]

In the account presented, the foundation worker refers to social activity as a way of addressing the integration problems of older people who form older people's clubs. What I attempted to grasp here by connoting these examples is a different starting point for the implementation of social active aging compared to the previous two sections, where the idea was an element of the organizations' or institution's interest or obligation. This section deals with a different perspective on the implementation of social activity, namely the perspective of aging societies and the individual perspective. Both from a societal and an individual perspective, social participation helps to mitigate the effects of this process, adapting the local environment to be more conducive to social participation of older people or, as in the case of the individual perspective, for whom social participation is a way to integrate and mobilize. These two perspectives of looking at the social activity of older people, that is, social and individual, are common in research on it, and were pointed out by me in an earlier part of the thesis—1.3 Urban Aging. Researchers point out the influence of social activity on individuals' self-satisfaction and stress reduction (Ahmad & Hafeez, 2011; Fu et al., 2018; Ho, 2017a), but also facilitates coping with problems (Pei et al., 2014) and aid maintenance of good health (Bilotta et al., 2012; Fu et al., 2018; Granbom et al., 2017; Tong et al., 2019). In the perspective of society, social activity is perceived by scholars as a measure to enhance financial independency of older people (Suzuki et al., 2021) or provide them with low-cost support of local community (Novak & Vute, 2013a). Thus, the results of my research are in line with the conclusions reached to date regarding the impact of socially active older people on society and the individual. But importantly, through my research I would like to point out that this attitude to the idea under study is relevant to the very formation of urban aging policies.

Reasons come by themselves

The implementation of social activity for older people in Poznan is not only induced by documents or the desire to attract customers or participants, but also by older people, who come up with initiatives:

> The Centre for Older Citizen Initiatives, which will soon be 10 years old, was not created because some politicians thought it up, but because older citizens came to the president and said: "We want such a Centre to be created." [D2]

For the director of the Centre, it is important to underline that the establishment was not just the decision of local authorities, but rather it came from the bottom, from older active citizens, who proposed such initiative and so they were heard.

This autogenesis of actions, among them social activity events, also reoccurs in other cases:

> Voices that these local clubs need a bit of support from someone who will devote a bit more time to them were linked to voices from the older citizens themselves. [...] The clubs themselves come to us with their doubts and problems, and this is probably the greatest joy of our work, that apart from the fact that we animate a little bit, they also stimulate themselves to give us some suggestions, ideas, and proposals, so it is interesting. [D1]

Once again, the fragment cited from the interview with the worker at the center suggests that initiatives to act for older people come from themselves. Therefore, the enactment of social activity, which could be carried out by the center, is also possible thanks to the already-existing social activity of older people. Those who came up with the proposal to establish the Centre for Older Citizens Initiatives or those who advance their problems and needs, which could be addressed by its workers.

However, there is also another aspect of this generative tendency of social activity. The following examples present two workers from NGOs, who were referring to the way they were arranging the activities:

> Let me explain. All activities come from the older peoples themselves, because every time we carry out a project, for which we receive funding, we first diagnose their needs. [D9]

And the second example also from nongovernmental organization:

> **Interviewer:** So, the ideas for your projects were from the bottom up?
>
> **Expert:** Yes, but we always try hard to listen to what they want, because it is quite important for us. We don't want to come with a ready-made offer, but rather to ask. [D8]

For some reason the opinion of older people is also important for them. As it appears, in the second case these consultations are in line with the model of local community animation, another element of the urban policy, which promotes a particular way of cooperation between local communities and NGOs. The idea behind it is that to make a change and improve the livelihood of some communities. NGOs, first, have to recognize community needs, but also available resources and possible ways to engage them. As for the first case where the foundation worker also declares to carry out the diagnosis, it is important to note that the context for it is the running of the project. For them, the need for participants' opinion may stem from requirements that come with every public task carried out within a project. Each public task is commissioned to the chosen entity based on competition, which in its regulations, also demands from a task implementer (nongovernmental organization) to conduct a diagnosis of needs and problems among a targeted group. The following table shows the requirements for potential project implementers selected through competitions held by the city. The projects refer to tasks received by the city as a result of its role as a municipality and a district. Among the criteria there is the necessity to conduct an analysis of needs and their problems (see point 1.4.).

Table 12: Criteria within the framework of the open call for proposals for activities related to people of retirement age

	Specific criteria for the selection of the offers	Maximum number of points
1.	The possibility of carrying out a public task:	34
1.1.	The offeror's experience in implementing tasks in: "Activities for people of retirement age."	8
1.2.	Size and characteristics of the audience, method of recruitment.	10

	Specific criteria for the selection of the offers	Maximum number of points
1.3.	The housing and material resources necessary for the proper implementation of the actions.	14
1.4.	The analysis of needs and the degree of problem identification.	12

Source: Translation from Announcement of the open competition No. 45/2021 for assigning the tasks of the City of Poznan in the area of activity for people of retirement age, <www.poznan.pl>. [D17]

In both cases, that is, of the OSL model and the project implemented by the organization as part of a commissioned public task, the need to address older people turns out to be dictated by the requirements of the program in which the surveyed organizations participated. What we can see is that both municipal entities, as well as for third-sector organizations, joined the network in reference to bottom-up information. It can be important as a justification of their actions or as a requirement from programs to which they apply. Referring to the title of this section—*Reasons come by themselves*—I wanted to show that for my interlocutors it was important, when talking about the social activities of older people, to show that its source comes from the older people themselves. As can be seen from the examples I presented, certainly for NGOs this desire also comes from the requirements of the programs they implement. As far as the director of the Centre and the staff members are concerned, such an assumption is inherent both in the statute of the organization and in the older citizens' policy they try to implement. Thus, the spontaneity of emerging ideas for social activism of older people is in fact written down, sometimes hidden in documents or programs. This means that the ideas contained in aforementioned documents, policies or programs are the starting point for the implementation of the analyzed idea of social activity. Such an idea is the concept of empowerment popular in public policies (O'Connor & Netting, 2011a; Olech & Kaźmierczak, 2011), and also in aging policies (Walker, 2002). It consists in empowering citizens and residents and giving them initiative and agency in the field of emerging social services and activities.

In summary, in this section I attempted to expound different points on the map of social activity implementation, which could be called starting points, at least for the events I observed. I tried to show what the perspectives of different actants might be when problematizing the social activity of older people. We are dealing with the interests of private companies, which are joining the social activity of older people and seeing benefits for themselves, such as creating a positive image of their company within the framework of CSR, reaching a larger group of potential consumers, or perhaps adapting their services to older consumers. Therefore, companies joining in become actants in the network's implementing social activity of older people by means of CSR or the silver economy.[14] These are further, as ideas of social activity, global ideas that have been developed at an international level and embedded at a local level (Cox, 2009). This shows what a mosaic the public philosophy (Mehta, 2011) behind policies can be. It is even more diverse if we consider the further elements of problematization presented in this section. In the part about obligations and reasons that come by themselves, there are further reasons why NGOs, cultural institutions, or informal groups (such as older citizens' clubs) get involved in making social activity a reality. Their willingness to do so may stem from documents, policies, statutes, or projects. We can call all these elements actants, which induce further actants in the network to realize the idea of social active aging. In turn, the mentioned documents, policies or statutes are pushed by again other actants, another idea such as the mentioned empowerment (Olech & Kaźmierczak, 2011), popular in social policies. Another reason for the emergence of social activism of older people is its practical function as a measure that can minimize the social and individual effects of the aging process, much emphasized by researchers of social activity for older people in cities (Ahmad & Hafeez, 2011; Ho, 2017a; Novak & Vute, 2013a; Suzuki et al., 2021).

In summing up this section, I answered the question—*Why do you care?*—to individuals, organizations and other actants who make social activity for older people in Poznan a reality. By looking for what binds them together,

[14] It is a concept developed within the paradigm of symbolic interactionism, relating to activity and continuity theory (Marshall & Clarke, 2010). At that time, in addition to the idea of successful or active aging, a parallel idea emerged for productive aging, which emphasized prolonging the usefulness of older people through their continued work but also active consumption. Hence the term silver economy, which refers to the offerings of companies focused on older consumers, often significantly profiling their activities (Klimczuk, 2015; Walker, 2008).

we see further actants, namely interests, ideas, legal documents that make the implementation of this idea beneficial to actants. This shows how complex local public philosophy is, but also how globally rooted it can be.

4.1.2. Entering the network

As a continuation of the previous section on the problematization, I will further trace threads of relations, which place actants within the network. Through four sections, I will show how the actants became part of a network making the social activity of older people a reality. Starting from the first section—*Looking for the support*—I discuss joining the network by the need to get resources for the organization's activities. The next section, *In search for sites*, focuses on another aspect of networking and bonding, namely the issue of space for social activity. In the next section, *Positioning*, I discuss the relationships in the network that make actants indispensable to each other. The final section, *Casting the net*, to show the formation of a network of connections between actants through the metaphor of casting a net.

Looking for the support

I will start with a description of how respective actants enter the network of social activity implementation. First, we can see different kinds of entities that enter the network of projects and programs formed by city authorities, to gain some funds for their activities with older people:

> We have started some form of cooperation with the city, but it is still a work in progress because I am not the kind of person who would say that I want to do this and it is a brilliant idea and everyone should support me and give me money. [D5]

As we can see from the aforementioned statement, the foundation leader seeks to find some resources for his ideas by applying for money from city projects. However, if his ideas for activities are not in line with the assumptions formed by the city, he cannot receive the municipal funding for it. It is important to add that getting a project is substantial for NGOs:

> We are NGOs, the third sector, and we operate mainly when we have grants [...]. Everything is connected to the source of our funding. If we do cultural activities, we apply for funds from the culture department (Poznan city hall), then we have to include in the application that we will go with a group of selected older peoples for example to a museum. [D9]

As a result of this fragment of the interview, NGOs need to apply for city projects in order to operate. This, in turn, allows local authorities the opportunity to influence what is going on in third-sector organizations, as they may not support the ideas of NGOs, whenever they are not compatible with the project agenda. Furthermore, social activity for older people can be enacted by various sources of funding and thus different assumptions toward older people's participation, causing the multiplication of social activities within one entity:

> However, last year some of the activities for older citizens came from CIL,[15] some came from the project of the Health Department project, and some came from the Department of Culture. Now we are going to try to submit some projects for re-granting, for small grants, and to do something at least in this direction, because generally there is a need, and those of our residents who have contact with us and our leaders call and ask if we are going to do something if we can do something together. [D8]

By these examples, I demonstrate how social activity implementation looks from the perspective of NGOs. Events that emerge as the result of their action must meet expectations given by the funds donor, which itself has some assumptions, such as promotion of culture in Poznan or empowerment of local communities.

Moreover, the need for finding support is also present within Older Citizens' Clubs, which, however, need not only financially support but also a legal one, as they are not a legal entity, thus they are not eligible for public benefit activities (according to the Law on Public Benefit and Volunteerism). However, what can happen is the Older Citizens' Club cooperates with NGOs, companies, local parishes, or housing councils, which have legal capacity, and through their support apply for funds. However, this condition forces Older Citizens' Clubs into an alliance with possible patrons.

However, what I observed more was that different entities decide to set up an Older Citizens' Club within their structures, rather than clubs starting the cooperation:

---

15 The Centre for Local Initiatives (pl. *Centrum Inicjatyw Lokalnych*) for further explanations, see p. 119.

> I don't know how it was, anyway, we belonged to the Centre Club, we were under the Association's care, and the Association wrote projects and received 10,000 or 15,000 (polish zloty) for older citizens. And we had to say what we wanted to do for those 15 000, what kind of workshops. The ideas were ours. There were trips, gymnastics. [D13]

So, we can see that social activity to be enacted by older people themselves also needs support, but even more complex than in the case of NGOs. However, there are also other possibilities for Older Citizens' Clubs, which as an informal group can apply for some dedicated to such groups. They can try to raise funds for their activities within grants:

> The leader of this club wanted, for example, to organise Christmas, but they did not have the funds. We thought together, I searched for the nearest grants, small ones, which would allow us to achieve this goal. After searching for it, we sat together to discuss what the plan is and the older citizen presented how she sees it [...] And, of course, the next step was to receive this grant, and the older peoples started implementing it, according to these guidelines. [D12]

The grants mentioned are a small amount of money that is transmitted to various informal groups for their actions. Money is dispensed by NGOs, which were chosen to do so within another municipal project.

It can be seen that *looking for support* is a way entities enter some networks of social activity implementation, impersonating into a role of contractor, who will deliver a task in exchange for necessary resources. Looking for financial support by getting involved in available projects is part of the phenomenon of projectization described in public policies (Godenhjelm et al., 2015; D. Hodgson et al., 2019) as a way of public management (Jałocha, 2019, 2021), of implementing policies (Jensen et al., 2018), also on the local level (Skórzyńska, 2018; Skrzypek-Prawelska & Jałocha, 2014; Snopko, 2014). The existence of this phenomenon, as researchers point out, on the one hand is an improvement (Jałocha, 2021; Snopko, 2014); however, on the other hand, it favors temporarily introduced policies, limits NGOs and imposes some ready-made ideas (D. Hodgson et al., 2019; Kuura, 2011; Skórzyńska, 2018).

However, as the researchers and my analysis indicate, such design promotes the temporality or one-off nature of politics. In return, policymakers receive a tool that is easy to manage, allocate money and seemingly more measurable.

However, according to my research, projects leave some grassroots initiatives created by local activists unrealized and focus on actions toward specific groups included in documents, omitting other locally relevant groups of people in need of support.

In search of sites

As was explained earlier, actants seek financial support to go on with their activities. However, there is one more significant element, namely, a site of action. It seems to play an active role in the social participation of older people's social participation. During my visit to CIS, I was acquainted with activities carried out by CIS, but also with the place itself:

> I will show you the centre, well, the heart of the centre is the information room, the first one, where there are brochures, information and where older peoples can come on their own, use, search, relax, and I think this is the best formula because there are older people who come to us every month and they know where to look and what to look for. [D1]

What is visible from that interview is that the sheer space of entities can enact social activity by welcoming in its visitors and *giving* them further information on what events they can attend. Furthermore, it seems that the center's activity focuses on exposing the sites available for older citizens in Poznan and, by doing so, enhancing their activity. There is a special program *Older People Friendly Place*, within which different firms, restaurants or other entities could get a certificate of such *Older People Friendly Place* if they will meet the conditions of the program, concerning the availability for older people and additionally offer some discounts. In exchange, such a place is given a certificate and recommendation, which in turn serve as an incentive for older people to visit.

Furthermore, tracing other programs that take place in Poznan, one could notice that they also sort of open the city space for its older citizens:

> Mr. President, together with us … We had the idea that one of Poznan's cinemas should be an older citizens' cinema, and that is what happened. After the renovation of the Muza cinema, we can boldly say that it is an older citizen cinema. On Wednesdays there are performances, you can go for 10 zloty, which is a good price, and there is also coffee, tea, cake, and the opportunity to talk. There is also the Palace cinema in the Castle (cultural centre), which is also an older citizen's

> cinema. There is also the private Rialto cinema, which also hosts screenings for older people, and there are crowds of people there. [D2]

The aforementioned city spaces and cinemas are examples of already-existing places that offer activities for all, but through a special name and dedicated service, they aim to attract older people to participate in social activities happening there. Another example of a place with a special role in the social activity of older people is an event called *Older Citizens Days (Senioralni).* It takes place every year in Poznan, usually at the beginning of autumn for one month, thus called a month of older citizens. For 30 days, older people are encouraged to participate in different activities available in the event's program. Moreover, for its opening, the President hands representatives of older citizens keys to the city, as from this time they are hosts of the city. This program was established based on a similar event called *Students' Day (Juwenalia)*, which is focused on younger citizens. During the month of older people, the city establishes a wide range of events. However, what can be seen is that a big part of events enlisted in the program are happening independently from this special event, they are regular meetings, workshops or one-time events open to the broad public. However, through events such as Older Citizens' Days, older people are becoming more frequent visitors to city spaces, for example, theaters, museums, cinemas, or simply parks and monuments in the old town.

Apart from being available for older people, city space is also an important element in social activity enactment by NGOs or Older Citizens' Clubs.

> We opened our club, then we started looking for a room. We found one in the kindergarten, which needed to be renovated, and we asked the president to finance it because the basement needed to be completely renovated and adapted. So, the club was set up in the kindergarten. And that is how the club operates. [D11]

> And the club started to have such a nice real activity, we had 40–50 members. Because there were 3 rooms, a social room, a computer room, a lecture room, and there we could develop, you know, in the sense that we could have all kinds of circles there. [D13]

Both examples show that space forms the foundation for action. Therefore, actants must ally with others to find a venue for their meetings. From the perspective of actants who have space, in turn, it can incline an engagement in the enactment of social activity:

> I always liked social work in some NGOs. And that contact led to some cooperation, where it turned out at some point that they were not able to serve so many interested older citizens. I said: "Why not, I have the room, I have days," and it is the case that two weeks in advance the place is full. [D5]

The space presented in this section is presented as an actant, which is a starting point for the realization of social activity, through its functions and characteristics, e.g., the free space of an NGO or the space of a cinema hall or a museum. As a result, activities such as Older People's Wednesdays, Older People's Cinema or museum visits appear. Furthermore, space is also needed to tie relations between participants so that their social activity lasts.

> We make friends with this group of older adults who come to us because there is no denying that relationships are formed. These meetings and workshops are always held over coffee and cakes, and they have a slightly different character. It is not about stressing anyone out, it is about creating a friendly atmosphere, and that is why it can have such a nice effect later on. [D3]

Within the data analysis process, the *search for a site* appeared to be an important action. Social activity is perceived as staying in spaces, particular places trigger actions and events, which allows implementation of social activity of older adults. Furthermore, we can see that actual space is an actant, which shapes social activities through its features, such as old buildings, interesting exhibitions, or spare space to drink coffee and chat.

The role of space in the social activity of older people has already been highlighted by various researchers, which is also included in my literature review (see Section 1.2—Urban aging) (Beard & Montawi, 2015; Dawidowicz et al., 2020; Xiong et al., 2020; Yung et al., 2016). Also in the environmental gerontology paradigm, researchers emphasize the strong relationship between space and older people, highlighting the mutual influence (Wahl & Gitlin, 2007). Moreover, the idea of Age-Friendly Cities, popular and promoted by the WHO, places great emphasis precisely on the city space, its accessibility, and adaptation for older residents (Moulaert & Garon, 2016; Rémillard-Boilard et al., 2020). However, in my research, the city space, fragmented into buildings of public institutions, cultural institutions, monuments or headquarters of companies or NGOs, becomes an actant, actively shaping social activity, influencing the forms it takes. Because it is also a permanent element of the city, it can foster more long-term activities and the involvement of the participants in given activities.

Positioning

In this section, I would like to demonstrate how in another way they enter the network and start to share a common interest with others to consolidate in a common aim, namely social activity of older people. Actants are *locked in* the network of social activity enactment by the support they receive or the space in which they stay, which I call *interposition*. It was visible in the declaration[16] between Polish cities:

> We declare our willingness to work together to develop the best possible solutions in the field of older citizen policy, which will foster the creation of an age-friendly environment while ensuring conditions for dignified and healthy ageing and preserving as much activity and independence as possible. [D16]

In addition to the Declaration between the mayors quoted earlier, international programs also play a similar role, offering membership in exchange for the adoption and implementation of specific objectives:

> In July 2016, the city of Poznan joined the World Health Organization's Age-Friendly Cities network, which brings together cities open to the needs of older people. This is, on the one hand, recognition of the City's activities to date in support of older citizens, but also acceptance of the assumption that actions to improve the quality of life of all residents should be integrated, giving them a common goal: making the city increasingly age-friendly. [D14]

Participation in such declarations can be seen as a frame within which actants, here the city, decide to function, it binds them to achieve common goals, among them social activity of older people. Interpositioning means that an actant is found among other actants with similar endeavors. Another example of it was, when actants entered the network of social activity throughout projects established by the city:

> We started, as far as I remember, with a grant-funded project, it was such a big project based on older volunteers work and that was the first thing that was done here. [D3]

---

16 Declaration is a common understanding between twenty cities. In it, presidents declare common effort for sake of better live of older people. It was signed on October 20, 2017.

Or by the Ministry:

> We participate in two different programs that are in September in Poznan. [...] Sometimes we also get proposals to join projects from the city or the Ministry. [D4]

In these examples I wanted to show the initiating role of the programs. As a result of their implementation, the museums mentioned earlier have taken further steps to activate older people. In the first interview, the museum worker describes how it all started, namely how the museum began the social activity of older people. The first trigger was some project, which helped to start cooperation with older visitors as volunteers. This allowed them to form relationships and get to know the needs of older people and to be able to offer next events for them. Similarly in the second interview, the worker referred to projects in which museums participate, which make them well-known actants in social activity for older people. Therefore, these projects place these entities on the city map of older people ventures.

Furthermore, it also happens that the actors decide to enter already exiting and working network:

> So, I called them, found out how it works and, in general, decided that we would be the coordinating point for Debiec,[17] that is, we collected volunteers, all their data, etc. We reported them to Caritas, and now the City Hall has a general telephone number that older peoples call if they want to buy something, they give their data and if the older person is from Debiec, they send this information to us, usually several orders in bulk, and we distribute it among the volunteers in Debiec who volunteered to help and do the shopping. [D8]

In the process of social activity implementation in Poznan, it seems that mentioned declarations, programs, and projects are powerful actants, gathering others, supplying them with necessary sources to take action in favor of mutual aims and at the same time fulfilling the interests of each actant separately. *Positioning* is the moment in the translation process when actants are grouped and weaved with each other, so they become dependent on each other. These conclusions allow us to develop the previously mentioned phenomenon of projectization (D. Hodgson et al., 2019; Skrzypek-Prawelska & Jałocha, 2014), noting the resulting links and dependencies between actants.

---

[17] It is the name of district in Poznan.

Thus, projects are not only a tool to facilitate the management of public policies, but they also foster the creation of commitments and dependencies between local actants, which appeared to be a part of the implementation of social active aging.

Casting the net

Finally, I want to focus on older people and on the process of becoming weaved into social activity. As the title of this section suggests, older people are sort of decoyed into the net:

> Reaching out to the group of older people with whom I was able to work, I started looking for environments where I could present what community animation is all about.[18] Do the organisations know anything about it, are they interested in cooperating in this area? The first such institution that I went to was the Day Care Centre (Dom Dziennego Pobytu) on Konopnicka Street, and it was there, after discussions with the staff, with the director, with the older citizens who were at the meeting, that I was able to identify their needs. [D12]

As we can see, for this activist, who aims at local community animation, to gain older members of the community, she strived to get to know their needs. The needs are what connects her with others, and common understanding of what is necessary for them can conduce to further common action:

> Every action, I would say, requires, apart from the fact that there is an action, an initiative, and it is ingenious or has a very noble goal in itself. It is always grassroots here through discussions, and then we think about how to do it, to make it happen, but it always requires a network of people to help us make it happen and to bring these people together to achieve a common effect. [D12]

She knows if any venture was to be successful, people engaged in it need to gather under a shared goal, so by *casting the net* construct, she strives to tie older people with social activity initiators. Sometimes activists also use a *trick to fill the net*:

---

18 She refers to OSL model, which is an abbreviation of *organizowanie społeczności lokalnej*, meaning animation of local community. It is a way of cooperation with local communities applied in Poznan by some public institutions, such as City Centre for Family Support (Miejski Ośrodek Pomocy Rodzinie).

> The Long Table is something we started even before the epidemic. We are doing it with an informal group called the Mutual Aid Society, and the main idea was that we would meet and cook together, and at the same time talk, build relationships, and so on. [...] It was also about involving as much as possible those people who would come to such meetings, including the fact that they would, for example, bring food. It was supposed to be a kind of spontaneous cooking, where everyone brings what they have at home, e.g., what they don't use at the moment or will have to throw away soon, so it is better to use it right away. [D8]

In this case, local leaders try to gather members of the community through joint cooking. The aim is to build relationships that will last and allow other initiatives to emerge. However, as it will be visible in the next fragment of the interview, it can be difficult to cast the net in such a way that all actants would be content with it:

> However, when the meetings were held in a closed space, more organized, it was much worse, as there were various conflicts because the children were too loud. After all, older people wanted to pour the wax first, etc. (laughs). So, the following year, we decided to divide it up, at least in part, and hold meetings specifically for older people. Because then you can devote more time to them, and this relationship is more convenient for them. [D8]

So, one can see that sometimes creating a network of participants requires adjustment, which in this situation meant separating a group of older residents from others to give them the space and time they needed. This allowed them to start forming relationships with each other, which are the basis for future activities. *Casting the net* is a section that illustrates how social activities impact on older people to win them over and keep them engaged. This type of activity highlights the need for networking between actants, so that their involvement is sustained and stays until the end, bringing new value, which was the aim of cooperation between actants, established within the network. This is the aspect of entering a network implementing social activity, which, unlike the previous ones, focuses on the sustainability of the activities carried out.

In Section 4.1.2—*Entering the network*—I wanted to show how actants become indispensable to each other. As M. Callon (1984) wrote, it is the moment when the actants involved prove to be important for each other, necessary for their goals to be achieved. Thus, in the *Looking for the support* part, the binding element is the projects, and more specifically the money behind them. For project implementers, the NGOs, it is important to get funding so that they can work. For the authors of the projects, on the other hand, the NGOs are important, because they have the resources, mainly personal, but also the knowledge to carry out such a project. Another indispensable element, presented in the section—*In search of sites*—to implement social activity of older people in Poznan turns out to be the space of the city, the buildings of organizations, cultural institutions, restaurants, or cinemas. Understanding the social activity of older people as just being in the public space of the city has already been noted by researchers (Beard & Montawi, 2015; Dawidowicz et al., 2020; Xiong et al., 2020; Yung et al., 2016), and moreover is an element of the concept of Aging Friendly Cities (Buffel et al., 2020; Rémillard-Boilard et al., 2020). However here, it is not only about the good influence of space, the environment on older inhabitants, but also about showing how important it is in creating urban policies. How having it or not having access to it can be an incentive to implement social activity network or for older people simply to take part in it. Another such indispensable element was described in the *Interpositioning* section, documents, declarations, which "produced" between actants commitment, making them mutually bound to perform a given task. What is more, such indispensability was sometimes also imposed on older people, which I tried to describe in *the Casting the net* section. It shows that some organizations, cultural institutions, or other entities try to include older people in social activities, also in a way that for them it is beneficial or even necessary to participate in this network, which can enhance to stay active for a longer time. The issue of indispensability of individual actants raised here will be relevant to the endurance of the emerging network and whether the stated objectives are achieved, and the network contributes to the creation of new value, as I will discuss in Section 4.1.4—Desired product.

4.1.3. Vehicles of social activity

Previously, I described how a social activity implementation network for older people can emerge and under what conditions actants enter it. But now I present an analysis of how they can carry out their tasks to bring about social activity. I will try to describe the different vehicles that bring about social activity for older people in Poznan. I will start with a mode of social activity that I have called *Seduction*. Its emergence is then associated with the efforts of various agents (NGOs, companies, or public institutions) to entice older people with their offer of events. The next section—*Engaged social activity*—shows how education, self-development or civic activity of older citizens can be the vehicles of social activity. Yet another way of making social activity more tangible is to delegate it from the city in the form of commissioned tasks to be implemented by NGOs—*Commission to actants*. The last way to realize social activism, presented in the final section—*To kill two birds with one stone*—is to realize social activism through previously created activities, accessible to a wider audience in the city.

Seduction

During my observations and interviews with people who organize events, I noticed that there is some desire to attract older people to an exact place. Thus, events are sort of presented as a service; the customers being older people. It is the case with the museum, where a worker describes its events and activities:

> I mean, we assumed that we wanted to create an offer for very different audiences and therefore we wanted to create an offer for older peoples. [D3]

It is similar for another entity, which is a nongovernmental organization, mainly dedicated to older people:

> Again, the second option is for active older people. We meet them at various places in Poznan, primarily in all older citizens' activity clubs, formal and informal older citizens' clubs, and very often we simply ask them what they would like, what activities they would like. Very often, the offer is simply educational, recreational, or cultural, or exercises that focus on improving mental or physical fitness. [D9]

Both fragments show a particular way of thinking about activities that take place in these entities.

The term *offer* seems to be a key word here, as it sets the relation between these entities, older people and also social activity in the end. Such a nomenclature was also very popular when talking about activities also within other events, described in *The Older Citizens Policy for Poznan:*

The trade fair presents companies for which mature consumers are important, which appreciate the challenge of meeting the expectations of determined, experienced, and wise consumers. The offer covers topics related to health, work and education, travel, sport, beauty and lifestyle, passions, new technologies and media, as well as law and finance. [...] The VIVA OLDER CITIZENS Fair is also a space for nongovernmental organisations and municipal units that work for the benefit of mature and older adults people and undertake efforts to activate them. During the two days of the fair, the organisations present their offer and show how many meetings, cultural events, social and civic activities are organised daily in and around the city. [D14]

When the two first examples illustrated seldom actants, who describe their activity in the field of older citizen policy as making an offer, the latter one describes a bigger venture—*The VIVA Older Citizens Fair*—which is an event for older peoples to acquaint with a rich offer of companies as well as NGOs, operating in Poznan location. In addition to more conventional stalls with leaflets and entity representatives, the exhibitors aim to lure visitors with activities available at their place:

For example, some of the members of the literary club arrived on the basis that I organised an open meeting, so everyone could come and see what it looked like, whether they liked it or not. [...] It was a kind of promotion of the foundation at a certain point. That we were doing something like that, like it or dislike it because it is obvious that one event is like that. [D5]

Another way of attracting older people issued by the center is monthly brochure with all events happening in Poznan, which could be interesting for the older citizens.

We also published our offer through the CIS, and many older citizens' clubs approached us to conduct activities that would improve, activate, and integrate them. [D9]

Furthermore, older people are also seduced into activities with such programs as Poznan Golden Loyalty Scheme[19] or Older Citizens-Friendly Places, which encourage them to benefit from discounts offered by a wide range of

[19] Card which entitles Poznan citizens aged 60 and over to discounts in selected restaurants, shops, and businesses.

companies, restaurants, shops, etc. and become their customers. However, here we notice a clear difference as older customers are not offered free activities, as is in the case of NGOs or public entities (such as museums, universities, etc.), but instead, they become more privileged customers.

By and large, the offer is a vehicle for social activity, used by both nonprofit and market players, and it is intended to seduce older people. According to it, older people become recipients or clients, and social activity is a type of service provided to them, which may or may not meet the interest of older people. Within this section, social activity for older people appears as a service, offered by companies but also by NGOs or public institutions. This way of referring to participants in social activity refers to the service approach present in social policy, related with New Public Management[20] (Guy, 2010; Jałocha, 2021; Szarfenberg, 2010). The aim of which is to create social services for residents which will respond to their needs, with high quality provided by professionals (Szarfenberg, 2010). Moreover, the form of services, which implies calling recipients as clients, mitigates the stereotypical image of a person using social benefits (Chaczko, 2021; Grewiński, 2009). Thus, social activity for older people is understood in this as a rich offer of events available for older people.

Engaged social activity

Following the implementation of social activities for older people in Poznan, I was looking for events that would be dedicated to them. I also wanted these events to aim at social activity of older people, consisting either simply in participating in events with a group, or in integrating with a community or acquiring skills to be socially active. In my observations and subsequent analysis, I noticed that one of the vehicles for social activity is educational cycles:

> And in the end, it worked and a lot of people were so interested in it that I decided to make a cycle "On the way of tea," last Friday we had more than 50 people, so you can see that there is a very big interest in this tea, there were three meetings […] I can also add that apart from "Icons of design," "On the way of tea" and "Meditation in the Museum" there is also a cycle "Graphic Concept," which also attracts a lot of older people. [D4]

[20] The trend of public management that emerged in the 1970s. It focused on increasing the effectiveness of public action, as well as more accurate monitoring of its results, and is also associated with the introduction of projects as a tool for carrying out public policy tasks.

Those few events invite people into the space of the Museum of Applied Arts and propose tours of its exhibitions. Another example of such an event comes from NGOs acting within the local community.

> It was a very popular activity, we even had whole cycles of hortiterapeutic[21] activities and it was very successful. [D8]

Moreover, the social activity of older people is also enacted through the development of their competencies:

> We cooperate with the Gorczyn[22] older citizens' club, where I was with Ewa, we were in the Academy of Women Leaders, we spent half a year there, we are always learning, you know, we laugh that we are eternal students (laughs). It is cool, there's always something new. [D13]

This example differs a little bit from the previous one as it involves further involvement of two older leaders in the animation of the older citizens' club. The development of competencies among older people is one of the activities also proposed by other NGOs:

> I: And these technology consultations, they are just one-to-one?
>
> E: There is a group of people who bought a smartphone for the first time out of necessity. And there we learn, so to speak, from the basics. Making calls, receiving calls, sending, receiving text messages. And these are total basics. [D5]

Education and self-development, then, are vehicles of social activity for older people, which are understood as an extension of their knowledge and competencies. For the first two examples, education is a trigger for older people to engage and maybe come back to museums or NGOs. The last three pieces of training dedicated to older people were supposed to arm its participants with abilities, which in turn could be used for their further engagement.

This leads to another way in which older people are activated, meaning that they are engaged in action taking place in the city, for example as supervisors:

---

21 It means therapy through work in garden.

22 It is a name of a district in Poznan.

> Fifteen representatives are elected to the Municipal Council of Older Citizens, all of whom must be over 60 years old. However, nine persons are represented by civic movements, various local councils, associations, foundations, and organizations working for the benefit of older citizens. The idea was to reach out to people who are active in the older citizen community so that we could work with them. The remaining 6 people were: three people were indicated by the President and three by the Poznan City Council. [...] People come to the Older Citizens' Council and say: "Let us do something for older people!" But we have no budget, we are not a legal organization, we have no legal standing, we cannot do anything for people. [D10]

Being a council member is another embodiment of social activity, which is less temporary than simply attending the event. Older people act as representatives of the older citizen community and try to advise local policy designs so that it will also serve them and their peers.

The vehicles of social activity for older people in this section were their involvement in educational, self-development or civic activities. These vehicles of social activity extend the dimensions of social activity I have identified in the literature, referring to areas such as self through educational and self-development activities (Fu et al., 2018; Ho, 2017a; Novak & Vute, 2013a; Pei et al., 2014), or sense of community (M. L. Chan et al., 2015; Pasquallie, 2018; Tong et al., 2019) in the case of civic activity. The identified areas of social activity of older people in Poznan illustrate how the implementation of one idea—social activity of older people—entails other ideas. The latter may be the carriers of the former, but this relationship may be two-way, that is, the social activity of older people serves to implement the idea of active citizenship. These conclusions illustrate the complexity of the implementation process within urban policy, drawing attention to important actants such as ideas about education or self-development, but also others absent in my case study.

Commission to actants

In the previous section, I trace social activities enacted by offers of various entities; here another term would be crucial, namely a task. In the previous section, I mentioned several projects, which are important actants forming the network of social activity enactment. However, the projects themselves are also the result of others' translations, which makes them so powerful. As I attempted to show earlier, projects are an important source of financing for entities engaged in the network of social activity enactment. Their description can be found in the Act of April 24, 2003 on Public Benefit Activity and Volunteerism:

> Project means a public task in the sphere referred to in Article 4, implemented by a project implementer in the manner referred to in Article 16a. [D18]

This extends the understanding of the project to public tasks, which are in turn defined in the same Act as areas of activities for third-sector entities; among them are tasks devoted to people in the retirement age. Such tasks are to be implemented by selected entities in the process of competition:

> An open offer competition is a way, defined by the Act on Public Benefit Activity and Volunteerism (Art. 13), to select organizations that receive grants from a local government unit to implement specific public tasks. [D17]

According to this, NGOs engaging in such a project will need to realize a task described in such offer competitions. Tasks, in turn, are transformed into planned results.

Table 13: The proposed results and their indicators

Proposed outcome	Planned level of result achievement (target value)	Means of results monitoring/source of information on the achievement of the indicator
Organization of a sports tournament for older people.	Number of older people who participated in the tournament.	E.g., attendance list, photographic documentation.
Organization of integration events for older citizens.	Number of events.	E.g., photo documentation, website article, newspaper article.

Source: Translation from Announcement of the open competition No. 45/2021 for assigning the tasks of the City of Poznan in the area of activity for people of retirement age, <www.poznan.pl>. [D17]

Table 13 is an excerpt from a competitive bid, announced by the city, for the implementation of activities for the retired. In the first column, the authors of the competition list the suggested results of the task, that is, specific forms of events. In the middle column and the third one, on the other hand, measures are proposed as evidence of the complete event. This is where the commissioned tasks materialize and become a list of attendees or photographs documenting the event. In the competition process, each participating entity must submit a bid that reflects the requirements introduced in the competition notice.

In the presented competition documents, social activity of older people was presented by means of suggested events, desired outcomes, and their measures, that is, photographs from the event or a social media post. Within this section it can be seen that social activity is realized through a network of documents, that is, laws, policies, or competition texts. Just as in the previous sections, the vehicles of social activity were the creation of an offer, the attraction of older citizens, the self-development of the individual, or their civic activity; here a new element appears. With *Commission to actants*, the social activity of older people is embodied in the content of acts or local documents, through which it materialized as a public task or project.

In this section, I show that a locally implemented idea is in fact weaved into networks created by policies at higher levels of government, and that local actants are its implementers. This complements my earlier findings (e.g., in *Reason come by themselves*), where I wrote about the bottom-up nature of social activity. This section, as if in counterpoint, shows that the activities carried out by the city are the result of commissioned tasks, which are passed on to organizations from the third sector.

To kill two birds with one stone

The events that I traced during my data collection were not only established for older people. It means that the social activity of older people was not their only desired goal. It happened that along with some events, older citizens had the opportunity to engage in activities for all citizens.

> During the inauguration, it was possible to obtain the Poznan Golden Card and vote for projects in the Poznan Civic Budget. [D15]

This is a fragment of the *Older Citizens Days' programme* that takes place annually in Poznan. During its inauguration in the courtyard of the Municipal Office, participants had the opportunity not only to participate in the activities of older people but also to participate as every citizen and decide what to spend the money on the Civic Budget.

During my observation, I attended a similar event, which was held within the *Older Citizen Days* program. The meeting I took part in was held at the

Centre for Older Citizens' Initiatives and was described as a meeting on air pollution in the city and the exchange of coal-fired boilers. However, during the meeting, it appeared that the meeting was devoted only to the program of coal-fired boiler exchange, whereas the topic of air pollution was not raised. It means that it was a regular meeting about the boiler exchange program. This is similar to the earlier issue described of inviting older citizens into city spaces by somehow making it dedicated to them, like an older citizens' cinema. In this way, sites available for everyone become known to older people too. Consequently, programs targeted at all citizens through dedicated agendas become familiar to the oldest members of the community. It also works the other way around, at least in the declaration of the municipality:

> As this is generally an Age-Friendly City, we have decided that these age-friendly cities are friendly to everyone. Not only do we prepare projects and activities typically dedicated to older people, but the projects and activities are dedicated to everyone to a large extent. [D2]

My interlocutor refers to the Age-Friendly Cities program, launched by the World Health Organization, to which Poznan also joined. The idea behind its action is that friendly city should be seen also a beneficial aim for all city groups, thus he would expect their engagement in its enactment.

What I also observed was that social activity was enacted with already available networks. The activity of Older Citizens' Clubs was waved with the life of other already-existing groups or entities:

> Today we went to a meeting with Caritas to ask about the groups that operate in parishes, which are also kind of like older citizens' clubs, only they are called something else, so we are already making some contacts with Caritas. [D1]

The worker of the center describing her daily work talks about extending the network of older citizens clubs into existing groups, gathered around a big religious organization. Instead of approaching those older people with her program or offer, she strives to link to a network that is already functioning. This type of web threading was present also in the action of people whose work was related to the earlier model of local community animation mentioned:

> I have managed to introduce older peoples to other environments, for example, I have associated them with the Forest Dwellers kindergarten, and now they are

> invited to all celebrations, for example, Christmas, Easter, Grandmother's Day, Grandfather's Day, so they are very well cared for in this kindergarten. [D12]

This kind of consociating between older people and children aims to fulfill the need of those two groups at the same time. For the older one, it provides social activity and a feeling of usefulness and belonging. For kindergarteners, it is a chance to meet with the older generation, embrace their experience, and maybe have step-grandparents if the real ones are not around.

Apart from introducing older people to existing in the city or local community networks, their social activity is also used by some activists, so it can bring good for others:

> I am also very keen to stimulate the older peoples themselves, those who are still fairly active, to help those who are less active, who are at home. I would like to build a self-help network, I started such activity last week, and already this week, I would say, we managed to meet the needs of one of the older people, who needed certain things because he was in a difficult situation, and I would like it to work like this. [D12]

Here, the need of older people to be active is displaced into their volunteering abilities to help those much older, for whom everyday duties are challenging. Both cases, the alliance with a kindergarten, as well as the devotion of spare time to those in need, show a kind of consolidation of relations and networks already existing. In general, undertaking social activity by older people can be described as a practice of reuse. This means that it carries events, encounters those that already exist but are only adapted as activities for older people. These are events open to the general public, that is, all residents, or meetings of groups, not necessarily older people, but for example, writing oriented. In this way, the social activity of older people takes place within the available resources and networks between actants who create events together. This can be seen as saving money and effort on the part of local policy makers on aging, but also as a way of integrating older people into existing communities and counteracting their isolation from other groups of residents.

In this Section 4.1.3—Vehicles of social activity—I presented four vehicles which takes part in implementation of social activity for older people. The idea was to show which methods are used by companies, NGOs, or municipalities to achieve the goal of social activity. In the beginning,

I referred to the seduction used by private actants, but also by third-sector organizations and cultural institutions in terms of their offers for older people. While it seems obvious for private companies to create offers and promote their activities, it is less obvious for public institutions or NGOs. However, such a service approach to the recipients of social activities is a well-known phenomenon in social policies from the 70s of previous century, especially in Western European countries (Guy, 2010; Jałocha, 2021; Szarfenberg, 2010), whereas in Poland it appeared with little delay (Chaczko, 2021; Grewiński, 2009). Under this approach, public institutions and entities implementing various types of projects provide social services, and their recipients become clients.

A different way of realizing older people's social activity was shown in the section—Engaged social activity, where older people were engaged in activity through education, development of their technological competences or engaging them as advisors to the older citizens' policy in Poznan. This is different to the previous section, as it draws more on the ideas of social activity as self-development (Fu et al., 2018; Ho, 2017a; Novak & Vute, 2013a; Pei et al., 2014) and participation (A. C. M. Chan & Cao, 2015; Novak & Vute, 2013a; Pasquallie, 2018; Tong et al., 2019). It is worth noting that within a single entity, social activity can be carried out in both ways.

The next section has already resounded several times in the previous sections where I wrote about projects and public tasks commissioned by municipal institutions to third-sector organizations. The commissioning of a public task of social activity for older people is a further consequence of this process. It is then operationalized into concrete results and measures. This is an interesting aspect of urban policy, whose form is limited then to available projects and grants, which addresses the problem of non-recurrence, limited by the project framework, that is, its duration, concrete results to be achieved, finances, etc. This issue I will address in the next section 4.1.4—Desired product, which deals with the sustainability of networks of social activity.

The last section—To kill two birds with a one stone—can be seen as contrast to this limitation imposed on urban policy by projects. It refers to the reuse of activities taking place in the city. When one of the events, turns out to also meet the criteria of activities for older people to activate them. While this may seem like a shortcut, on the other hand, it promotes the inclusion of older people in the city's existing social activities, while at the same time realizing the idea of intergeneration cooperation, which is a premise of aging policies.

The vehicles of social activity implementation, presented in this section, illustrate the mechanisms of this urban policy. Although, the service-approach (Guy, 2010; Jałocha, 2021; Szarfenberg, 2010), participation approach (Beresford & Carr, 2018; Taylor-Gooby, 2018) and projectification of policy (D. Hodgson et al., 2019; Kuura, 2011; Skrzypek-Prawelska & Jałocha, 2014) are not new phenomena in social policy. What is new, however, it is identified diversity of actants engaged in the implementation process within urban policy, such as ideas about education or self-development. Moreover, in this section I present the other side of the bottom-up approach to urban aging policy, presenting public tasks commissioned by successive levels of government as a vehicle of social activity toward older people. This implies the co-occurrence of these two directions of policy formation in the urban policy of Poznan I have studied. Furthermore, the results presented in this section draw attention to the reuse of the city's activities and different organizations resources to involve older people in existing communities. These issues of how to make social activity for older people a reality will be developed in the next section, which will focus on the effects of social activity networks.

4.1.4. Desired product

In this section, I wanted to focus on the last moment of translation, which is mobilization. The aim is to see how networks, weave together to implement a social activity, last, and if, what entities they bring about, in other words, what result we can observe. In the first section, *Life full of events*, I refer to the large number of events for older people in Poznan, which is precisely the result of making social activity a reality. Another effect of the social activity network could be *Acting for others*, where the aim of the event is for older people to act for others. So social activity is transformed into a new form of activity. The duration, or rather the *Endurance of relations* within a network, will be described in the next section. In it I will look at the endurance of relationships between actants as they bring some social activity events among older people. The last section—*Proliferation of networks*—will continue, in which I will discuss the issue of proliferation of networks that form the social activity of older people in Poznan. These four sections lead to the conclusions presented in the last section, suggesting a distinction between networks that create social activity of a one-off nature or of a long-term nature.

Live full of events

Along with data collection, I experienced a great number of events to attend. It seems that at nearly every public entity, namely museum, university or library, as well as private ones—cinemas, restaurants or sport centers—have something to offer. My observation was also shared by others:

> When you talk to them, older people are very busy in Poznan. I also have an older friend, who I wanted to ask for help in one project, she is a specialist in Russian, but she said that she would love to, but she doesn't have the time. [...] I am saying: maybe it is because Poznan is doing so much for older people that you can choose an event for free, or for a small price. [D5]

This involvement of an older friend, although disappointing for a foundation worker, can reflect the network aimed at establishing social activities for older people and their participation. The intensity of events in Poznan for older people was also claimed by the director of CIS, who said that older citizens are *sick and tired of* activities, as there are so many of them. Moreover, he considers all this richness of events as a cause for change in the thinking of older people about themselves.

> So, to say older people, returning to the fact that not everyone identifies with this, it is no longer so passe, many people feel very good about it, they are proud of it. That maturing into old age is also an important part of the city's activities, and we manage to do this. [D2]

We can see that the efforts of municipal entities focus on noticing older people as an important local group. To this mission also refers a worker of the center:

> We are interested in finding out about all activity for older citizens. [...], we provide information on what is interesting in the city, I recommend associations, places that cooperate with us, older citizen-friendly places, these are reliable places, foundations, but we also perform an informational function, because older peoples call us with various questions. These are often different kinds of problem. [D1]

This was also an observation of a museum worker, with whom I talked:

> I have the impression that older people are very well informed, there are some older people here who come to almost all our meetings. [D4]

Keeping older citizens informed seems to reflect the work of social activity. A life full of events is the picture that emerges from the excerpts presented.

At least this is the kind of life older citizens are offered by NGOs, companies, or CIS. What emerges is an image of an active older person who has no time to get involved because he or she is so busy. Thanks to this abundance of events, being an older person is not a negative thing, it breaks down negative stereotypes. So, social activity made real by information of events mobilizes an older person, present at the events of the city. This is a new finding with respect to my research review. Among the articles I found, being socially active was not equated with being informed. Some researchers, however, referred to social participation as an individual right, and emphasized the need for accessibility for people of different socioeconomic profiles (Afacan, 2013; Ahmad & Hafeez, 2011; Barrett & McGoldrick, 2013; Beard & Montawi, 2015; Carr et al., 2015; Chiribuca & Teodorescu, 2020). However, this area remained hidden in my study. Visible are those older people who are at events, who have personal space to get involved. However, as the leader of the older citizens' clubs and a long-time activist for older people mentioned, there is little interest in dependent people who are confined to their homes. One can conclude that their social activity in the form of information does not reach them.

This image of older people is in line with the idea of active aging, which focuses on being active and promoting a positive image of older people in society (Boudiny, 2013; Foster & Walker, 2015). However, according to research (Katz, 2000a; Nadobnik et al., 2021), for older people themselves, activity is not enough to mitigate the process of aging, and these are the sense of the activities undertaken, usefulness or finding oneself.

Acting for others

One more example of successful social activity translation between actants was aimed at in the process of creations. When older people do something:

> We managed to hold a larger meeting, a culmination of our first year of work, which was a Christmas meeting in December 2017, where we met at the Pireus club, in Lazarz[23] and there was a meeting about Christmas. Such a meeting, in which we jointly prepared Christmas decorations, were invited in addition to older people, people with disabilities, young people from schools, of course, also the local community, and together here, with our forces, we produced such basic decorations for Christmas. [D12]

---

[23] It is a name of a district in Poznan.

Photograph 3: The members of older citizens' club produce charity greeting cards. They do it during VIVA Older Citizens Fairs.
Source: Private collection.

Furthermore, it could be something they create for others' benefit:

> The first concept we did, when the club was founded, was to make Christmas decorations, which were sold for the benefit of a sick boy with a tumor in his head. So, that is where we do our social work, as a club. [D10]

These two examples can be extended with my observation during *VIVA Older Citizens' fairs* when on many stalls older citizens' clubs were promoting themselves as producing various decorations and crafts, which can give to charity. The process of creation was then used as an integration of the group and a way of engagement in the local community. Moreover, creative work appeared to attract older people, even if only for its utility:

> However, to my surprise, the literary group, i.e., older peoples who write, came as a very pleasant surprise. We started with three people, now we have 11, and this is the maximum, because such a meeting lasts about two hours, so to process what we create, well, this is the optimal group. [D5]

By developing their literary skills, older people also become home-based writers, which kept them engaged with the group and meeting, as opposed to an earlier attempt of foundation workers to form with them a reading club.

In this section, I have shown examples of how the social activities of older people can develop into activities for others. This process of translation is an important aspect that seems to be important for research on the development of urban aging policies. On the one hand, it refers to the researchers' perception of older people's social activity as voluntary work (Carr et al., 2015; Gawron, 2017; Ho, 2017a). On the other hand, it points to a possible outcome of social activity, that is, the weaving of its participants—older people—in successive networks of activities and their connection with other actants. Such interconnectedness of networks can foster their persistence and maintenance of activity, as will be discussed in the next two sections.

Endurance of relations

Another effect that was important for my interlocutors was to cause a formation of relations between participants of social activity, so the network could endure and become more permanent, fulfilling the need for activity. Such endurance was seen as a challenge by one leader of the older citizens' club.

> And the fact that it came into being is good because having a baby is easy. A club and that's it, for me it is a piece of cake! Sit down, invite people, the club is there. But keep it now and give them what they want. [D13]

From her statement, we can see that setting up a club, which is gathering people to meet, is easy. However, it can be hard to keep everyone happy and involved in the club later on. In conversation with me, she recalls that there are still clubs that are chaired within a strong division between club leaders and their members, and then they first decide in the name of all, what to do. However, she perceives them as old-style clubs that survive as long as the leaders are active, then they will be shut.

The relations seen as a chance of endurance for the network formed between the participants in the social activity were also observed by the activists of one of the foundations:

> We did such a project that we conducted integrating activities for one and a half to two hours, which were supposed to stay with these older people for longer so that after we left, when they meet up with us in a month or two, they could carry out these activities on their own and they would still be fun. [D9]

> The matter of links between participants is also important for those who have fewer networking actions, such as tours or training. They observe a self-evolving net of communication between older visitors.

> Anyway, I see how many people come here again and again, and these are often familiar faces; I see how they recommend various events or tours to other friends. [D4]

Thanks to the exchange of information between participants, the events have a greater popularity, which is desirable for their organizers. Such word-of-mouth is an engine of events that drives more and more people. It can also influence a course of technology training:

> In this second group, I have to tell you that there are fads. That is, if theoretically the first person in a given week comes and throws the slogan "WhatsApp," it means that for a fortnight we will talk about WhatsApp. Because they mutually: "aha, because you have WhatsApp, and what is it, how to use it?" And that kind of circle goes on later and they want to learn this WhatsApp. [D5]

These relations, about which we speak both previously mentioned individuals, were also observed by me. During museum or old town tours I could see people who see each other there regularly, exchange news and information. Although it was not a fundamental assumption of such events, for sure it was very often a side effect of it, which displaced one-time events, or even cycles of events into lasting relations.

The issue of network endurance is related to the *Engaged social activity* or *To kill two birds with one stone* sections described in an earlier section. The described ways of implementing social activities, whether by involving older people in self-development or civic activity or including them in activities already taking place in the city, promotes the endurance of social activity. In my study, this is the social activity of older people. That is, the activity enacted by the actants after through the network of connections between them (Callon & Latour, 2015) is likely to create new value within the intended purpose. In the case of my study, this is the social activity of older people. The aspect of sustainability of social activity is new in relation to research on the social activity of older people, but it is part of a new trend in social policies, especially local policies (Beresford & Carr, 2018; Taylor-Gooby, 2018; Theiss, 2017) aiming to create a support network around older people, which could respond to these needs in the event of problems, relieving public institutions that lack resources and staff.

Proliferation of networks

This section is sort of a continuation to the previous one, as it stems from endurance of relation, which favors its further proliferation. Very illustrative is an example of one older citizens' club which has grown so much that it was split into three new ones:

> You know what, when there are too many leaders, they want to split up. The most beautiful thing is that they parted in harmony, with blessings such as love. [...] When there are three leaders in this club, three strong personalities, they have to part, because everyone has a different vision. [...] Each one has a different vision, and it is impossible to work together. Now we can work together. [D13]

The evolution of one club into three separate is seen by a leader as a successful and natural course of events. It seems that the interests of all members could not be satisfied anymore, so the split could bring more benefits. In the perspective of translation, we can see how one network of negotiations ended and at the same time make a ground for new alliances. A similar mechanism can be observed between two NGOs:

> A place that is made available to us by a befriended foundation as part of the so-called CIL, which it runs. We rent a room there, free of charge, of course, as part of our partnership. [D9]

From this statement, I think the functioning of the speaker's foundation, more exactly an event *Older Citizens Wednesday, would not* be possible if not for the help of other NGOs. This case illustrates that the enactment of social activity is based on the rule of continuation. This attitude was also shared by the activist, who worked with local communities, with the already mentioned model of local community animation (OSL):

> But over time, as I got to know the older people community, it was not just the Day Care Centre, but there were also meetings during festivals, picnics, I would say informal ones, where I met various older peoples, and these, for example, were already members of a club, and then they invited me to come and talk about

> community animation, about volunteering for older people, and that is how I got into these environments. [D12]

She talks of sequences of events and activities, which allowed her to weave into the local environment and derive from it for the next events and ventures. In this section, I wanted to draw attention to the mechanism of continuation, which was present in the data. I find this unusual as it is difficult for third-sector organizations to pursue such a goal, as the public tasks they are commissioned to undertake are usually funded as short-term projects. This point has been made by me several times in the section—Commission to actants or Interpositioning. This is a new value that is emerging alongside social activities for older people carried out as part of a commissioned public task. In the case of the activities presented in this section, social activism tended toward long-term involvement of older citizens. This trend is a countervailing force for the activities of NGOs, which are known to struggle precisely with the short-term nature of their activities (Godenhjelm et al., 2015; D. Hodgson et al., 2019; Skórzyńska, 2018), due to the project framework that governs their activities, which is unfortunately due to the way the third sector is funded. However, it is worth noting that the city authorities are aware of this limitation. In their report[24] on the cooperation between NGOs and the city, they showed that some of the tasks were commissioned in the framework of long-term projects, aiming for better effects of the activities. Another indication, based on the research conducted, could be the just-mentioned reuse of activities taking place in the city anyway.

In all four sections, I strove to present a reflection on mobilization, meaning this moment in translation between actants when goals they aimed for becoming visible and entities not visible before emerged (Callon, 1984). In this case, those entities would be the endurance of relationships between older people, taking part in various activities, and the possibility for its repetition or better long-term engagement, presented in sections *Acting for*

---

24 *Report on the implementation of the annual program of cooperation with nongovernmental organizations*. -<https://bip.poznan.pl/bip/wydzial-zdrowia-i-spraw-spolecznych,32/news/sprawozdanie-z-realizacji-rocznego-programu-wspolpracy-miasta-poznania-z-organizacjami-pozarzadowymi-za-2020-rok,c,8840/sprawozdanie-z-realizacji-rocznego-programu-wspolpracy-miasta-poznania-z-organizacjami-pozarzadowymi-za-2020-rok,164910.html> (Date of access 22.03.2022).

other, Endurance of relations and *Proliferation of network*. However, there also were events that occurred once. They were aiming more at practices creating a rich offer and positive image for the older citizen among the others, like in the section *Life full of events*. The diverse effects of social activity for older people in Poznan are linked to the different intentions of the actants. It is about the goals of the actants, the networks in which they were involved, but also how they perceived the older residents, that is, as a client, participant or perhaps co-organizer. This last section will lead to conclusions about social activity which I encountered during my research in Poznan. I present its two types in the conclusion to this section. The issue of the perception of older people, on the other hand, is related to the different narratives present in the urban policy of aging in Poznan, which I discuss in the next section 4.2—Ontologies of social activity implementation.

4.1.5. Conclusions

In this section I presented the moments of translation of social activity for older people in Poznan. In section—*Why do you care?*—I identified the key starting points for its implementation. Next, in *Entering the network*, I presented the ways in which the actants in a network of activities become interdependent. The next moment of translation, the enrollment, is described in the section *Vehicles of social activity*, in which I showed how, in the cognition I had investigated, the actants are carrying out the activities assigned to them. So that in the last section—*Desired product*, I described what the result of the weaving of the network of urban aging policy by the actants is. The characteristics described of social activity enactment can be divided into two types, that is, a one-off activity that aims at the realization of a given event or an activity with long-term effects which aims at generating relations and involvement between participants.

In the initial phase of social activity enactment, the actants decide to engage in social activities for older people. They are driven to do so by the possibility of self-interest (*Interests*), by obligations resulting from documents that oblige them, that is, laws, statutes, policies, or projects (*Obligations*). They may also be motivated by other ideas, such as CSR, empowerment (*Reasons come by themselves*), or active aging (*Measures*). At this point, whether a social activity is a one-off or a long-term activity depends on the mosaic of these elements and the ideas that shape them.

At the next stage, the actants become dependent on each other. An important element of this dependence is the question of funding (*Looking for the support*). For NGOs, this is an important issue, because for those without their own budget, the question of raising funds for activities is crucial. What funding they manage to obtain will also have an impact on the nature of their activities, such as a one-off guided tour of the old town or a series of integration workshops for older citizens' clubs. In turn, a certain degree of financial independence, which cultural institutions such as the Museum of Applied Arts can boast, can influence more long-term activities that maintain the social activity of their participants over the course of a year or years. Another element binding the actants at this stage of social activity may be the attitude toward space (*In search for sites*)—its possession, lending, needing, or lacking. A more permanent relationship with the urban space favors long-term social activity. Permanent does not necessarily mean being there all the time but can also refer to a certain cyclicality of being there in the framework of weekly meetings. Decisive in this phase of becoming socially active may also be the location of the actants (*Positioning*), which results from their contracts, documents, or policies. The more actants become dependent on each other, the more densely the network of social activity is weaved. This means that one activity does not only involve one foundation and a group of older people, but also the kindergarten children for whom the older people will act. Another example is the city's commitment to a policy on aging, by embedding it in other specific policies. At this stage, older people are also targeted in order to make the social activity beneficial for them (*Casting the net*) and to encourage them to stay involved for longer.

The next phase of the implementation of social activity describes how the actants perform their activities that fall to them within the given network. One of the possible ways is to create an interesting and appealing offer for older people (*Seduction*). This marketing approach is valid not only for companies, but also for second and third-sector actants, such as museums and foundations. This way of making social activity a reality builds relationships between consumers and service providers. This is the service approach in politics, which does not aim to involve the citizen, but rather to fulfill his or her needs and expectations. The more participatory role of older people in social activity is described in the next section (*Engaged social activity*). Here again the idea of empowerment but also of participation comes into play and older people are involved in further networks through self-development or civic activity (membership of a municipal older citizens' council). This is the kind of social activity that will promote its long-term sustainability. The same is true of reusing events and activities that have already taken place (*To kill two birds with a stone*), where older people's activities are interwoven into the existing networks of organizations and institutions in the city. On the other hand, a certain limitation that contributes to the one-off character of the activities is the task-based nature of the implemented social activities (*Commissioned to actants*). In this case, the project framework implementing a given public task has a limiting effect on its long-term impact and the social involvement of older people. This is due to limited time, funding and rigidly limited measures and results (Durczak et al., 2019; D. Hodgson et al., 2019; Jałocha, 2021).

In the final stage, when the event takes place, a sustainability created by the network may emerge (*Acting for others, Endurance of social activity and Proliferation of social activity*), which will foster participants' re-engagement. It can also turn out to be a rather one-off event, which an active older citizen can enjoy without commitment (*Life full of events*).

Based on the data collected, I presented two types of social activity for older people: one-off and long-term. The former describes activities that aim to deliver an event. In the second type, the activity is aimed at long-term participant involvement, by creating support networks between them and integrating them into existing networks. These two types reflect the attitude toward social activity among the organizations, public and cultural institutions I studied. The types of social active enactment in Poznan presented are not negative and positive. Rather, they are types of social activity for older people implemented in Poznan. Representing two different approaches to policy implementation, one-off social activity refers to service approach (Guy, 2010; Szarfenberg, 2010), which can suit a certain group of recipients who do not want to commit or bind themselves permanently to a particular organization or community. The second type, favoring long-term social commitment, will pursue the ideas of empowerment (Dudgeon et al., 2017; Olech & Kaźmierczak, 2011) and participation (Taylor-Gooby, 2018). In addition, it will allow for the creation of a support network for older people, present in case of problems and limitations due to age (Beresford & Carr, 2018).

The kind of activity that will take place depends on which actants are involved, what other ideas and values influence their approach and goals, and how, and with what resources. In the following Section 4.2—Ontologies of social activity implementation, I will try to organize this multiplicity of social activity by presenting ontologies of its implementation and scales that describe relations between actants.

4.2. Ontologies of social activity implementation

In the previous section (4.1—Social activity enacted), I showed how, based on a process of translation, social activity for older people in Poznan is enacted. In recreating this process, I drew on four moments of translation (problematization, interessement, enrollment and mobilization) to explain how actants bind together to form networks of activity, then negotiate their tasks. Based on the data collected, I also presented two types of social activity for older people: one-off and long-term. The former describes activities that aim to deliver an event. In the second type, the activity is aimed at long-term involvement of the participants by creating support networks between them and integrating them into existing networks. These two types reflect the attitude toward social activism among the organizations, public cultural institutions I studied.

In this chapter, referring to the features of social activity of older people that I have identified, that is, all the categories with which I have described the different moments of translation, I will present the ontologies (4.2 Ontologies of social activity implementation) involved in the implementation of social activity. It refers to the ANT, which uses ontologies to describe the process of implementation of a phenomenon by actants (Blok, A., Farias, I., & Roberts, 2019; Galis, 2011; Mol, 2002). The researcher aims to isolate realities that co-construct the phenomena in question in parallel, complementing but also excluding each other (Blok, A., Farias, I., & Roberts, 2019; Galis, 2011; Iskandarova, 2017).

Presented in the previous chapter, moments of translation were aimed at illustrating the formation of social activity implementation network. In this section, my aim will be to present ontologies that describe the process of implementing social activism for older people in Poznan. In line with the ANT analytical theory, which I adopted in my study, I aim to uncover the networks of relationships and the ways in which these networks are constituted between actants, which in turn create practices. Composed of networks of actants, practices form realities—ontologies—that co-create a given phenomenon (Law, 2008, 2019; Mol, 2002). Therefore, it can be assumed that exposition of my ontology will help to structure the process of implementation of social activity for older people in Poznan, and to look at it from a broader perspective of urban aging policy. As I mentioned in the section describing the analytical framework of my study (Section 2.1—Actor-network theory), ANT researchers perceive the investigated reality as a network of relations which are difficult to describe using the order of things, because they are the result of the mentioned practices, composed of complex networks. The separation of ontologies will allow seeing realities constructing the studied urban policy. Their application also relates to the theoretical concept of this thesis, namely DI, which within economics seeks to understand the complexity of policies and decisions made by individuals. An essential element of this approach is discourse, understood as the narrative through which the ideas that make up a given policy move (Schmidt, 2010). Thus, recreating an ontology will allow us to understand how urban aging policies are made.

The application of ontologies within ANT had had place also in the policy research (Galis, 2011; Iskandarova, 2017). In the study on renewable energy policy (Iskandarova, 2017) ontologies were used to explain different regulations, which formed a distinct network of actants in the implementation of this policy. However, in research on policy toward the needs of people with disabilities (Galis, 2011) application of ontology, understood as separate realities, helped to combine the implementation of this policy, taking into account the experience of disabled people and the relations of power that influence the policy.

Based on my data, I was able to distinguish four ontologies of social activity enactment. In Table 14, I describe distinct characteristics, taken from A. Mol (2002) research on ontologies of medical practice enacting atherosclerosis. Such ideas behind them, socio-material practices, and actants engaged in this ontology establishment, perception of older peoples as the desired product of social activity and finally meanings ascribed to social activity.

Table 14: Ontologies of social activity for older people implementation

	Weaving the network	**Providing a service**	**Responding to the aging crisis**	**Using space**
Engaged actants	- Older people, - Communities, organizations, and programs existing in the city - Individuals or organizations that can utilize the resources of older people, such as children or dependent individuals - Municipal institutions	- Companies, - NGOs, - Public institutions (museums, universities, schools), - Older people needs, - Policymakers	- Policy documents, - Strategic plans - Third sector organizations, - Local authorities, - Strained economy - Aging societies	- Public space, Buildings, - Parks, - Private buildings: cinemas, restaurants - City events
Socio-material practices	- Working for others - Connecting different actants (NGOs, cultural institutions, informal groups, kids, etc.) - Integrating older people - Using of already available resources, e.g., cities events, programs	- Creation of offer; - Recognition of older people's needs. - Promotion practices—discounts, dedicated offers	- Data presentation - Taking actions, initiatives. - Planning. - Developing strategies. - Reporting	- Visiting the city and museums. - Creating age-friendly places. - Renting of premises - Lending space between organizations - Organizing events, festivals, meetings for older people

(Continued)

Table 14: *(Continued)*

	Weaving the network	Providing a service	Responding to the aging crisis	Using space
Perception of older people	- Volunteers - Partners - Source of knowledge and experiences, - Citizens, - Members of the local community	- Customer, - Receiver, - Brand ambassador	- Retired person, over 60 years. - Reason of society aging	- Citizen, - People in the need of safe environment
Social activity meaning	Social activity implies the agency of older people within a group, relations emerging between older people.	Service provided to older people, an event.	Solution for the aging process, task with assigned results.	Meeting with other people in the public space, taking part in a common activity within public space or organizations and institutions' space.

Source: Own elaboration.

4.2.1. Weaving the network

To start explaining the qualities of this ontology, I will relate to the perception of older people held by actants enacting it. This somehow involves ideas behind used practices and clarifying relations between actants. Therefore, older citizens are seen as volunteers, who have time, knowledge, and experience to engage for their own sake or others benefit:

> But then the Older Citizens' Initiatives Centre just left us, the volunteers, to do things, packing leaflets and various other things there, helping at the Fair, helping at the Older Citizens' Days. For what CIS needed us there, we were open. [D13]

This is how one of the older activists, who set up four older citizens' clubs and was a member of the Older Citizens' Council, describes her role and activities while cooperating with the CIS. Next example similarly shows the engagement of older people as helpers for others:

> Among other things, they also had more manual therapy, which was introduced alternately with these classes. This consisted of the fact that older peoples, who themselves also have some cognitive problems, using their resources: sewing machines, hands, and all the other products they needed, we simply bought them and sewed 20 such specialised sensory aprons, which we later donated to the Wielkopolska Association for People with Alzheimer's Disease. [D9]

Apart from being volunteers for others, older people are seen as partners in action, citizens of their local communities, and sources of experience and knowledge, which could be passed on to others:

> I think this is a very valuable group of people to work with because we can also learn a lot from each other, they are a rich source of knowledge and experience. [D3]

The older people are then weaved into various networks. The activities proposed for them lead to more long-term involvement in Older Citizens' Club, local NGOs or some dedicated group led by a public institution. Within this ontology, it is useful to recall the section entitled *To kill two birds with one stone*, in which I described how the enactment of social activity is inscribed into existing resources, such as networks in local communities or NGOs. Here is another example of weaving practice, which reflects this reality:

> I mean, I will put it this way, as an example, when we were doing one of the initiatives, I was approached by the leader of an informal group of older citizens, and I invited her to one of the events, I organized a meeting with the local community and the youth, and with people with disabilities, and she was very pleased not only that she could participate in the meeting, but also that I met her with other people, representatives of particular organizations, institutions. This was also very important to her, and it helped her make those first contacts, to get to know the environment, to get to know who is from non-governmental organisations, that there is a psychologist from this school, or that there is a teacher, for example, or that there is a clergyman, for example, so that she would also have contacted so that she would know who to contact if she needed to. [D12]

This description of how my interlocutor introduced an older leader into her environment underscores that this ontology is about cooperation and partnership, and older people are just another group that can weaved themselves into these networks of relations. On the one hand, such inclusion of older people is beneficial for them, promoting their activity and consequently their well-being (Bilotta et al., 2012; Coll-Planas et al., 2017; Granbom et al., 2017). On the other hand, their inclusion is dictated by the resources they possess which may be useful to others. We are talking here about time, knowledge, experience that can be devoted to those who need help (Alzheimer's patients) or time (children in kindergartens).

In such reality, social activity implies an agency of older people, who as partners or volunteers are encumbered with obligation and responsibilities, such as recall one of older leaders:

> I ran all the activities, in terms of lists. We had to elect a treasurer because we had a statute. The director of the Association helped to write the statute so that it was all official. And we had to have our contribution, so we could participate in projects. And if money from the local government came in, we would write a project on health and life, what we wanted to do in the club in a given year, and we'd get money. [D13]

The similar empowerment of older people was mentioned in the previous section—Vehicles of social activity (section on *Engaged social activity*). It is once more reflected in the local documents, namely in the *Older Citizen Policy of Poznan 2017–2021*:

> Older people community, represented by the City Council of Older Citizens and—nongovernmental organisations, will be involved in monitoring activities, expressing their opinions, comments, and proposals. Monitoring will be a continuous and constant process of observing quantitative and qualitative changes aimed at providing information on the effectiveness of the actions undertaken and the results achieved. In this way, current and phased control over the degree of implementation within the outlined tasks will be ensured. [D14]

This kind of deliberate recognition of older citizens as advisers, written in policy documents, aims at the inclusion of older people in matters concerning them which are decided in the particular municipal departments.

Weaving the network is an ontology within which social activity is enacted through older people's networking. Within this ontology, it is important to see social activity as a set of practices that connect actants to each other. The ideas behind it, such as empowerment, the creation of relationships of dependency between actants or the use of available resources result in the networking of the urban policy of aging in Poznan, in which the older person has agency and the possibility of influencing their environment.

On the one hand, this ontology refers to the social activity of older people, which empowers them, engages them, and weaves them into local communities. The presence of such ontologies in the urban policy of aging in Poznan, which I researched, fits in with the more popular trend in the west toward the welfare state, which seeks to create networks of support between citizens (Beresford & Carr, 2018; Olech & Kaźmierczak, 2011; Taylor-Gooby, 2018). In this way, a part of the responsibility for meeting needs is shifted to local communities and support networks. This is a solution that allows for a reduction in state expenditure on social objectives. On the other hand—*Weaving the network*—raises another issue, namely intersectorality in the management of local social policy (Rémillard-Boilard et al., 2020; Theiss, 2012, 2017). This is a practice trend related to local social policy, which perceives policy to be more effective if it is built on a support network of different actants. This means a move away from a sectoral approach to a more networked or even informal one. In the case of my research, a similar tendency can be seen in the activities of city authorities, which try to incorporate activities for older people into already-existing networks, programs, and city policies. What is more, they try to make sure that the policy on aging is also perceived as beneficial by other residents.

4.2.2. Providing a service

The implementation of this ontology is linked with the transformation of social activity into service provided to older citizens by various entities. For the private companies, this kind of approach is rather understandable, as for third-sector organizations and public institutions it is not so clear-cut. They also offer their services to older people, at least so they speak about it; however, they do not charge them for that.

For the market-based organizations, older people were seen as customers, with specified needs, within their need for social activity. This was used by them, so the older customers were displaced into the role of brand ambassadors, who in exchange for a discount or specially designed services were supposed to encourage others to also use their services. During my observation on *The VIVA Older Citizens' fairs,* I also saw a great number of companies, such as tourist offices, language schools, or sports centers, which even decided to dedicate their endeavor to older people. Following is a leaflet from a travel agency that caters exclusively to older people.

Among trips to various places in Poland and abroad, there are also offers of trips to sanatoriums.

Photograph 4: Photographs of leaflets collected during the VIVA Older Citizens' Fair. They advertise a tourist office dedicated to older people, which offers domestic and foreign trips. Their clients are active older people.

Source: Private collection.

This market-based enactment of social activity for older people is consciously accepted by a municipal worker:

> So, business needs to sell, it needs some CSR, it needs some promotion, and it needs to study the needs of older peoples to create a product tailored to them. [...] I don't think we should be afraid of business to the very end, I mean, of course, we are a municipal unit, so we don't accept everything that comes along. Because it is also true, I have to say directly that if we wanted to open ourselves completely for business, we would not have financial problems. Because many companies come and say: 'we will throw you this money, promote us'. [D2]

However, as he later notes, this approach to older people may involve some risks for them:

> We also know that many companies view older peoples typically as business customers and sometimes apply unfair rules, mechanisms, and schemes, and we must avoid this and warn older peoples against it. [D2]

As the director of the Centre for Older Citizens' Initiatives recalls, they need to be careful with such cooperation, as it can be harmful for older people, by tricking them into buying expensive products or services or by exploiting their lack of knowledge of, for example, technology. However, he also notes the benefit of involving private companies as they provide additional financial support and extensive lists of possible social activities in Poznan. In any case, as I mentioned, public institutions and NGOs import from private companies the service-based approach toward older people, which is expressed in the establishment of *offer* and thus market diagnosis:

> I process them to a large extent through myself and through what interests me, and also through what I know interests other people because I observe all kinds of trends, needs, I read, I watch what is happening in other museums in the world and I see what catches my fancy and what does not. [D4]

To respond accurately to the needs of older visitors and prepare the most suitable for the offer, the museum worker performs reconnaissance of what might attract them. One more example, from another museum, illustrates the tailoring of services, to mold the offer:

> So, the offer has evolved over the years, but at the beginning, when it was created, it was also created in consultation with the City Older Citizens' Council, i.e., with the older peoples themselves, so that we knew what interest them and what would be good for them. [D3]

This gentle process of the need to diagnosis in the form of consultation can be juxtaposed with an opinion on older people's satisfaction.

> I always say to the president, to anyone, to older peoples: Recall that an older citizen needs three things: to eat, to have fun and to go out, these are the three basic things that will satisfy an older citizen. And we are moving in this direction. [D11]

This practice of probing the needs and problems of older people is crucial to grasp the values in this ontology, which is *to provide* an event, entertainment, or some form of development. Referring to the quoted statements of an employee of an NGO, a museum, or an organizer of an older citizens' club, it can be noted that the practices used also transform older people into customers, recipients of services. In creating a given activity, their expectations are taken into account, but, as we see in the last section, they can sometimes be reduced to very basic ones, such as free food and entertainment. This determines the relationship between them as provider and client, which can be satisfying or irritating. This relationship is shattered by the gratuitousness of events organized for older people. As the organizers themselves explain, it stems from a desire to include all older peoples, regardless of economic status. This is why the vast majority of events organized for them are free of charge. For some community organizers, this is normal, but during the survey it was also claimed that the absence of fees causes disrespect on the part of participants, e.g., by not turning up at events where there was a registration requirement, or by taking food out of events. These reflections of my interlocutors support the earlier conclusion of a more service-oriented relationship between the event provider and the audience, lack of commitment and responsibility.

Furthermore, practices of this ontology also involve dividing older people according to their special needs and then the formation of proper offer:

> Usually, these activities are two-fold—for more active older peoples who may want more from life and who want more, we try to stimulate them to want more, to be more independent and to stay independent for longer. We also divide older peoples into a group of more dependent ones, mainly those with dementia, for whom we usually have other activities. [D9]

Such profiling of older people shows that social activity is also a type of service not only in the market but also in the nonprofit sector, to meet these needs. Within such reality, relations which emerges between actants were more strictly defined and occasional, which can be once a week, and usually, they were limited to some period:

> It is usually the case that they sign up for a whole series of classes, so we are together for, say, six months or a whole year, depending on how our schedule is laid out. [D3]

To conclude the ontology of providing a service, I would like to emphasize that the practices that comprise it, that is, creating an offer, identifying the market and the needs of older people, encouraging customers in the form of free products or discounts, lead to social activity understood as a service. For market players, this understanding of the activities undertaken is linked to their approach to business. This form of providing services is an opportunity for them to promote or implement CSR strategies (Freitag, 2008; Latapí Agudelo et al., 2019). As noted by the director of the CIS, the involvement of companies in aging policies in the city are beneficial, because it allows companies to offer more to older residents at lower cost. This is a form of public-private partnership, which, as described in the literature, refers to the joining of forces of public and private institutions in meeting the needs of the residents. However, this is a quantitative rather than a qualitative response to the problems of an aging population and older people.

Within this ontology, organizations from the II and III sectors also present a service character. This is related to the service approach in social policy I already mentioned in the previous chapter (Guy, 2010; Jałocha, 2021; Szarfenberg, 2010). Its premise is to approach people using state aid as service recipients. The aim of this approach is to reduce the stigmatization of persons benefiting from various forms of state aid (Chaczko, 2021; Grewiński, 2009; Guy, 2010; Theiss, 2017). In the case of my research, however, one can also see a problem resulting from such a relationship between the public entity and the service recipient, namely less involvement of the participants or a demanding attitude toward the services received. This may also result from a misconception of what social activity events are supposed to be for older people and moreover indicate a lack of satisfaction of basic needs such as food, financial independence, or lack of funds for paid social and cultural activities.

4.2.3. Responding to the aging crisis

Within this ontology, there are practices involved in depicting the aging process with data that illustrate its impact on the functioning of the state and the economy. Older people are then seen as the causes of this phenomenon, and their very social activity is seen as an opportunity to deal with this problem. It therefore takes on a new dimension, which goes beyond the local activities of organizations and institutions to become an action to counter the demographic challenge, which can help to minimize the problem of the large number of older people in relation to the working population, the problem of the efficiency of social, health or long-term care systems.

Presented statistics were placed within city policy and aimed at illustrating the problem of enlarging a group of older people in comparison to decreasing in other social groups and imposing its effects on society and economy:

> A commonly observed demographic phenomenon is the aging of societies worldwide. Also in Poznan, a phenomenon that will intensify in the coming years is the ageing of the population. According to data from the Central Statistical Office, covering the state and demographic structure of Poznan in 2016, the indicator of demographic old age, determining the share of people 65 years and older (103 291), is 19.1 % (in 2000—13.6 %). (…) The only group in which there will be an increase in numbers (by 20.1 thousand, or 19 %) is the population in the post-working age. According to the Central Statistical Office forecast, in 2035 the number of people in all age groups up to 24 years of age will fall. However, the number of older people will increase. The population over 65 years of age will increase by 32 %, including those 85 years and over by 87 %. [D14]

As it can be seen, the statistics are triggers in this reality for action; however, before action is taken, the authors of policy depict challenges, which come with a defined problem:

> Poznan's current demographic situation and projections indicate a need to continue the current and plan and take further measures, in particular, to introduce increasingly effective instruments to ensure the best possible living conditions for Poznan's older citizens. [D14]

What comes from these short declarations are a few practices, which are employed in this ontology, namely *planning, taking measures,* and *introducing effective measures*. What is worth noticing is that these practices are limited with desired results, which need to be reported. In such a reality, social activity is a closed cycle, precisely described and divided into pieces, a tool of local policy, along with others, such as putting up apartments adjusted to the needs of older peoples, promoting preventive healthcare or prolonged labor activity.

Moreover, social activity is also one of the conditions to achieve established plans and linked with their results. In the policy documents the authors claimed that determined tasks were realized and, in their results, leads to desired future:

> The Program 'Older Citizenship Policy' of the City of Poznan for 2017–2021 identifies actions, tasks, and initiatives that shape the conditions for dignified and healthy ageing. [D14]

During my data analysis, I came across offers which were answers to competition for the delivery of public tasks, carried out by The Municipal Office.

Within these documents, social activity was enacted also by practices linked with tasks, measures, and results:

> Synthetic description of the task
>
> Meetings at the club will be held a minimum of twice a week. During this time, older people will be able to benefit from various types of social activity, including, among others: physical, educational, cultural, and recreational and, indirectly, care activities.
>
> Results
>
> Social activity of older people with visual impairment. [D21]

The ontology presented shows that in implementing the idea of social activity of older people in Poznan, it was important to recognize the significance of the problem of aging and the resulting threats to society and the economy. This type of representation of the problem presents older people, on the one hand, as the source of the problem and, on the other, as the recipients of activities undertaken in relation to it. A similar reality emerges from research on the social activity of older people (Carr et al., 2015; Granbom et al., 2017; Ho, 2017a; Novak & Vute, 2013a; Pei et al., 2014; Rezaeipandari et al., 2020; Suzuki et al., 2021), identified by me within the framework of the presented review (see Section 1.2—Urban aging). The ontology identified provides an understanding of why the city engages older people. Previously emerging ideas of empowerment, fostering participation or networking local social policy could indicate that the implementation of social activism is an embodiment of these very ideas. However, within the framework of the ontology described in this section, I wanted to show that social activity of older people is an activity which is a response to the pressing problem of aging. Moreover, it is an activity undertaken based on public tasks, defined in laws and strategic documents, and finally it is also the result of the activities mentioned earlier, included in documents, programs and strategies at the local but also national level. Social activity is therefore implemented through all these activities, and by combining them it becomes the impetus for creating an urban aging policy.

4.2.4. Using space

Within this last ontology, I present a group of practices that refer to the city space, but also to the buildings of public institutions, restaurants, or

NGOs. The use of space is therefore one of the realities responsible for the implementation of social activity for older people. Within this ontology, the politics of aging acquires a spatial character, and the focus is not on the activity itself or on older people, but rather refers to practices that describe different kinds of interactions with space, not only of older people, but also of organizations and informal groups that do not have this space. My aim is to bring within this ontology of local politics the material perspective that is the city, its buildings, and streets. This is particular to this level of policy-making, because the projected actions are made real, among other things, also by the place in which they take place, but also by the relations to it of the participants or organizers of the action.

The following photo is an advertisement for the University of the Third Age, organized by the local University of Life Sciences. This is also offered by other universities. Following is a quote from an interview with the director of the CIS, who notes that creating such a space is important for older people, as it gives them a space to meet and have fun together.

Photograph 5: Fragment of a leaflet of the University of the Third Age, organized by the Poznan University of Life Sciences.
Source: Private collection.

Photographs of older people in the role of students further capture the imagination of the audience, emphasizing the belonging of older people to the university space and giving them the role of students.

> On the other hand, they [older people] sometimes need information support, who need space for entertainment, and this is what the University of the Third Age offers. [D2]

The very fact of having a place to stay triggers social activity among older people. For an organization that does not have its own premises, it is necessary to find such a free space to carry out an activity. The following excerpt refers to this situation, where the activities of one organization can be triggered by borrowing space from another:

> This room is located in the Old Town and this is where we came up with the initiative so that every Wednesday older people could come to us if they wanted. [D9]

In these examples, space appeared as a site for meetings. They draw attention to social activity as staying somewhere because it involves activities of going out, making acquaintances, and performing various activities. Without the space, no matter if it is a museum, cinema, or public park, activities do not have any embodiment and this chance to interact with others.

Photograph 6: A tour of the Museum of Applied Arts in Poznan, organized as part of the Older Citizens' Days.
Source: Private collection.

Photograph 7: A tour of the Museum of Applied Arts in Poznan organized as part of the Older Citizens' Days.
Source: Private collection.

The photographs opposite show a tour of the Museum of Applied Arts, by a group of older people, organized by the museum as part of Older Citizens' Days. The space actually makes social activity a reality by providing a place to meet and, with the exhibits on display, creates content for the activity itself. It can therefore be said that through programs and activities of various public entities, space is given to older citizens.

The pictures preceding illustrate social activities that rely on older people being in some kind of space. This could be the enclosed space of a local cinema, which becomes a dedicated space for older people once a week. In the second case, the ad concerns a more open and extensive public space. It is an advertisement for walks in and around Poznan with the Poznan Tourist Organization, which offers tours specifically for older citizens.

Furthermore, apart from social activity enactment by the sheer activity of staying in some common space, it can be enacted by space ownership, which could be seen in the examples of older citizens' clubs and NGOs, which need space when planning some activity or even regular group meetings. Space seems to be right, without which it is difficult to act.

Photograph 8: Leaflet advertising the Muza cinema as the Older Citizen's cinema.
Source: Private collection.

Photograph 9: Excerpts from the bulletin of the Poznan Local Tourist Organization, offering trips in and around Poznan for older people.
Source: Private collection.

It is also visible in the ventures of municipal workers and their program *Age-Friendly Spaces*. Within it, older people can visit local restaurants and cafes, on a low budget:

> But we also provide information on what is going on in the city, recommend associations, places that work with us, places that are friendly to older peoples. [D1]

As part of this, private companies are also opening up to older people and taking part in social activities. Like stated by a CIS employee, thanks to these activities older people were better informed about what was happening in the city, where they could stay and where they could meet, which may encourage them to undertake other less formal social activities.

In general, just being in a space can be a trigger for social activity, such as visiting a museum or an old town. But space is also an essential element of social activity, sometimes unnoticed. This point is the context of social activity discussed in the literature (Beard & Montawi, 2015; Dawidowicz et al., 2020; Xiong et al., 2020; Yung et al., 2016), discussed by me in earlier parts of the thesis (see Section 1.2—Urban aging). This ontology can be seen as the distribution of older people's social activity across the available public and private spaces. Researchers emphasize the need for equal access to this space. Equal in terms of financial and infrastructural accessibility. The Older Citizens' Friendly Places action, which certifies places based on their accessibility for older residents, is one such action.

However, this ontology also includes the complexity of the relationship between the city space, including public institutions, and residents, NGOs, or informal organizations such as older citizens' clubs. It is worth noting that social implementation gives older residents a right to it, through dedicated events and adapted infrastructure. However, it also draws attention to organizations' right to have space in order to function. The same is true of older citizens' clubs, which, as sometimes informal groups, are forced to seek space in friendly associations or public institutions. This shows a certain friction in the process of giving space to the inhabitants. On the one hand, this takes place in the form of various events, but on the other hand, the lack of such space for use by local NGOs results in this space being taken away. Similar issues are raised by research on local initiatives, also in Poznan (Durczak et al., 2019), but above all by the current contemporary urban studies referring to the phenomenon of gentrification or the right to the city (Domaradzka, 2018; Harding & Blockland, 2014; Jayne & Ward, 2017). However, these studies emphasize the commercialization of urban spaces, even for the purposes of policy, with the result that they become too valuable, too expensive for the average resident. These findings can also be applied to urban policies on aging in Poznan. Where, on the one hand, the city opens up to residents, in the framework of one-off events, but remains difficult to access for organizations wishing to work on behalf of older people.

The materiality of the city and its role in policymaking are also strongly evident. Space is crucial and necessary for any activity. Besides enabling social activities for older citizens, it is also something permanent, and even if an activity is a one-time event, space is a carrier for further similar activities, a link for equal interests. If there is an event somewhere that activates older people socially, then a relationship is created with that place.

Conclusions

In this section, I strove to introduce four ontologies of social activity implementation. They represent different realities of this process. Each of them is enacted within different socio-material practices, which would refer to the earlier mentioned moments of translation (Mol, 2002). Although they form separate realities, distanced in their interests, and relations between actants, they interact with each other (Mol, 2002). Their prevalence is not to be exactly described, but they rather form four threads, which can connect, complete, or dominate over each other within implementation of social activity for older people (Mol, 2002). As an example, I will mention the case of the Porta Posnania Museum, which systematically creates offers of events for older people (*Providing a service*). As a museum employee comments, older people are one of the groups that are important for the museum because of the mission it has adopted. Therefore, they cannot imagine not having an offer of events for older people. Within this ontology, we can see the practices of public institutions aiming to deliver social activity as a service to one of their audiences, which corresponds to a service approach in social policy. However, at the same time, within each cycle of events created by this museum, more lasting relationships are established between the participants, some of them stay and get involved in subsequent projects, which already indicates social activity seen in the perspective of *Weaving the network* ontology, where the agency of the older person emerges and the social activity itself aims to network its participants and include them in support networks.

Another example that will illustrate the implementation of social activeness of older people is the senior policy of the city authorities, which in its content presents the need to take action in the face of the problem of aging societies (*Responding to the aging crisis*). Among the measures proposed by this policy is the promotion of social activity of the oldest inhabitants. Moreover, as the director of the CIS, who was the co-creator of this policy, mentions in an interview, the aim is for the policy to draw on the resources and activities of specific policies, such as infrastructure policy, spatial policy, or social assistance (*Weaving the network* and *Using space*).

The aim of identifying these ontologies was to understand the implementation of social activity of older people at the level of urban aging policy in Poznan. Although the identified ontologies refer to well-known trends, ideas and approaches in social policy, including local social policy, that is, the ideas of empowerment (Dudgeon et al., 2017; Klimczuk, 2018; Olech & Kaźmierczak, 2011), participation and networking (Beresford & Carr, 2018; Taylor-Gooby, 2018), public-private partnership (Jałocha, 2021; Snopko, 2014), the phenomenon of projectization (D. Hodgson et al., 2019; Skrzypek-Prawelska & Jałocha, 2014), distinguishing these concepts within the presented ontologies allows to understand the complexity behind the creation of local aging policy, and even local social policy. Above all, because the coexistence of these ontologies means the coexistence of practices that can be mutually exclusive, when more emphasis in a given policy is placed on providing a service, that is, social activity, which is monitored by the number of activities undertaken (*Providing a service*), and less on networking older people (*Weaving the network*). Both ontologies will result from a different understanding of social activity, which will also imply different intended outcomes. In my study of urban aging policies in Poznan, I identified two types of social activity, described by me in the previous chapter. Their existence may be indicative of the twofold directionality of measures taken in Poznan toward older people. I do not assess this but rather point to it as a result of the implementation of social activity through the ontologies I have identified.

Furthermore, referring to local social policy research (Czupich, 2018; Klimczuk & Tomczyk, 2016; Kutsar & Kuronen, 2015a; Theiss, 2017), which focuses on analyzing economic, political, cultural or structural factors, the ontologies I propose provide a new perspective for further local social policy research. Using the approach of DI, I have searched for certain discourses (Hall & Taylor, 1996; Schmidt, 2008, 2010), which, within the analytical approach of ANT, I have just called ontologies (Galis, 2011; Iskandarova, 2017; Latour, 1993; Schmidt, 2008). Together they form a picture of the dominant narratives in a given policy, while touching on the aforementioned areas previously analyzed separately as concrete factors shaping local social policy. Thus, referring to the mentioned need for a more comprehensive approach to the study of local social policy (Theiss, 2017), I propose to understand it through dominant ontologies, which are the result of different practices and the ideas and interests behind them that push actants to act.

4.3. Scales of Social activity Implementation

Until now, I have presented the outcome of my research, which came from the application of ANT. The goal was to comprehend the nature of social activity for older individuals in Poznan (4.1. Social Activity Enacted) and the methods used to implement it (4.2. Ontologies of Social Activity for Older People Implementation). I introduced four ontologies, with the aim of understanding and clarifying the implementation process based on my data. In this section, I extend the emerging data process of social activity implementation with the concept of glocalization, described in detail in Section 3.2—Glocalization. The application of glocalization serves as an additional theoretical framework for examining decentralization processes in social policy, particularly in the context of aging policy (Bdowski, 2016; Theiss, 2007; Urbaniak, 2018). These processes present a novel set of relationships that deviate from traditional vertical governance and respond to the hierarchical implementation process (DeLeon & DeLeon, 20In my research, I interpret glocalization as the upward movement of the state to the international level and the downward movement to the local level of governance due to globalization (Cox, 2009; Swyngedouw, 1996, 2005). 09; Swyngedouw, 1996, 2005). Hence, the formation of local policies is not a simple result of a hierarchical system of administration; it is subject to the action of both global and local forces resulting from economic, social, political, and territorial circumstances (Kutsar & Kuronen, 2015; Swyngedouw, 1996; Theiss, 2017; Wathen, 2020).

Within the concept of glocalization, researchers use the concept of scale to understand local policymaking in the age of globalization (Swyngedouw, 1997). Scales are elements of the glocalization concept widespread in policy research (Farías & Bender, 2010; Latham & McCormack, 2010; Nygren et al., 2005; Smigiel, 2019; Sun et al., 2017; Swyngedouw, 2005; Wathen, 2020) and they are elements that allow to capture these shifting directions of policy formations on the local level, which become significant as an outcome of welfare decentralization (Andreotti & Mingione, 2016; Kutsar & Kuronen, 2015). They are represented in the data by dominant values and leading actants, which influence relations in the political process (Wathen, 2020).

In this part of the book, I introduce the scales I have identified in the data, describing them by the extreme values they use. I begin with a scale known as "Initiation of Social Activity," which pertains to the origin of the social activity. This refers to whether the activity originates from the ground up or if it is the result of external ideas. Next, I will introduce the 'Execution of Social Activity' scale. In this scale, I concentrate on delineating the range of social activity implementation methods, ranging from project-based endeavors to those executed through local initiatives or informal means. The "Embeddedness of Social Activity" is another scale that assesses the activity's integration into an organization or community. Finally, I will present the last scale, "Resource Mining," which deals with the resources involved in the implementation of social activity, from individual to public to market.

4.3.1. Initiation of social activity

Within this scale, I will discuss the issue of initiating social activity among older people in Poznan. The aim is to show what forces influence their implementation and, more specifically, what prompts actions taken at the level of the policy examined. Based on the collected data, I distinguished two extreme values of the presented scale. The first signifies *the grassroots* inception of social activity, whereas the second, on the other hand, stems from *external forces* within the local communities.

Grassroots initiatives

I will start by discussing the bottom-up aspect of initiating social activism among older people. The director of the Centre for Older Citizens' Initiatives generally mentions this approach to social activity enactment and policy:

> It is difficult to say that the policy is established from the top down because it has been prepared from the bottom up. It is established by the president, he coordinates it and watches over it together with the city council, while the policy itself was created from the bottom up. And the initiatives are bottom-up. In my view, the city policy's success stems from its grassroots approach, where no one imposes any changes, and it undergoes constant updates and adaptations. [D2]

He emphasizes that the process of designing policies for older citizens follows a bottom-up approach, where older citizens and activists shape it. Furthermore, he demonstrates:

> Or she comes and says: "Listen, my mother has problems moving around the cemetery. She won't disclose this to anyone due to feelings of shame and her inability to communicate. "But it is such a voice: "do something about it." The city pays attention, leading to the creation of Handyman,[25] which provides free transportation to the cemetery, facilitates movement around it, and renovates graves, among other initiatives. [D2]

This is a recognition of relations between the Centre for Older Citizens' Initiatives, the Municipal Office, and the older people, the receivers of their actions. However, a bottom-up flow of initiatives was also present in the relationship between NGOs and older citizens' clubs.

> Older Citizens Clubs and older individuals in Poznan are familiar with us, and they frequently approach us with requests for activities aimed at enhancing their cognitive abilities. We could also undertake a project that would introduce them to the cultural offerings in the Old Town. [D9]

The speaker emphasizes that the crucial element in determining who directs actions for older individuals is their approach to us. Other NGOs or older citizens' clubs have also emphasized this bottom-up approach. The bottom-up direction of initiatives seems to be their significant advantage.

The described aspect of the scale refers to the grassroots implementation of social activity among older people. This issue has already been addressed in earlier parts of this book, when I referred to the idea of empowerment

25 It is a program in which older people can use the services of a handyman, a taxi, or the repair of minor defects at home. All services are funded by the city; you just need to apply to CIS.

or participation in social policymaking, which were the actants responsible for the implementation of social activity for older people. These ideas aim to increase residents' involvement and their influence in policymaking. According to my interviews, the organizers of activities for older people believe that these initiatives originate from the interested parties themselves. However, given the presence of the aforementioned concepts aiming at citizen empowerment in policies, the bottom-up approach to these activities appears to be driven by existing policy approaches and strategies.

External forces

There is also the other side of the scale, which, in contrast to the bottom-up character of initiating social activity, refers to more top-down forces shaping a given initiative. It consists of the values that guide the actants, those at the local level, but also the values adopted by higher-level policymakers. It can be illustrated with the Older Citizens' Animator (Animator Senioralny) project, an instructional program dedicated to people who work with Older Citizens' Clubs. It aims to give them tools to successfully develop their clubs' functioning, enhance their independence, and help them solve problems. Two interviews highlighted this project. The first interview was conducted with a worker from the Centre for Older Citizens' Initiatives and the second one was with the leader of a foundation that primarily serves older people. However, both individuals present their perspectives on the program in unique ways. For the center worker, the project aims to empower older people in their role as leaders of Older Citizens' Clubs. The foundation worker recalls these workshops and comments on her accounts' low number of young participants. He believes that young people should work for older people, a viewpoint that differs slightly from the program's goal of empowering older individuals to become local leaders. This conflict in the perceptions of older people highlights the potential for younger individuals to take the initiative of social activity. Another example also demonstrates this reconfiguration of scale.

> **Activists:** As part of this "older person to older person" cooperation, we used to go there for Valentine's Day; there was a May party; there was a ball; it's all in the archives. We continued this tradition at Older Citizen's Corner until the city took over and no longer wanted our presence.

Interviewer: But where didn't you want to be?

A: No, the president took over the patronage of these "Ugory"[26] events, and he organised other breakfasts there, ones on a larger scale. So, our club went .... [D13]

Another type of external influence on the implementation of social activism is the programs, policies, or strategies that feed this process. An example of such a program within the framework of Poznan's urban aging policy that I researched is the AFC, run by the World Health Organization (WHO), which Poznan joined in 2016. It relies on the certification process. It means that the city that joins the network of AFCs receives a certificate which attests to their age-friendliness. However, to become a member, a candidate must fulfill specified WHO criteria and make future commitments. The Poznan data revealed that a group of local older activists partially initiated the AFC's membership by bringing the idea to the President's Office. Municipal workers, obligated by their membership in the AFC network, had to develop an older citizens' policy that aligned with the WHO guidelines.

We formulated an application, which the president also drafted and forwarded to the WHO. In this application, we detailed the city's efforts and accomplishments in the realm of older citizens' policy. Additionally, he conveyed the city's responsibility to develop a new plan, specifically one focused on older citizens' policy. Such an action plan has been in place for several years. Later, the city will consider the needs of older people in all policies, including "small" ones like roads and construction, and will adopt a strong stance on this issue. We submitted an application, received acceptance into the network, and Poznan became the second city in Poland to join the network of ageing-friendly cities. We have a certificate confirming the city's acceptance into the network. And now, this is it: There were specific tasks and obligations that the city needed to fulfill. Our main task was to prepare a plan; the President decided following the resolution of the city councillors because the procedures are such that for a city to be admitted to the network, the councillors had to agree that the city should apply, and such an agreement was given by the councillors; in other words, it was an authorization for the President. The President issued a special request and drafted a commitment from the city, which included preparing this plan and incorporating the needs of older citizens into local policies, among other things. We proceeded to implement the commitments made. Our basic commitment is to prepare a plan. [D2]

---

[26] The event took place in the nursing home for older people.

This commitment to the program encourages a specific approach to designing policies for older citizens, including a sectoral approach that focuses on specific aspects such as city infrastructure and housing. The director of the Centre for Older Citizens' Initiatives stated that these measures aimed to improve the city's friendliness for older people, potentially motivating them to engage in social networks and feel secure.

Within this scale, I aimed to focus specifically on the issue of initiating social action, a topic not explicitly addressed in Poznan's urban policy on aging. Thus, this scale encapsulates the process of initiating action for older people. It acknowledges the residents' grassroots efforts but also acknowledges the influence of external factors like NGOs, city-adopted programs, strategies, and policies, which hold certain assumptions about the conduct of activities in a specific area. Therefore, the scale presented here illustrates certain tensions existing within the framework of initiating social activity. Referring to the literature, however, it is possible to view these two opposing points on the scale as complementary (Putnam, 1995). This is because the bottom-up element is considered by researchers to be an important social element in the creation of local social policy, which allows for increased relevance and effectiveness, as well as a quicker response to emerging problems (1995). As a result, it complements external ideas implemented in local policies. The organizers of social activity may place emphasis on its initiation from below to gain credibility and trust from citizens, who, by participating in the decision-making process, can supervise the actions and enforce the declarations made by the decision-makers (Theiss, 2017).

4.3.2. Execution of social activity

While in the previous section I referred to the driver of events concerning older people and politics in general, here the scale allows us to frame how activity is realized. My goal was to understand the categories within which social activity is realized. Based on the information I collected, I was able to differentiate between two levels of this scale. The first one refers to activities implemented based on projects and the guidelines they contain. The second level includes activities implemented locally by NGOs or older citizens' clubs. Implementation of social action is a broad concept that includes funding, action planning, and expected outcomes.

Carried within a project

Within project-based activities, social activities obviously differ from one another, depending on the task the project is to carry out, the results it proposes, and the metrics. However, these elements provide some constant in facilitating social activity for older people:

> As far as I recall, we initiated our work here with a funded project, a larger initiative that relied on older volunteers. And then it turned into a second project, which involved older men and women running classes for families with children in cooperation with our educator, which were created together, with a common scenario. Because we gathered a group of people who are very diverse, willing to cooperate, and who also work in different professions in this project, we created a series of classes during which, for example, veterinarians talked about their work. [D3]

The example shown illustrates the process of creating social activities for older people within the Porta Posnania Museum. According to the museum worker, older people's activities were based on the museum's early projects. The museum's initiatives were framed by the subsequent projects. The project-based implementation of social activities set the entity's activities on track and provided it with the necessary tools. Unfortunately, it also happens that such assistance is needed, as was the case with the ideas for action in one of the foundations:

> Yes, I wrote two projects, one for the Ministry, at the end of last year, when I already knew more or less what to do here. The other was for the city. Unfortunately, neither one nor the other got funding. [D5]

Applications, both for municipal and ministerial funds, have failed. This example shows a grassroots initiative put forward by a given foundation, which, however, cannot come into being because it does not meet the conditions of available projects. We can therefore see the interpenetration of the two scales of initiating and implementing community activity. Their interplay in the quoted example, on the one hand, points to the grassroots character of the activities undertaken, or more precisely, of the ideas, but if they do not fit into the framework of available projects, their implementation is impossible. Therefore, we can conclude that the realization of a bottom-up initiative requires its integration into external and top-down programs and projects. This was the case with ventures designed for older activists.

> We wanted to support a project for older people who do not go out at all and are trapped. The Municipal Council of Older Citizens provided a lift for one individual, but deemed it excessive for the others. [D13]

Similar to the previous example, it can be seen that people working for older residents in some way need the project as a legitimization of their activities and ideas, and as a source of funding for planned activities. Regrettably, the resources available to activists through projects do not include assistance for older dependents. By focusing on the project-based level of social activity implementation, we were able to identify a discrepancy between the bottom-up initiation of social activity, as outlined in the previous scale, and its execution within projects commissioned by the city or the ministry.

Carried out locally

Such a failure in carrying out the desired actions leads to the opposite side of the Executing *Social Activity* Scale, which is called *Carried out Locally and* refers to ventures completed with the local forces of an NGO:

> Because at the very beginning we also received such opinions "from below," and we also had such observations ourselves, that in general there were a lot of older people on the street, in the market, and in the shops, and that maybe it would be good to organise such a shopping campaign for older people so that they would sit at home. [D8]

This example demonstrates that it is feasible to conduct social activities for older individuals within the constraints of the organization, which includes the community members and their available time. Another example could be the actions implemented by the local older citizens' club:

> That's when we thought about how to help people in these difficult circumstances, and that's when we came up with the idea of sewing masks together with older citizens and volunteers. We organized a group to sew masks for older people who were unable to leave their homes due to the pandemic, and we personally delivered these masks to their homes, providing them with a sense of safety. [D12]

Moreover, the initiators themselves, whether an organization or an informal group like an older citizens' club, determine the implementation of a given project, its purpose, and its success. This leads to the conclusion that social activity realization is largely dependent on the resources available within the organization. They provide a certain level of independence in the activities undertaken. However, due to a lack of financial resources, organizations often rely on volunteers to handle their work, resulting in them forgoing their salaries, which can pose a threat to their survival. Consequently, this may rather limit the independent willingness of organizations and informal groups to initiate or implement activities, as it deprives them of the means to maintain their organizations. This problem is part of the phenomenon of the dominance of grants and projects in locally implemented policies (D. Hodgson et al., 2019; Jałocha, 2021; Skrzypek-Prawelska & Jałocha, 2014). While so far, I have mentioned the limitations resulting from this, related to the duration of the project, which can be a hindrance to the long-term effects of the activities undertaken, here another issue appears, namely the problem of matching the activities envisaged in the project. The commissioning of public tasks within the framework of projects is one way of giving local organizations responsibility by transferring funds for the realization of specific goals. However, as it results from the data, the tasks commissioned for implementation result from the assumptions of top-down policies and laws regulating the tasks of a given unit, and they may not be in line with the activities that local organizations and groups want to undertake based on their experiences and observations.

4.3.3. Resources mining

In my description of the previous scale, I brought up the issue of resources that fall under this scale's purview. They are an important component of social activity implementation. In the collected data, the word resource does not refer only to financial resources but also to time, needed space, qualifications, or knowledge. The scale's framework elucidates the resources utilized by participants in social activities for the older people. I have classified them as those coming from the market (brand-based resource) as well as those belonging to individual organizations or individuals (individual-based resource), and public institutions (public-based resource).

Market-based resources

The reference to resources coming from companies also implies the presence of another actant, in the case of my research, it was a public institution. This kind of combination is called a public-private partnership (Jałocha, 2021; Snopko, 2014), in which it is possible to see social activities carried out with resources coming from companies and initiated by public institutions:

> But that is not the point. We have our own rules; we have this campaign, "Older Citizens-Friendly Places." We promote only those businesses that are older citizen-friendly, that is, certified older peoples ... We have a committee, a group, we visit, we see what it all looks like, and we certify them, and we can only promote the certified ones. [D2]

As mentioned in the fragment earlier, the program I described earlier is called *Older Citizens' Friendly Places.*[27] It is a great example of mining resources to carry out social activities for older citizens. Based on the mutual benefit of companies, who have a chance of promotion, and older people, who enjoy discounts in cafes and restaurants, the city program establishes an activity within already available resources. Cooperation with private entities expands the potential for ventures.

> This is also a good moment to promote them. They may not be a city unit, any entity with which we cooperate, or any nongovernmental organisation; they are an institution, as if it were a private company, but this is a good moment to promote such cooperation. [D6]

Such a compromise between private and public entities implies negotiations and triggers, which will attract both sides. However, the concept of corporate social responsibility (CSR) frames cooperation between the private sector and public entities. It is a concept that tends to belong to management studies, however, through the decades, it has been incorporated by various agencies of the United Nations and European Union to make it a standard for international and national corporations (Latapí Agudelo et al., 2019). In short, it is a concept that aims to encourage companies to include social aspects in their ventures. It prompts them to feel responsible for the environment in which they are functioning by supporting social equality and development. Workers at the Centre for Older Citizens' Initiatives in this study cited CSR as a rationale for private companies' involvement in initiatives for the older people. Their need for CSR explained their support for various ventures and their desire to participate in older citizens' programs, among other reasons.

---

[27] It is a program whereby restaurants, cinemas, sports facilities, etc. can apply to be certified as age-friendly places.

Public-based resources

Within this level of resource mining scale, I refer to public resources, which are not necessarily money but also museums or universities that are engaging in the enactment of social activity, along with their resources such as their history, monuments, and know-how. Those are actants that form a great number of events, which can be found in bulletins for older people. The connecting element here is the mission of these places, which obliges them to disseminate cultural heritage:

> This is organized by the city, and if we can, we get involved in various such initiatives. I also keep a watchful eye on the city's ongoing events and initiatives, targeting a diverse range of audiences, not limited to the older people, in an effort to expand our reach. [D4]

In this case, I would argue that resources include not just buildings or the people who work in them, but also the commitments enshrined in their statutes and missions. Within the framework of these commitments, cultural institutions or other public entities, such as universities, decide to enter networks that implement the social activity of older people by deploying their resources. Similar to museums, these networks consist of spaces and exhibits. However, in the case of universities of the Third Age, the focus is on academics and their knowledge, which serve as resources in a specific social activity, such as a lecture or a debate.

Another public source is the financing of social activities that take place within the framework of commissioned public tasks or projects from other sources. When talking about implemented activities, my interlocutors referred to several sources of public funding, such as municipal projects allocated through a bidding process, national older people's policy projects allocated by the relevant ministry, or EU project funds. Of course, the availability of these funds depends on specific requirements. Municipalities, for instance, might not be able to utilize national resources due to their allocation to less developed municipalities with less developed older citizen activities. However, municipalities successfully apply for projects from the European Union to finance part of their initiatives. Within this level of resource mobilization, we can identify some stratification. It is about the use of public resources from the perspective of the city, NGOs, and informal groups such as older citizens' clubs use public resources. For the former, they turn to national and international institutions, such as the European Union, to obtain funding for their activities that go beyond their budgets. Third-sector organizations have the option to apply not only for city funds but also for national and international projects. These funds can come from the EU, as well as from other institutions that support NGOs. This is the case of the Flanders Foundation, which works in partnership with a Belgian foundation to draw resources in the form of ideas and statutory assumptions. The fact that both city institutions and NGOs can apply for resources from national or international agencies makes them equal in a way, giving the third sector a chance to act more autonomously.

Individual-based resources

The more extreme end of this scale pertains to a person's individual resources, which in my data included time, knowledge, and experience. The following quote is an example of the use of individual resources. Members of an older citizens' club described an action they took to collect products for Christmas parcels intended for more vulnerable older people with mobility problems. They therefore volunteered their free time to collect the products, including walking around shops and restaurants and encouraging people to join in:

> Some signed up, some did not, and we collected. I was in three places among those who gave. Several shops reported that they did not allow entry. But three places joined; it was Orange, Petit Paris, and Kahawa, or something like that, which I don't remember anymore. Anyway, when we announced that these dispensaries were located upstairs at CenterMed, the doctors actually brought cartons with them. I had to add cartons for two days because even some of these patients brought a packet of coffee or chocolate. These were articles, not monetary donations. [D13]

This example of involvement demonstrates the realization of a social activity based on the individual's resources, specifically their free time. Globally promoted ideas, such as active or productive aging, recognize this as a valuable resource (Walker, 2009b). These ideas emphasize the need to involve older people in the life of the community and maintain their productivity, not only by extending their work, but also precisely by volunteering for the benefit of others.

CIS also used this type of resource as part of the Older Citizens Fair, where older volunteers helped organize the fair, kept watch over participants, and supported the event. In addition to this, however, some actors also benefit from the knowledge and experience of older people:

> During this project, we brought together a diverse group of individuals who were willing to collaborate and came from a variety of professions. Based on this, we developed a series of classes for children where veterinarians shared their work experiences and we discussed various topics. Allow me to guess that the topic was ancient animals. Alternatively, there were individuals with a passion for letters, telegraphs, stamps, and other forms of postal communication. They engaged in discussions about communication in the past, during their youth, and also about these telegrams, a topic that modern-day children may not be familiar with. [D3]

The preceding excerpt highlights a museum project where older individuals shared their professions and passions with children. The next quotation, on the other hand, also refers to an activity by older people for the benefit of children, in which members of an older citizens' club use their storytelling skills:

> The manager of the club, Czarek, has recently developed a successful project named "Older Citizens Read to Children." This project is presented in kindergarten. Our members dress up in Winnie the Pooh costumes and visit kindergartens with a story. [D11]

The last level of the presented scale allows us to see social activities carried out precisely based on individual resources. On the one hand, it shows older people as useful individuals who can be useful to other members of the local community, but on the other hand, it supports their inclusion, strengthening their subjectivity and sense of belonging (A. C. M. Chan & Cao, 2015; Katz, 2000; Nadobnik et al., 2021; Pasquallie, 2018; Tong et al., 2019).

This section aimed to identify the scale that traces the resources used in the implementation of social activity for older people. Within the framework of the collected data, I was able to distinguish three points of this spectrum, namely *market-based, public-based, and individual-based resources*. However, the needs of local social policy, which include a high task load due to decentralization and limited resources, appear to drive the availability of diverse resources for social activity implementation. Therefore, policymakers seek resources that can aid in policy implementation through public-private partnerships and from the recipients themselves, who can serve as their own resources through voluntary work. For all parties involved, the situation appears to be advantageous. For companies, it presents an opportunity for further promotion, while for older individuals, it presents a chance for social engagement through volunteer work. This type of social engagement is well-known in research on the idea of social activity in the city (Carr et al., 2015; A. C. M. Chan & Cao, 2015; Ho, 2017). However, the researchers also emphasize that social activism in the form of volunteering may not be accessible to everyone due to their physical and economic limitations (Carr et al., 2015).

Resource mining from the perspective of third-sector organizations, as well as other public institutions, allows us to draw attention to an alternative way of raising funds by the aforementioned organizations through international organizations or foreign partner organizations. However, a limitation of my study is the lack of information regarding the extent to which organizations and institutions in Poznan utilize this assistance. Supporting such a flow of resources is desirable to support the independence of their activities, which, as illustrated by previous scales (*Initiation* and *Execution of social activity*), is often problematic. Fundraising's connection to specific project objectives may hinder bottom-up initiatives within a given policy.

4.3.4. The embeddedness of social activity

One of the ontologies focuses on the use of space, a topic that contrasts with this scale. However, this case involves more than just the spatial aspect. By highlighting this scale, I aimed to demonstrate the profound influence of the projects within the district or organization, or conversely, their absence. The aim was to determine how much social activism for older people in Poznan is linked to the actants' affiliation and how vertical this relationship is. This embeddedness applies to both the participants of the organized events and their organizers.

Lack of affiliation

Within the analytical framework of activities for older people, I came across events whose setting was difficult to define. The NGO, located in the center of Poznan, organizes events that attract a diverse group of older individuals.

> **I:** And as if you were to say, are you more of the local activity in this neighbourhood or more on a city scale?

> **N:** As far as older people are concerned, it is rather non-local because, to be honest, looking at this literary group, I don't even know if there is anyone from Jezyce[28] here. More like Piatkowo,[29] Poznan in general. [D5]

In this example, embedding coincides with the origin of the event's participants. They can be a group of locals from the nearby neighborhood or a group coming from different districts. Thus, the activities carried out by the foundations in question do not have a neighborhood dimension, but rather can be classified as aimed at older people with literary interests. So, the activity has escaped territorial classification. Another example involves a foundation that lacks a registered office, leading to its classification as a mobile foundation. Its target audiences are specific groups of residents from city districts, while its affiliation is unspecified, allowing for a wide reach:

> **Interviewer:** So, you are such a mobile foundation?
>
> **Expert:** Yes, yes, exactly. I think that is a big benefit because it also stems from the fact that we listened to the older people, saying that it is fine; they would like to come to the classes that I run, but not everyone finds the city centre convenient, so we suggested that they could try to get to a given place, and it works very well. I believe it garners more positive feedback than having all classes in one location, as it fosters a stronger commitment to the local community, enabling us to expand our reach beyond the old town, where we have a presence, to encompass numerous districts. [D9]

Whereas in the previous example, the activity was not embedded in any specific district, the earlier statement applies the district distinction; however, it rather moves around them than inscribes itself into a particular one. Although its operations have a temporary foundation, the implementation of social activities remains somewhat unclear. A sort of combination of these two examples is the older citizens' club, described by its leader in the following quote. It was founded in the city center by the Polish Medicine Association and brings together older residents from different parts of Poznan. The only thing they have in common is the fact that they are older. However, over

---

28 It is a district of Poznan.

29 It is a district of Poznan.

time, the number of members has grown so much that the club has split into smaller ones:

> We first met twice a week, on Thursday and Tuesday, and then once a week. It was the end of 2016–17 because other clubs started to spring up closer to where our members lived, and out of those 53—even on the list, we had 120—it was too many. Only that, not everyone attended, as some chose to participate in gymnastics, others in bridge, and still others in lectures. s no room. [D13]

The development of the older citizens' club and its growth in members resulted in division and the establishment of new clubs, placed within the neighborhoods of participants.

In general, at this scale, the implementation of social activities shifts from being for everyone, with the primary aim of activating older residents, to activities embedded within a neighborhood, for example. Within this range of scales, social activity appears to be an activity primarily aimed at older people. Its neighborhood focus is secondary, or a further step in the development of an organization or a local community.

Belonging

The second dimension of the presented scale relates social activity to the affiliation of its participants or organizers. This may be an affiliation within a neighborhood or profession. We can view these markers of belongingness as catalysts for social activity, as they guide individuals from a specific neighborhood, region, or possessing other shared traits to participate in activities. Here, the question of being an older person is not a connecting element, as it was in the previous dimension. The election of members to the Municipal Council of Older Citizens is an illustrative example of belonging. Older citizens in Poznan appoint its members for a four-year term. Some members of the Council are representatives of organizations that are active in Poznan; others are representatives of the City Council and the Mayor. Its goal is to represent the voice of Older citizens in shaping city policy. The Council collaborates with the CIS, which, as an agency of the City Council, undertakes a variety of activities for older people:

> A year later, I joined the Council, having been placed on the additional list due to a single point deficit. And a year later, I started. However, I joined the Council

> on behalf of the Polish Medicine Association and worked there, primarily with CenterMed, which established a facility for older people. [D13]

In this statement, the concept of belongingness is unique, as it involves an NGO or a private firm that provides older citizens with a mandate to participate in elections. Cooperation within cities is another example of embeddedness. The classification of the area as a city determines the level of belonging, which varies. The cited example highlights specific concepts that Poznan adopts after borrowing them from another city:

> I remember for sure that a taxi for older people, which is in Poznan, was probably brought to us from Siemianowice Śląskie as an example. The box of life in Poznan, for example, and Łódź have an envelope of life, so it is as if the cities are observing each other and taking these ideas from each other. [D1]

Moreover, Poznan is a place of activity for a great number of NGOs. Some of them work in conjunction with the local community animation mode, which suggests a specific way of working with local communities, focusing on partnership and drawing on local resources.

This example demonstrates the integration of social activity for older individuals within the city. The point is to show that not only the activities of organizations or older peoples themselves can be associated with an area or group, but also the city itself through the affiliation of social activity with city activities. As a result, activities for older people are the subject of cross-fertilization between different urban centers.

In addition, Poznan is a place of activity for many NGOs, which direct their activities to a specific group of inhabitants in a given district and only later define their affiliation with such categories as age or needs. Their activities are based on the OSL model,[30] which proposes a specific way of working with local communities, focusing on partnership and drawing on local resources. The neighborhood, its spatial and human resources, as well as its constraints and problems, strongly influence the activities of these organizations or individuals.

The last scale covers issues of integrating social activism with older people. On one hand, it pertains to activities primarily characterized as social inclusion for older individuals. On the other hand, it includes those social

---

[30] Abbreviation means organization of local community.

activities that in some other way link the actants involved in its implementation, e.g., a partner organization, a neighborhood, or a type of territorial unit. Observing the diverse features within this scale, we can assert that certain events occur beyond local networks, potentially rendering them sporadic and transient (as detailed in Chapter 4.1—Social activity enacted). On the other hand, it provides a non-committal engagement opportunity for individuals who prefer not to be part of a community. Then, this affiliation serves as a gathering point for the event participants; it anchors them and provides them with the opportunity to further engage themselves, thanks to the relationships they have formed.

Conclusion

Through the scales I present in this section, I wanted to show the tension between the actants involved in the process of implementing social activism for older people within the framework of the urban policy of aging in Poznan, which I have studied. The reason why I looked for these relations was the decentralization of social policy, including the policy of aging, commonly defined in the literature. By framing my research within the concept of glocalization, I also wanted to address the issue of globalization, which causes a kind of collapse of the temporal vertical hierarchy in policymaking (Roudometof, 2015; Swyngedouw, 1997; Wathen, 2020). Causing greater influence of global actants and ideas within local communities and giving these local levels greater responsibility for dealing with global challenges (Andreotti & Mingione, 2016; Kutsar & Kuronen, 2015).

The first of the two scales identified relates to the issue of initiating and implementing social activism. The conclusions from these scales indicate a tension between these two approaches. The question also emerges as to the feasibility of the bottom-up approach I identified, which both municipal unit employees and NGOs strongly emphasized. This is because even grassroots ideas and initiatives, if they are to be realized with public funds, have to fit into the framework of a given source of financing, that is, a project. On the other hand, the scales that exist in the local politics I have studied show the possibilities that third-sector organizations and public institutions have in raising funds, bypassing the vertical model of policymaking, and applying for support from international organizations or other foreign partner organizations.

Furthermore, the scales illustrate the diversity of participants based on their affiliations. This has an impact on the activities and values of the described organizations or companies. On the one hand, this diversity represents an opportunity for local social policy because it offers different resources and possibilities, which is necessary as a result of the underfunding of policies at the local level (Błędowski, 2016; Theiss, 2017). On the other hand, this diversity can result in differing perspectives on the implementation, potentially obscuring its effects and even leading to mutual exclusion, depending on the perception of older people's social activities and their role in the aging process. An example of such tensions is the cooperation between the Centre for Older Citizens' Initiatives and private companies. They come together to organize social activities, but each has different goals and values. The city established the CIS as an institution for older people. A travel agency, for example, is a private enterprise, and although it organizes trips for older people, the aim is to make a profit. Older citizens' clubs serve as another example, functioning as informal groups without affiliation. Alternatively, they could have affiliations with an NGO or a parish. Then, their activities are linked to the umbrella organization.

4.4. Conclusions

Aging is a challenge for modern societies and their economies. This is not a new problem, as in the 1970s, researchers already predicted the influence of aging process on economy and the functioning of social systems (Achenbaum, 2010). Moreover, throughout the twentieth and twenty-first centuries, scholars have put forward different conceptualizations of old age, and thus of older people and their role in society (Foster & Walker, 2015; Hooyman & Kiyak, 2017; Klimczuk, 2017; Marshall & Clarke, 2010; Phillipson & Estes, 2007; Wahl & Gitlin, 2007). One contemporary research approach is the critical perspective (Estes & Grossman, 2007; Estes & Portacolone, 2009), which pays attention to the construction of old age by society, the policies pursued, and the ideas behind them (Estes & Grossman, 2007). Although the process of aging has been in the minds of researchers and politicians for several decades, it is gaining new relevance today. In the result of globalization aging become a global problem but strongly diversified within local communities. Within the economic crises, in turn, public policies, responding to the effects of aging issue, have to face with savings in social expenditure. Furthermore, the decentralization of social policy and the devolution of its implementation to local policies (Andreotti & Mingione, 2016a; Błędowski, 2016b; Kutsar & Kuronen, 2015a; Theiss, 2017), as well as the recognition of the local level as the one which most accurately responds to the diverse problems of older people's communities. As a result, regional and urban policies gained in relevance. These factors make it desirable to know how measures that are part of aging policies are implemented at the micro-level.

Therefore, the subject of my research was how urban policies on aging are implemented. Since the concept of aging policy is very broad, I set out one area, that is, the implementation of the idea of social activity of older people, which is derived from the idea of active and happy aging (Council of the European Union, 2012; Walker, 2008; World Health Organization, 2002). These are concepts which originated in the last century, and which promote the most active way of spending old age, benefiting both the individual, by supporting his or her mental and physical health, and society. From the latter perspective, active aging means being useful in the form of volunteering, continuing to work, and being involved in the social life of the local community. These ideas are still part of the policies and strategies developed at the level of international organizations, such as the European Union and the WHO, as well as at the level of national policies. However, their practical implementation remains the responsibility of local politicians and other actants (Álvarez-García et al., 2018; Joy, 2018; Perek-Białas et al., 2006). Therefore, to understand the urban aging policy implementation, I studied the implementing of social activity ideas for older people in Poznan. In order to address this problem, I formed two research questions. With the first question I aimed to understand *what the idea of social activity* for older people *and hence aging* is in the case of Poznan. To achieve it I applied ideational analysis and seek to explore how idea reflects studied reality (Wildavsky, 2018). The answer to the second question, in turn, concerned how the idea is implemented by urban aging policy. As a result I strived to know *how political actions occurs and form urban policy.* In this question I referred to DI and explored practices, which introduce political change, as well as values and norms forming them (Schmidt, 2008).

The empirical chapter I have presented provides insights into urban aging policies. This was possible by following the implementation of the idea of social activity of older people in Poznan. The collected data, analyzed using ANT, allows us to follow the formation of an urban policy.

4.4.1. What?

In the beginning I wanted to explore what actually social activity for older people is. One of the answers comes from a way the sheer aging process was perceived by local actors. It was seen as a phase of inactivity with good health and available resources of knowledge, practical skills, and time. Therefore, social activity was aimed at managing older people's resources through volunteering, community engagement or education through events such as museum tours or telephone learning. Whereas the aging phase, characterized by dependency and physical limitations, was missing in my data. Hence, aging does not apply to the *third-floor prisoners*. For them, the social activity I encountered would be difficult due to physical limitations or lack of personal space.

Exclusion within the social activity of older people is the subject of research (Afacan, 2013; Ahmad & Hafeez, 2011; Barrett & McGoldrick, 2013; Beard & Montawi, 2015; Carr et al., 2015; Chiribuca & Teodorescu, 2020). Scholars emphasize that this is a policy element available to people of high socioeconomic status. Based on my research, in turn, it is apparent that this also focuses on people with good physical and mental health. This is an important conclusion, as social activity at the local level should accurately diagnose the needs and barriers of older people. Also, those, and perhaps especially those, who find it difficult to express their voice and to fight for it. In summary, aging in the perspective concerns people who are physically active, willing to get involved and develop. It refers to a critical perspective in gerontology that was a conceptual framework of my research here. It emphasizes the need to examine how aging policies are made and what ideas feed into them. Furthermore, critical perspective perceive aging as a product of struggle between influential political and social actors (Estes & Grossman, 2007). As a result, this may lead to a focus on meeting the needs of older people, whose need to be socially active is different from those with less power to influence and influence policymaking, that is, the less able.

On the basis of the findings I have presented, conclusions can also be drawn in the context of research on social activity itself implemented at the city level. In previous research, social activity was understood as activity in public space (Dawidowicz et al., 2020; Xiong et al., 2020; Yung et al., 2016), volunteering (Carr et al., 2015; Ho, 2017a), action for the local community (Pasquallie, 2018; Tong et al., 2019; Yung et al., 2016) or self-development (Fu et al., 2018; Ho, 2017a; Novak & Vute, 2013a; Pei et al., 2014). All these dimensions of social activity have been identified in my study. Additionally, my research found that social activity is also a kind of *commodity*. The need for social activity is exploited by companies, restaurants, and other private enterprises, which offer discounts to encourage older people to take advantage of their offers. I understand the commodification of social activity as a transformation process of some non-market activity into a commodity that can be offered in exchange for market value (Tittenbrun, 2014). The literature on aging (Endo, 2020; Klimczuk, 2016; O'Rand et al., 2010; Phillipson & Estes, 2007) has already recognized this issue, called 'aging enterprise.' This phenomenon refers to biomedical industries' commodification of aging, which propose mostly expensive healthcare solutions for older individuals (Phillipson & Estes, 2007). Furthermore, many researchers draw attention to the idea of productivity, which is often a part of active aging policies and strategies. Researchers have criticized coercion to lead an active and productive life (Endo, 2020; Katz, 2000; Lakom, 2023) because such commodification of aging can cause stigmatization of older adults and isolation for other groups (Klimczuk, 2016). In my data, we observed that various companies included social activity as part of their offerings, encouraging older people through discounts and targeted events. For them, social activity was a way to attract new customers and promote themselves as socially engaged restaurants, cinemas, shops, sports centers, or companies. However, private organizations were not the only ones to adopt this market-oriented perspective. Public institutions and NGOs also viewed social activity as a component of their offerings and treated older people as clients. These circumstances favored a one-time type of event rather than a longer engagement. My data indicates that social activity can be viewed as either a one-time event or a long-term commitment. We claim that some activities are only one-time events that do not aim at any further engagement of older individuals. Others, in turn, can be perceived as long-term relationships. As they strive to establish networks between participants, build relations between them, and provide them with a sense of belonging, those two trends in social activity could be understood as reflections on older people's heterogeneity (Nadobnik et al., 2021; Vidovićová, 2018). Simply put, some individuals may exhibit a greater desire for prolonged engagement, while others may favor less socially demanding activities. However, there are several studies pointing out the fact that older people need connectedness with others and the feeling of having some support in life (Bruggencate et al., 2018; Morgan et al., 2021; Teater & Chonody, 2019).

To sum up, the commodification of social activity (Tittenbrun, 2014; Ziółkowski, 2004) offers opportunities for its wider implementation through the involvement of actors who may find it beneficial to have such a commodity in their offerings. Thus, increasing the offer of such events. However, there is an issue of the aforementioned effects that a given activity may bring. It is about the one-time and long-term nature of social activity. In the case of commodification of social activity, there is less chance for longer engagement, as this is not the purpose of such events.

Finally, my data revealed that public space, within the using space ontology, served as a strong foundation for social activity among older individuals. Social activity events often focus on inviting older people to various places (such as museums, city monuments, cinemas, shops, etc.) or creating dedicated spaces for older citizens. This issue is not new in the field of urban aging; numerous studies have examined the impact of mobility, transportation, and accessibility to social activities on the mobility of older individuals (Alidoust et al., 2019; Bosch-Meda, 2021; Li & Wang, 2024; Wood et al., 2023). This is also an important issue within the AFC Community framework promoted by WHO and implemented in Poznan. In the AFFC framework, space plays a crucial role in making cities more suitable for their older inhabitants (World Health Organization, 2023). However, my research primarily links the significance of space to the ability to access it and the sense of community it fosters. It means that to create social activities, organizers must invite participants into some space; it can be a public park, a museum's exhibition, a cinema, or a local community club. Therefore, space plays a crucial role in fostering social activity among older individuals, particularly when the focus is on long-term engagement and networking. This issue was also the focus of a study that examined the availability of third places (public spaces) that are available for common use and confirmed the positive influence of these spaces on the social activity of older people (Alidoust et al., 2019). We claim that not only is accessibility of third spaces important, but also more space within communities and neighborhoods to support local initiatives and activities. Some of my interviewees expressed concern about the lack of space for their activities, such as NGOs that assist older people and support their cognitive development. For older people, in turn, going to some space regularly can evoke a feeling of belonging and connectedness with others. This implies that the openness of city spaces could potentially support social activity for older individuals. This aligns with the Right to the City movement (Domaradzka, 2018), which advocates for granting citizens access to the city.

Another important aspect of urban aging that is present in my research concerns relations between the private and public. I could observe that the private and public sectors play a crucial role in co-creating social activities for older people. Such cooperation enhances the accessibility of certain consumption activities for older individuals and contributes to the development and attractiveness of the urban aging policy. However, cooperation with private companies was also a matter of concern among city hall workers. Cooperation between the public and private sectors serves to establish policies for older people, especially in the absence of public finances, and is also known in the literature as the privatization of social services. Based on my case study, I observe that the private and public relations sectors significantly contribute to the implementation of urban policies, and it could be beneficial to incorporate their contributions into existing policy frameworks like the AFC Network. So far, the AFC framework (2023) mentions the private sector as an important partner that can share knowledge on technological innovations and economic constraints. Based on our findings, we propose further research on the role of the private sector in aging urban policy formation and the development of practices that would support private and public sector cooperation while securing the rights of older citizens.

4.4.2. How?

The other aim of my research was to see how social activity for older people is implemented by urban aging policy. My study reveals that enactment of urban aging policy is fueled with projects, already-existing ideas, space, public-private partnerships, or bottom-up initiative.

In the case of projects, my data referred to the well-known issue in the literature of projectization in public policies (Godenhjelm et al., 2015; D. Hodgson et al., 2019; Jensen et al., 2018). The literature shows this phenomenon as an element which facilitates policy management, but also as a time and financial constraint on policy implementation (Jałocha, 2021; Skórzyńska, 2018; Skrzypek-Prawelska & Jałocha, 2014). However, based on my research, projects could also be defined as means of support, commitment or bonding between actants. These words describe the types of relationships between the actants involved in the urban aging policy in Poznan. Projects provide support to NGOs and other actants who are looking for resources to implement their activities. However, entering into and carrying out a project implies a certain commitment, which consists in fulfilling set goals and achieving certain results, as defined in the project. Moreover, projects bind the actants involved in them, making them interdependent. An example is the participation of the Porta Posnania Museum in a project involving older people as volunteers. As a result, after the project ended, the cooperation between the volunteers and the museum remained, generating further activities for older residents.

Thus, as my research has shown, projects are not only a tool for efficient management in public policies, but they are also responsible for the emerging relationships between the actors of the created policies. However, the question is what are these relationships? That is, to what extent do projects support NGOs and other organizations, and to what extent do they limit their own grassroots initiatives? Based on my research, it can be said that while the bottom-up nature of the activities was strongly emphasized by the employees of municipal institutions (*Reason comes by themselves*). It can be seen from the interviews with third-sector organizations and employees of cultural institutions that the grassroots initiative has to meet the assumptions of the available projects (*Looking for the support* and *Commission to actants*). This is interesting in the context of the decentralization of tasks in aging policies, which is dictated among other things by the better accuracy of local policies in diagnosing community problems. In reality, however, projectization in such policies is an obstacle to bottom-up initiatives.

Moreover, my research shows that policy implementation at the city level is supported by mosaic of interests, strategies, statutes, as well as other political ideas. The latter are the links between policies, feeding one policy into those already-existing policies. This included the idea of empowerment, social investment, or CSR. Their presence is visible, for example, in the activities of private enterprises which decide to organize social activities within the framework of CSR. This shows how the implementation of ideas by city policies, in the case of my research the idea of social activity of older people, is connected to already present and influential ideas. Thus, it could be said that the formation of an urban policy on aging is dependent on an already established array of ideas and the influences exerted by them. This might be named as the *ideational background of urban policy*.

The diverse background of ideas feeding into the policy I have studied, has also influence on diverse practices evident in the ontologies I have identified—*Weaving the network, Providing a service, Responding to the aging crisis* or *Using space*. Practices are part of trends in politics such as empowerment (Dudgeon et al., 2017; Klimczuk, 2018; Olech & Kaźmierczak, 2011), participation (Beresford & Carr, 2018; Taylor-Gooby, 2018), public-private partnerships (Jałocha, 2021; Snopko, 2014), the phenomenon of projectization (D. Hodgson et al., 2019; Skrzypek-Prawelska & Jałocha, 2014) or the service approach in politics (Chaczko, 2021; Grewiński, 2009; Guy, 2010; Szarfenberg, 2010). Other practices may not be captured by a single concept, but they relate to the urban space and its accessibility for older residents as well as activity organizers. Identifying these practices and therefore the concepts they represent allows for an important conclusion about urban aging policies. The urban aging policy, then, is a collection of practices, coming from different approaches to the realization of social policy. We can see, for example, the service approach, which was present in the social policy of Western European countries back in the last century. However, it is still valid within a Polish context. It is reflected in the implementation of social activity as a service, which is visible in the creation of event offers by companies, but also by NGOs or public institutions, that fosters the creation of customer-service-provider relationships. However, some of the practices of the policy I studied were related to participatory approaches, which see older people as co-participants and co-creators rather than just customers. These findings point to the diversity of urban aging policy measures. That means, on the one hand, urban aging policy can be seen as positive, as it increases the possibility of reaching different audiences, but on the other hand, the implemented policies lose strength. The reason being is that these approaches pursue different goals, for example, promoting empowerment and creating services.

Also, the city space is important for the implementation. According to research, but also to emerging programs such as Age-Friendly Cities, space is important in policymaking, and moreover, being in public space is important for older people, having a positive impact on their well-being and independence (Beard & Montawi, 2015; Dawidowicz et al., 2020; Xiong et al., 2020; Yung et al., 2016). However, space is, like a project, an element of urban policy that affects the relationships between its actants. The ownership of a space, by public organizations or institutions, can make them organizers of social activity. For organizations and informal groups, such as an older citizens' club, the lack of a space encourages them to search for it and to cooperate. Thus, urban policy on aging has materialized through space. Such a connection, in turn, may lead to further questions for next research, namely how does access to public space affect the creation of local policies?

Urban aging policy in Poznan can be an array of single and independent actions, or a network of actions. On the one hand, there were events that seek networking within the urban policy. This applied both to the entities organizing the events and to the participants themselves. For the organizers, this meant forming relationships of cooperation. NGOs, public or cultural institutions and the Older Citizens' Club were supporting each other in organizing events, e.g., by exchanging ideas or exchanging resources, such as space or free time of older people. For older people, in turn, long-term social activity meant an establishment of social ties. It was achieved through older people's long-term commitment within a community or organization. In turn, the engagement of older people in the local social networks, is benefit as being part of a community can be a source of support for an older person and unweighting for social systems. The question of the formation or absence of relationships between recipients and organizers of urban policies offers a new perspective on local policy research. It is about looking at local politics from the perspective of the networks it creates.

The scales I have identified relating to the concept of glocalization also indicate a certain divergence in the urban policies I have studied. Scales within glocalization in the policy and urban study (Latham & McCormack, 2010; Mehta, 2011; Sun et al., 2017; Swyngedouw, 1996, 2005; "Urban Assemblages. How Actor-Network Theory Changes Urban Studies," 2010; Wathen, 2020) reflects narratives of ruling strategies and relations between actants. They nest actions of actants within a socio-spatial context, linking it to the local, national, or international levels.

Scales, within my study, show the great diversity of actants and thus of their affiliations. This means that the forces influencing their actions and values are influenced by different levels of organizations or companies. On the one hand, this diversity represents an opportunity for local social policy and its actors, because it offers different resources and possibilities, which is necessary as a result of the underfunding of policies at local level (Błędowski, 2016b; Theiss, 2017). On the other hand, it can lead to a divergence of visions as to what is being implemented, so that its effects are not very visible and may even turn out to be mutually exclusive, depending on the understanding of the social activity of older people and its role in the process of aging.

My study of urban aging policies also contributes to debate on the process of decentralization of aging policies (Błędowski, 2016b; Buffel & Phillipson, 2018; Kutsar & Kuronen, 2015a; Theiss, 2012, 2017; Urbaniak, 2018). One of the reasons for decentralizing aging policies is to diagnose the needs of residents more accurately, by getting in closer contact with them. However, according to my research, the bottom-up nature of the policy is not fully realized. Policies in the city are the result of adopted strategies or concepts. Moreover, grassroots activities of third-sector organizations or older citizens' clubs have to fulfill predefined criteria to get funding. This means that it is not entirely true to diagnose the needs of the inhabitants more accurately, as certain needs have already been identified at the stage of creating policy documents. An exception are the mini-grants available to informal groups to support their daily activities. So, my study raises the questions, how much bottom-up action is possible in urban policies and how is it feasible in practice? Is a complete bottom-up in politics possible?

Another practical implication of my research is the question of accessibility to public space by activists, informal groups, or NGOs. My research shows that for the activities of these groups to be possible, while at the same time independent, it is necessary to have access to a space that can be a certain constant in their activities. Policies implemented at the urban level are materialized, among other things, by the space in which they are implemented. Moreover, the relationship between space and its users, that is, its absence or possession, reflects the relationship between political actors and their power of influence (Durczak et al., 2019).

The participation of NGOs in the creation of policies for the older people is an element of the current policy[31] mentioned in Section 1.2 Social Activity

[31] "Social Policy for Older Persons (2030): Safety-Participation-Support."

of older people within aging policy. However, as experts comment (Komisja Ekspertów ds. Osób Starszych przy Rzeczniku Praw Obywatelskich, 2018) the authors of the document invoke the principle of subsidiarity in relation to third-sector organizations. However, it is misunderstood by policymakers, who present the actions of NGOs as complementary to the actions of the state. When in fact, subsidiarity should involve the state supporting the actions of local authorities, organizations, and the communities themselves (Kamiński 2013). Based on my research, the significant role of NGOs is evident, as they act as contractors implementing policies for the older people. Unfortunately, their activities are limited by the form of this cooperation, which consists of projects, as I mentioned earlier. Therefore, the question arises about what relationships between local entities (public, private, and third sector) are beneficial for residents? What follows is how a given policy can support these relationships?

Another issue raised in the experts' report on the current policy is the lack of consideration for public-private partnerships, which they believe play a significant role. This is also an important conclusion from my research. Private companies in Poznań, such as cafes, cinemas, swimming pools, and stores, are getting involved in policies toward the older people. Of course, their participation is based on market principles, that is, they gain the opportunity for promotion, but it is also an important part of the lives of older residents. As mentioned in an interview by the director of the Older Citizens Initiatives Centre in Poznań, the range of assistance offered by private companies is vast. However, such cooperation is not always beneficial for the older people. Therefore, including private entities in the creation of aging policies could help develop such cooperation.

4.4.3. New research perspectives and practical implication

The cooperation between actants responsible for the implementation of the urban aging policy is also based on the formation of relationships between the actants. It is about what influence they have on each other, or what they can do for each other, or why they are important to each other. It turns out that in the urban aging policy I studied, projects and space played an influential and binding role.

Referring my findings to local social policy research (Czupich, 2018; Klimczuk & Tomczyk, 2016; Kutsar & Kuronen, 2015a; Theiss, 2017), which focuses on analyzing economic, political, cultural, or structural factors, the ontologies I propose provide a new perspective for further local social policy research. The conclusion concerns effects of local policy implementation, which I defined as one-off or long-term implementation of social activity. These are the different products of social activity for older people. They aim either for long-term effects, in the form of continuity of the activities carried out and the emergence of lasting relationships between their participants or providing a one-off event that results in a single event. This duality of activities within urban policy on aging illustrates its nature

The types of policy implementation I proposed can complement the division of policy implementation created by E. Matland (1995) (see Section 1.3—The idea and the process of policy implementation). He used two perspectives. The first, described as ambiguity, concerns the question to what extent the implemented measure responds to a clearly defined problem. The second one, in turn, concerns the extent to which implemented actions may cause conflicts among the actors of a given policy. The types of implementations I have identified concern not so much the assumptions and activities undertaken in the implementation of the policy, but its effects. Moreover, they refer to a narrow group of policy actions, namely social activity of older people. However, they can be treated as complements to the division proposed by E. Matland. One-off implementation will concern clearly defined problems, the implementation of which does not create conflicts among policy actors. On the example of my research, these are events aimed at ensuring social activity of older people. Longer-term implementation, on the other hand, will involve fewer clear-cut goals, the implementation of which requires greater involvement of individual actors. This involvement may not necessarily be beneficial. In the case of the social activity I investigated, its long-term effect, that is, the continued activity of older people in the community, is not an obvious and desirable outcome for all actors. Its introduction involves more work, which may not be beneficial or cost-effective. To sum up, the conclusions I proposed may help policy scholars and practitioners look at the implementation process not only from the perspective of its assumptions and activities, but also of its effects. This is an important element, because often the subject of research on policy implementation is its success or lack (Schmidt, 2008).

Limitation

The study deals with one element of aging policy, although the narrowing was necessary because the scope of aging policy itself is too broad. Therefore, further research in the field of urban aging policy may help to understand even more fully what such a policy is and what other elements constitute it. Furthermore, as my study focuses on one case study of Poznan, there is a need for comparative studies. It can inform researchers and practitioners of local policy on local circumstances influencing the dominance of practices and ideas.

The study I present was mostly conducted before the COVID-19 pandemic and does not take into account some of the changes that have taken place in the way older people carry out social activities, namely moving them online. However, based on other research I have conducted, which referred to the issue of using social media as a tool for activation of older people during the COVID-19 pandemic (Nadobnik, 2021), it can be seen that the ways in how events are communicated and delivered have gained new modality, through the inclusion of social media. However, the understanding of social activity idea remained the same. In turn, practices and ontologies, identified in my research, used in policy formation are also applicable within online policy actions. The question for further inquiries is It this way of policy realization will appear as long-term solution?

Although the data I have collected comprises 300 pages of transcripts and documents, 12 hours of interviews and 20 hours of observation, the data I have presented do not cover all organizations and actors working for older people in the field of social activism in Poznan. However, the collected data allows us to explore the very implementation of the idea of social activity, its practices and relationships. They constitute a basis for further research, which may verify the adequacy of the identified ontologies and practices in the case of activities carried out by other entities and organizations.

Bibliography

Achenbaum, W. A. (2010). Past as Prologue: Toward a Global History of Ageing. In D. Dannefer & C. Phillipson (Eds.), *The Sage Handbook of Social Gerontology* (pp. 20–33). SAGE Publications UK: London, England.

Adolino, J. R., & Blake, C. H. (2010). *Comparing Public Policies: Issues and Choices in Industrialized Countries.* CQ Press, a division of Sage.

Adu, P. (2019). *A Step-by-Step Guide to Qualitative Data Coding.* Routledge.

Afacan, Y. (2013). Elderly-friendly inclusive urban environments: learning from Ankara. *Open Hous International*, *38*(1), 52–63.

Ahmad, K., & Hafeez, M. (2011). Factors affecting social participation of elderly people: A study in Lahore. *The Journal of Animal and Plant Sciences*, *21*(2), 283–289.

Álvarez-García, J., Durán-Sánchez, A., Del Río-Rama, M. de la C., & García-Vélez, D. F. (2018). Active Ageing: Mapping of Scientific Coverage. *International Journal of Environmental Research and Public Health*, *15*(12), 2727. <https://doi.org/10.3390/ijerph15122727>

Andreotti, A., & Mingione, E. (2016a). Local welfare systems in Europe and the economic crisis. *European Urban and Regional Studies*, *23*(3), 252–266. <https://doi.org/10.1177/0969776414557191>

Andreotti, A., & Mingione, E. (2016b). Local welfare systems in Europe and the economic crisis. *European Urban and Regional Studies*, *23*(3), 252–266. <https://doi.org/10.1177/0969776414557191>

Asadollahi, A., Hoseinzadeh, A., Tabrizi, A. M., & Nabavi, A. (2013). Urban Lifestyle and Social Participation of Aged Citizens of Ahwaz City: A Regional Survey. *Journal of Applied Sociology VO - 49*, *1*, 1.

Atchley, R. C. (1989). A Continuity Theory of Normal Aging. *The Gerontologist*, *29*(2), 183–190. <https://doi.org/http://dx.doi.org/10.1093/geront/29.2.183>

Barrett, G., & McGoldrick, C. (2013). Narratives of (in)active ageing in poor deprived areas of Liverpool, UK. *International Journal of Sociology and Social Policy*, *33*(5), 347–366. <https://doi.org/10.1108/IJSSP-09-2012-0084>

Bauman, Z., Bauman, I., Kostera, M., & Kociatkiewicz, J. (2017). *Zarządzanie w płynnej nowoczesności.* Fundacja Bęc Zmiana.

Beard, J. R., & Montawi, B. (2015). Age and the Environment: The Global Movement Towards Age-Friendly Cities and Communities. *Journal of Social Work Practice*, *29*(1), 5–11. <https://doi.org/10.1080/02650533.2014.993944>

Béland, D., & Cox, R. H. (2011). Introduction. Ideas and Politics. In D. Béland & R. H. Cox (Eds.), *Ideas and Politics in Social Science Research* (pp. 3–20). Oxford University Press.

Bengtson, V. L., & DeLiema, M. (2016). Theories of aging and social gerontology: Explaining how social factors influence well-being in later life. In M. Harrington Meyer & E. A. Daniele (Eds.), *Gerontology: changes, challenges and solutions* (pp. 25–57). Praeger.

Benjamin, W. (1999). *The Arcades Project*. Belknap Press; Harvard University Press.

Beresford, P., & Carr, S. (2018). Introduction. In P. Beresford & S. Carr (Eds.), *Social policy first hand. An international introduction to participatory social welfare.* (pp. 1–11). Polity Press.

Berman, S. (2001). Ideas, Norms, and Culture in Political Analysis. *Comparative Politics*, *33*(2), 231–250.

Betancur, J. J., & Arciniegas, C. O. (2018). Urban assemblages and dis-assemblages Medellin's hegemonic and counter-hegemonic forums. In E. L. Sweet (Ed.), *Disassembled Cities Social and Spatial Strategies to Reassemble Communities* (pp. 113–137). Routledge.

Bilotta, C., Bowling, A., Nicolini, P., Casè, A., & Vergani, C. (2012). Quality of life in older outpatients living alone in the community in Italy. *Health and Social Care in the Community*, *20*(1), 32–41. <https://doi.org/10.1111/j.1365-2524.2011.01011.x>

Błędowski, P. (2002). *Lokalna Polityka Społeczna wobec Ludzi Starych.* Oficyna Wydawnicza Szkoły Głównej Handlowej.

Błędowski, P. (2016a). O polityce społecznej wobec ludzi starych w Polsce. *Problemy Polityki Społecznej, 1*(32).

Błędowski, P. (2016b). Samorząd terytorialny i organizacje pozarządowe jako podmioty polityki senioralnej. In *Polityka wobec Starości i Starzenia się w Polsce w latach 2015–2035.* (pp. 83–105). Instytut Pracy i Spraw Socjalnych.

Błędowski, P., & Kubicki, P. (2014). Lokalna polityka społeczna wobec nowych wyzwań. Od interwencji do aktywizacji. *Polityka Społeczna, 3,* 34–38.

Błędowski, P., & Szweda-Lewandowska, Z. (2016). *Polityka wobec starości i starzenia się w Polsce w latach 2015–2035. Aspekty teoretyczne i praktyczne.* Instytu Pracy i Spraw Socjalnych.

Blok, A., Farias, I., & Roberts, C. (Eds.). (2020). T. R. C. to A.-N. Theory. <https://doi. org/10. 4324/9781315111667>. (2019). *The Routledge Companion to Actor-Network Theory* (A. Blok, I. Farías, & C. Roberts, Eds.). Routledge. <https://doi.org/10.4324/9781315111667>

Blumer, H. (1969). *Symbolic Interactionism: Perspective and Method.* Englewood Cliffs.

Blyth, M. (2002). *Great transformations: economic ideas and institutional change in the twentieth century.* Cambridge University Press. <https://doi.org/10.5860/choice.40-4719>

Blyth, M. (2010). Ideas, Uncertainty, and Evolution. In D. Beland & R. H. Cox (Eds.), *Ideas and Politics in Social Science Research* (pp. 83–100). Oxford University Press. <https://doi.org/10.1093/acprof:oso/9780199736430.003.0005>

Blyth, M. (2018). *Austerity. The History of a dangerous idea.* Oxford University Press.

Boudiny, K. (2013). “Active ageing”: From empty rhetoric to effective policy tool. *Ageing and Society, 33*(6), 1077–1098. <https://doi.org/10.1017/S0144686X1200030X>

Bratich, J. (2017). Observation in a Surveilled World. In K. N. Denzin & S. Y. Lincoln (Eds.), *The SAGE Handbook of Qualitative Research* (Fifth). SAGE Publications UK: London, England.

Brenner, N. (1999). “Globalisation as Reterritorialisation: The Re-scaling of Urban Governance in the European Union.” *Urban Studies*, *36*(3), 431–451.

Buffel, T., & Phillipson, C. (2018). A Manifesto for the Age-Friendly Movement: Developing a New Urban Agenda. In *Journal of Aging and Social Policy* (Vol. 30, Issue 2, pp. 173–192). <https://doi.org/10.1080/08959420.2018.1430414>

Buffel, T., & Phillipson, C. (2023). Ageing in place in urban environments. In *Ageing in Place in Urban Environments Critical Perspectives* (1st ed., pp. 3–14). Routledge.

Buffel, T., & Remillard-Boilard, S. (2019). Age-Friendly Cities and Communities: New Directions for Research and Policy. In D. Gu & M. E. Dupre (Eds.), *Encyclopedia of Gerontology and Population Aging* (Issue September). <https://doi.org/10.1007/978-3-319-69892-2>

Buffel, T., Rémillard-Boilard, S., Walsh, K., McDonald, B., Smetcoren, A.-S., & De Donder, L. (2020). Age-Friendly Approaches and Old-Age Exclusion: A Cross-City Analysis. *International Journal of Ageing and Later Life*, *14*(2), 1–29. <https://doi.org/10.3384/ijal.1652-8670.1470>

Burgess, E. W. (1960). *Aging in Western Societies*. The University of Chicago Press.

Caldarice, O. (2018). *Reconsidering welfare Policies in Times of Crisis. Perspectives for European Cities*. Springer.

Callon, M. (1984). Some Elements of a Sociology of Translation: Domestication of the Scallops and the Fishermen of St Brieuc Bay. *The Sociological Review*, *32*(1_suppl), 196–233. <https://doi.org/10.1111/j.1467-954X.1984.tb00113.x>

Callon, M., & Latour, B. (1981). Unscrewing the big Leviathan : how actors macro-structure reality and how sociologists help them to do so. In K. Knorr & A. Cicourel (Eds.), *Advances in Social Theory and Methodology* (pp. 277–303). Routledge and Kegan Paul.

Callon, M., & Latour, B. (2015). Unscrewing the big Leviathan: how actors macro-structure reality and how sociologists help them to do co. In K. Knorr-Cetina & A. V. Cicourel (Eds.), *Advances in Social Theory and Methodology* (pp. 277–304). Routledge. <https://doi.org/10.5840/intstudphil198618185>

Campbell, J. L. (2002). Ideas, Politics, and Public Policy. *Annual Review of Sociology*, *28*(1), 21–38. <https://doi.org/10.1146/annurev.soc.28.110601.141111>

Carr, D. C., Fried, L. P., & Rowe, J. W. (2015). Productivity & Engagement in an Aging America: The Role of Volunteerism. *Daedalus*, *144*(2), 55–67. <https://doi.org/10.1162/DAED_a_00330>

Carstensen, M. B., & Schmidt, V. A. (2016). Power through, over and in ideas: conceptualizing ideational power in discursive institutionalism. *Journal of European Public Policy*, *23*(3), 318–337. <https://doi.org/10.1080/13501763.2015.1115534>

Castells, M. (1977). *The Urban Question: A Marxist Approach*. Edward Arnold.

Chaczko, K. (2021). Czy usługi społeczne wskrzeszą większe nieba? *Magazyn Kontakt*, *46*, 158–163.

Chan, A. C. M., & Cao, T. (2015). Age-Friendly Neighbourhoods as Civic Participation: Implementation of an Active Ageing Policy in Hong Kong. *Journal of Social Work Practice*, *29*(1), 53–68. <https://doi.org/10.1080/02650533.2014.993947>

Chan, M. L., Gustafsson, L., & Liddle, J. (2015). Mandatory retirement for older professional drivers: An exploration of experiences for older Singaporean taxi drivers. *Ageing and Society*, *35*(7), 1384–1409. <https://doi.org/10.1017/S0144686X14000257>

Chen, Y. J., & Chen, C. Y. (2012). Living arrangement preferences of elderly people in Taiwan as affected by family resources and social participation. *Journal of Family History*, *37*(4), 381–394. <https://doi.org/10.1177/0363199012440948>

Chiribuca, D., & Teodorescu, A. (2020). Digital leisure in later life: Facebook use among Romanian senior citizens. *Revista de Cercetare Si Interventie Sociala*, *69*(June), 156–175. <https://doi.org/10.33788/rcis.69.10>

Ciesielska, M., Wolniak-Bostrom, K., & Ohlander, M. (2012). Obserwacja. In D. Jemielniak (Ed.), *Badanie jakościowe t. 2* (pp. 41–67). Wydawnictwo Naukowe PWN.

Coll-Planas, L., del Valle Gómez, G., Bonilla, P., Masat, T., Puig, T., & Monteserin, R. (2017). Promoting social capital to alleviate loneliness and improve health among older people in Spain. *Health and Social Care in the Community*, *25*(1), 145–157. <https://doi.org/10.1111/hsc.12284>

Connolly, W. (1983). *The Terms of Political Discourse.* Princeton University Press.

Council of the European Union. (2012). *Guiding Principles for Active Ageing and Solidarity between Generations. December,* 1–11.

Cox, K. R. (2009). "Rescaling the state" in question. In *Cambridge Journal of Regions, Economy and Society* (Vol. 2, Issue 1, pp. 107–121). <https://doi.org/10.1093/cjres/rsn029>

Creswell, J. W. (2007). *Qualitative Inquiry and Research Design. Choosing among five approaches.* Sage Publication.

Cumming, E., & Henry, W. E. (1961). *Growing Old: the Process of disengagement.* Basic Books.

Czarniawska, B. (2000). Organizational Translations: From Worlds to Words and Numbers—and Back. In H. Kalthoff, R. Rottenburg, & H.-J. Wagner (Eds.), *Facts and Figures. Economic Representations and Practices.* (Issue August, pp. 117–142).

Czarniawska, B. (2002). *The Tale of Three Cities.* Oxford University Press.

Czupich, M. (2018). Level of Social Participation in the Creation of Urban Regeneration Programmes—The Case Study of Small Towns in Poland. *European Spatial Research and Policy, 25*(2), 81–98. <https://doi.org/10.18778/1231-1952.25.2.05>

Dannefer, D., & Phillipson, C. (Eds.). (2010). *The SAGE Handbook of Social Gerontology.* SAGE Publications Sage UK: London, England. <https://doi.org/10.1016/B978-1-4160-6231-8.10031-5>

Dannefer, D., & Settersten, R. A. (2010). The Study of the Life Course: Implications for Social Gerontology. In D. Dannefer & C. Phillipson (Eds.), *The Sage Handbook of Social Gerontology* (pp. 3–20). SAGE Publications UK: London, England.

Dawidowicz, A., Zysk, E., Figurska, M., Źróbek, S., & Kotnarowska, M. (2020). The methodology of identifying active aging places in the city—Practical application. *Cities, 98,* 102575. <https://doi.org/10.1016/j.cities.2019.102575>

de Oliveira, S. M. L., Pessa, S. L. R., Schenatto, F. J., & de Lourdes Bernartt, M. (2019). Cities and Population Aging: A Literature Review. In *Advances in Intelligent Systems and Computing* (Vol. 824, pp. 1395–1404). Springer Verlag. <https://doi.org/10.1007/978-3-319-96071-5_141>

DeLeon, P., & DeLeon, L. (2002). What Ever Happened to Policy Implementation ? An Alternative Approach. *Journal of Public Administration Research and Theory*, *12*(4), 467–492.

Denzin, K. N., & Lincoln, S. Y. (2005). Introduction: The Discipline and Practice of Qualitative. In K. N. Denzin & S. Y. Lincoln (Eds.), *The SAGE Handbook of qualitative research. 3rd edition* (pp. 1–32). Sage Publication.

Denzin, K. N., & Lincoln, S. Y. (2017). Introduction: The Discipline and Practice of Qualitative Research. In K. N. Denzin & S. Y. Lincoln (Eds.), *The SAGE Handbook of Qualitative Research. 5th edition* (pp. 1–26). Sage Publication.

Domaradzka, A. (2014). *New Urban Movement Entrepreneurs Re-Negotiating the Public—Private Borderland : The Case of Polish Urban Politics New ! Urban ! Movement ! Entrepreneurs ! Re4Negotiating !! the ! Public—Private ! Borderland :! The ! Case ! of ! Polish ! Urban ! Politi.*

Domaradzka, A. (2018). Urban Social Movements and the Right to the City: An Introduction to the Special Issue on Urban Mobilization. *VOLUNTAS: International Journal of Voluntary and Nonprofit Organizations*, *29*(4), 607–620. <https://doi.org/10.1007/s11266-018-0030-y>

Douglas, H., Georgiou, A., & Westbrook, J. (2017). Social participation as an indicator of successful aging: An overview of concepts and their associations with health. *Australian Health Review*, *41*(4), 455–462. <https://doi.org/10.1071/AH16038>

Drori, G. S., Höllerer, M. A., & Walgenbach, P. (2014). Unpacking the glocalization of organization: from term, to theory, to analysis. *European Journal of Cultural and Political Sociology*, *1*(1), 85–99. <https://doi.org/10.1080/23254823.2014.904205>

Dudgeon, P., Scrine, C., Cox, A., & Walker, R. (2017). Facilitating empowerment and self-determination through participatory action research: Findings from the national empowerment project. *International Journal of Qualitative Methods*, *16*(1). <https://doi.org/10.1177/1609406917699515>

Durczak, K., Ławrynowicz, M., Nadobnik, H., & Sławecki, B. (2019). *Odkrywanie loklanego Poznani*. <https://www.researchgate.net/publication/339948439_Odkrywanie_lokalnego_Poznania>

Eckstein, H. (2000). Case Study and Theory in Political Science. In R. Gomm, M. Hammersley, & P. Foster (Eds.), *Case Study Method*. Sage Publication.

Estes, C. L., & Grossman, B. R. (2007). Critical Perspectives in Gerontology. In K. S. Markides (Ed.), *Encyclopedia of Health & Aging* (pp. 130–133). Thousand Oaks, CA: Sage Publications.

Estes, C. L., & Portacolone, E. (2009). "Maggie Kuhn: social theorist of radical gerontology.' *International Journal of Sociology and Social Policy*, *29*, 15–26.

European Commission. (2018). *The Ageing Report. Underlying Assumptions & Projection Methodologies* (Vol. 065, Issue November 2017). <https://doi.org/10.2765/40638>

Evans, A. B., Nistrup, A., & Pfister, G. (2018). Active ageing in Denmark; shifting institutional landscapes and the intersection of national and local priorities. *Journal of Aging Studies*, *46*(May), 1–9. <https://doi.org/10.1016/j.jaging.2018.05.001>

Farber, A. (2020). How does ANT help us to rethink the city and its promises? In A. Blok, I. Farias, & C. Roberts (Eds.), *The Routledge Companion to Actor-network Theory.* (pp. 264–272). Routledge.

Flick, U. (2017). Triangulation. In K. N. Denzin & S. Y. Lincoln (Eds.), *The SAGE Handbook of Qualitative Research* (5th ed.). SAGE Publications UK: London, England.

Flyvbjerg, B. (2006). Five Misunderstandings About Case-Study Research. *Qualitative Inquiry*, *12*(2), 219–245. <https://doi.org/10.1177/1077800405284363>

Foster, L., & Walker, A. (2015). Active and successful aging: A European policy perspective. *Gerontologist*, *55*(1), 83–90. <https://doi.org/10.1093/geront/gnu028>

Freitag, A. R. (2008). Staking Claim: Public Relations Lenders Needed to Shape CSR Policy. *Public Relations Quarterly*, *52*(1).

Fu, F., Liang, Y., An, Y., & Zhao, F. (2018). Self-efficacy and psychological well-being of nursing home residents in China: the mediating role of social engagement. *Asia Pacific Journal of Social Work and Development*, *28*(2), 128–140. <https://doi.org/10.1080/02185385.2018.1464942>

Galis, V. (2011). Enacting disability: how can science and technology studies inform disability studies? *Disability & Society*, *26*(7), 825–838. <https://doi.org/10.1080/09687599.2011.618737>

Gao, J., Zheng, P., Jia, Y., Chen, H., Mao, Y., Chen, S., Wang, Y., Fu, H., & Dai, J. (2020). Mental health problems and social media exposure during COVID-19 outbreak. *Plos One*. <https://doi.org/https://doi.org/10.1371/journal.pone.0231924>

Gawron, G. (2017). Senioralna koprodukcja? Analiza wybranych przypadków lokalnych inicjatyw na rzecz seniorów w krajach o niskich i średnich dochodach. *Praca Socjalna*, *5*(33), 29–53.

Gilleard, C., & Higgs, P. (2016). Gerontology versus Geriatrics: Different Ways of Understanding Ageing and Old Age. In G. Scarre (Ed.), *The Palgrave Handbook of the Philosophy of Aging* (pp. 31–48). Palgrave Macmillan UK. <https://doi.org/10.1057/978-1-137-39356-2_3>

Giulianotti, R., & Robertson, R. (2007). Forms of Glocalization : Globalization and the Migration Strategies of Scottish Football Fans in North America. *Sociology*, *41*(1), 133–152.

Godenhjelm, S., Lundin, R. A., & Sjöblom, S. (2015). Projectification in the public sector—the case of the European Union. *International Journal of Managing Projects in Business*, *8*(2), 324–348. <https://doi.org/10.1108/IJMPB-05-2014-0049>

Goggin, M. L., Bowman, A. O., Lester, J. P., O'Toole Jr, L. J., & Glenview, I. (1990). *Implementation Theory and Practice: Toward a Third Generation.* Scott, Foresman/ Little.

Goldstein, J., & Keohane, R. (1993). *Ideas and Foreign Policy: Beliefs, Institutions and Political Change.* Cornell University Press.

Golinowska, S. (2015). Polityka społeczna adresowana do grup ludności w cyklu życia. Wyzwania dla teorii i praktyki. *Problemy Polityki Społecznej. Studia i Dyskusje*, *28*, 15–43.

Granbom, M., Kristensson, J., & Sandberg, M. (2017). Effects on leisure activities and social participation of a case management intervention for frail older people living at home: a randomised controlled trial. *Health and Social Care in the Community*, *25*(4), 1416–1429. <https://doi.org/10.1111/hsc.12442>

Grewiński, M. (2009). *Wielosektorowa polityka społeczna. O przeobrażeniach państwa opiekuńczego.* Wydawnictwo Wyższej Szkoły Pedagogicznej TWP.

Gudkova, S. (2012). Wywiad w badaniach jakościowych. In D. Jemielniak (Ed.), *Badanie jakościowe t. 2* (pp. 110–130). Wydawnictwo Naukowe PWN.

Guy, P. B. (2010). "Meta-governance and Public Management." In S. P. Osborne (Ed.), *The New Public Governance?* Routledge.

Guy, P. B. (2018). Introduction. In A. Wildavsky (Ed.), *The Art and Craf of Policy Analysis*. PALGRAVE MACMILLAN.

Guy, P. B. (2019). *Institutional Theory in Political Science* (Fourth). Edward Elgar.

Habermas, J. (1996). *Between Facts and Norms: Contributions to a Discourse Theory.* Polity.

Hagestad, G. O., & Dykstra, P. A. (2016). Structuration of the Life Course: Some Neglected Aspects. In M. J. Shanahan, J. T. Mortimer, & M. Kirkpatrick Johnson (Eds.), *Handbook of Life Course Perspective. Volume II* (pp. 131–160). Springer.

Hall, P. A. (1993). Policy Paradigms, Social Learning, and the State: The Case of Economic Policymaking in Britain. *Comparative Politics*, *26*(2), 549–573. <https://doi.org/10.1017/S175577390999021X>

Hall, P. A. (1997). The Role of Interests, Institutions and Ideas in The Comparative Political Economy of The Industrialized Nations. In M. I. Lichbach & A. S. Zuckerman (Eds.), *Comparative Politics: Rationality, Culture and Structure.* (pp. 174–207). Cambridge University Press.

Hall, P. A. (2013). Tracing the Progress of Process Tracing. *European Political Science*, *12*(1), 20–30. <https://doi.org/10.1057/eps.2012.6>

Hall, P. A., & Taylor, R. C. R. (1996). Political Science and the Three New Institutionalisms. *Political Studies*, *44*, 936–957.

Hammersley, M., & Atkinson, P. (2000). *Metody badań terenowych* (S. Dymczyk, Trans.). Zysk i Sk-a.

Harding, A., & Blockland, T. (2014). *Urban Theory: A Critical Introduction to Power, Cities and Urbanism in the 21st Century.* Sage.

Hardy, C. A., & Williams, S. P. (2008). E-government policy and practice: A theoretical and empirical exploration of public e-procurement.

Government Information Quarterly, *25*, 155–180. <https://doi.org/10.1016/j.giq.2007.02.003>

Harvey, D. (1989). *The Urban Experience*. Blackwell.

Havighurst, R. J. (1961). Successful Aging1. *The Gerontologist*, *1*(1), 8–13. <https://doi.org/10.1093/geront/1.1.8>

Heaven, B., O'Brien, N., Evans, E. H., White, M., Meyer, T. D., Mathers, J. C., & Moffatt, S. (2016). Mobilizing resources for well-being: Implications for developing interventions in the retirement transition. *Gerontologist*, *56*(4), 615–629. <https://doi.org/10.1093/geront/gnu159>

Ho, H. C. (2017a). Elderly volunteering and psychological well-being. *International Social Work*, *60*(4), 1028–1038. <https://doi.org/10.1177/0020872815595111>

Ho, H. C. (2017b). Elderly volunteering and psychological well-being. *International Social Work*, *60*(4), 1028–1038. <https://doi.org/10.1177/0020872815595111>

Hodgson, D., Fred, M., Bailey, S., & Hall, P. (2019). Introduction. In D. Hodgson, M. Fred, S. Bailey, & P. Hall (Eds.), *The Projectification of the Public Sector*. Routledge.

Hodgson, G. (2004). *The Evolution of Institutional Economics. Agency, Structure and Darwinism in American Institutionalism*. Routledge.

Hodgson, G. (2018). Ekonomia instytucjonalna. In L. Fischer, J. Hasell, J. C. Proctor, D. Uwakwe, Z. W. Perkins, & C. Watson (Eds.), *Pomyśleć ekonomię od nowa.* (pp. 89–110). Wydawnictwo Ekonomiczne Heterodox.

Holstein, J. A., & Gubrium, J. F. (2005). Interpretive practice and Social Action. In K. N. Denzin & S. Y. Lincoln (Eds.), *The SAGE Handbook of qualitative research. 3rd edition* (pp. 483–507). Sage Publication.

Holstein, M. B., & Minkler, M. (2003). Self, Society, and the "New Gerontology." *The Gerontologist*, *43*(6), 787–796.

Hong, P. Y. P., & Song, I. H. (2010). Glocalization of social work practice: Global and local responses to globalization. *International Social Work*, *53*(5), 656–670. <https://doi.org/10.1177/0020872810371206>

van Hoof, J., & Kazak, J. K. (2018). Urban ageing. *Indoor and Built Environment*, *27*(5), 583–586. <https://doi.org/10.1177/1420326X18768160>

van Hoof, J., Kazak, J. K., Perek-Białas, J. M., & Peek, S. T. M. (2018). The challenges of urban ageing: Making cities age-friendly in Europe. *International Journal of Environmental Research and Public Health*, *15*(11), 1–17. <https://doi.org/10.3390/ijerph15112473>

Hooyman, N. R., & Kiyak, H. A. (2017). *Social Gerontology: A Multidisciplinary Perspective*. Pearson Education Limited.

Hsieh, H. F., & Shannon, S. E. (2005). Three approaches to qualitative content analysis. *Qualitative Health Research*, *15*(9), 1277–1288. <https://doi.org/10.1177/1049732305276687>

Immergut, E. M. (1998). The Theoretical Core of the New Institutionalism. *Politics and Society*, *26*, 5–34.

Iskandarova, M. (2017). From the idea of scale to the idea of agency: An actor-network theory perspective on policy development for renewable energy. *Science and Public Policy*, *44*(4), 476–485. <https://doi.org/10.1093/scipol/scw075>

Jałocha, B. (2019). The European Union's multi-level impact on member state projectification in light of neoinstitutional theory. *International Journal of Managing Projects in Business*, *12*(3), 578–601. <https://doi.org/10.1108/IJMPB-09-2018-0198>

Jałocha, B. (2021). Projekty w kontekście przemian sektora publicznego. In *Projektyzacja sektora publicznego w Polsce.* (pp. 19–61). Wydawnictwo Naukowe PWN.

Jayne, M., & Ward, K. (Eds.). (2017). *URBAN THEORY: New critical perspectives*. Routledge. <https://doi.org/10.1017/CBO9781107415324.004>

Jensen, C., Johansson, S., & Löfström, M. (2018). Policy implementation in the era of accelerating projectification: Synthesizing Matland's conflict–ambiguity model and research on temporary organizations. *Public Policy and Administration*, *33*(4), 447–465. <https://doi.org/10.1177/0952076717702957>

Joy, M. (2018). Problematizing the age friendly cities and communities program in Toronto. *Journal of Aging Studies*, *47*(September), 49–56. <https://doi.org/10.1016/j.jaging.2018.10.005>

Julien, H. (2008). Content analysis. In L. Given (Ed.), *The SAGE Encyclopedia of Qualitative Research Methods.* (pp. 120–121). Sage Publication.

Kaljonen, M. (2006). Co-construction of agency and environmental management. The case of agri-environmental policy implementation at Finnish farms. *Journal of Rural Studies*, *22*(2), 205–216. <https://doi.org/10.1016/j.jrurstud.2005.08.010>

Katz, S. (2000a). Busy Bodies: Activity, aging, and the management of everyday life. *Journal of Aging Studies*, *14*(2), 135–152. <https://doi.org/10.1016/S0890-4065(00)80008-0>

Kingdon, J. W. (2014). *Agendas, Alternatives, and Public Policies.* Pearson Education Limited.

Klimczuk, A. (2012). *Kapitał społeczny ludzi starych na przykładzie mieszkańców miasta Białegostoku*. Wiedza i Edukacja.

Klimczuk, A. (2015). *Economic Foundations for Creative Ageing Policy, Volume 1: Context and Considerations*. Palgrave Macmillan. <https://doi.org/10.1111/j.1728-4457.2016.00117.x>

Klimczuk, A. (2017). Economic Foundations for Creative Ageing Policy. Putting Theory into Practice. Volume II. In *Economic Foundations for Creative Ageing Policy, Volume II: Putting Theory into Practice: Vol. II*. Palgrave Macmillan U.S. <https://doi.org/10.1057/978-1-137-53523-8>

Klimczuk, A. (2018). Polityka publiczna wobec starzenia się ludności. Przegląd pojęć i podejść teoretycznych. *Studia z Polityki Publicznej*, *4*(4), 67–94.

Klimczuk, A., & Tomczyk, Ł. (2016). Inteligentne miasta przyjazne starzeniu się—przykłady z krajów Grupy Wyszehradzkiej. *Rozwój Regionalny i Polityka Regionalna*, *34*, 79–97.

Komisja Ekspertów ds. Osób Starszych przy Rzeczniku Praw Obywatelskich. (2018). „Analiza programu: Polityka społeczna wobec osób starszych 2030. Bezpieczeństwo. Uczestnictwo. Solidarność." *Studia z Polityki Publicznej*, *5*(4), 169–176. <https://econjournals.sgh.waw.pl/KSzPP/article/view/2675>

Kotus, J. (2013). Position of the Polish city on the ladder of public participation: Are we going the right way? The case of Poznań. *Cities*, *35*, 226–236. <https://doi.org/10.1016/j.cities.2013.08.001>

Krzyszkowski, J., & Przywojska, J. (2010). Lokalne strategie rozwiązywania problemów społecznych jako instrument decentralizacji polityki społecznej. In M. Gerwiński & A. Karwacki (Eds.), *Strategie w polityce społecznej.* Mazowieckie Centrum Polityki Społecznej.

Kubiak, M. (2018). Gminne rady seniorów z perspektywy lokalnej polityki senioralnej. *Wrocławskie Studia Politologiczne*, *25*, 101–117. <https://doi.org/10.19195/1643-0328.25.7>

Kutsar, D., & Kuronen, M. (2015). *Local Welfare Policy Making in European Cities* (D. Kutsar & M. Kuronen, Eds.; Vol. 59). Springer International Publishing. <https://doi.org/10.1007/978-3-319-16163-1>

Kuura, A. (2011). Policies for projectification: support, avoid or let it be? *Discussions on Estonian Economic Policy*, 47–55.

Kvale, S. (2010). *Prowadzenie wywiadów* (A. Dziuban, Trans.). Wydawnictwo Naukowe PWN.

Lambooy, J. G., & Moulaert, F. (1996). The economic organization of cities: An institutional perspective. *International Journal of Urban and Regional Research*, *20*(2), 217–237. <https://doi.org/10.1111/j.1468-2427.1996.tb00312.x>

Latapí Agudelo, M. A., Jóhannsdóttir, L., & Davídsdóttir, B. (2019). A literature review of the history and evolution of corporate social responsibility. *International Journal of Corporate Social Responsibility*, *4*(1), 1–23. <https://doi.org/10.1186/s40991-018-0039-y>

Latham, A., & McCormack, D. P. (2010). Globalizations Big and Small. Notes on Urban Studies, Actor-Network Theory, and Geographical Scale. In I. Farías & T. Bender (Eds.), *Urban Assemblages: How Actor-Network Theory Changes Urban Studies.* (pp. 53–72). Routledge.

Latour, B. (1993). *We Have Never Been Modern*. Harvard University Press.

Latour, B. (2005). *Reassembling the Social: An Introduction to Actor-Network-Theory*. Oxford University Press.

Latour, B., & Woolgar, S. (1986). *Laboratory Life: The construction of scientific facts* (2nd edn wi). NJ: Princeton University Press.

Law, J. (2008). Actor Network Theory and Material Semiotics. In B. S. Turner (Ed.), *The New Blackwell Companion to Social Theory* (pp. 141–158). Wiley. <https://doi.org/10.1002/9781444304992.ch7>

Law, J. (2019). *Material Semiotics*. 1–19.

Lefebvre, H. (2004). *Rhythmanalysis: Space, Time, and Everyday Life*. Continuum.

Lieberman, R. C. (2002). Ideas, Institutions and Political Order: Explaining Political Change. *American Political Science Review*, *96*(4), 697–712.

Linder, S. H., & Peters, B. G. (1989). Implementations as a guide to policy formulation: a question of "when" rather than "whether." *International Review of Administrative Sciences*, *55*, 631–652.

Łuczewski, M., & Bednarz-Łuczewska, P. (2012). Analiza dokumentów zastanych. In D. Jemielniak (Ed.), *Badanie jakościowe t. 2* (pp. 163–188). Wydawnictwo Naukowe PWN.

MacManus, S. A. (2010). The Politics of Aging. In D. Dannefer & C. Phillipson (Eds.), *The Sage Handbook of Social Gerontology* (pp. 641–652). SAGE Publications Sage UK: London, England. <https://doi.org/https://doi.org/10.4135/9781446200933.n50>

Marshall, V. M. (1999). Analyzing Social Theories of Aging. In V. L. Bengtson & K. W. Schaie (Eds.), *Handbook of Theories of Aging* (pp. 434–455). New York: Springer Publishing.

Marshall, V. M., & Clarke, P. J. (2010). Agency and Social Structure in Aging and Life-course Research. In D. Dannefer & C. Phillipson (Eds.), *The Sage Handbook of Social Gerontology* (pp. 294–306). SAGE Publications UK: London, England.

Martinson, M., & Berridge, C. (2015). Successful aging and its discontents: A systematic review of the social gerontology literature. *Gerontologist*, *55*(1), 58–69. <https://doi.org/10.1093/geront/gnu037>

Matland, R. E. (1995). Synthesizing the Implementation Literature: The Ambiguity–Conflict Model of Policy Implementation. *Journal of Public Administration Research and Theory*, *5*(2), 145–174.

McFarlane, C. (2011). Assemblage and critical urbanism. *City*, *15*(2), 204–224. <https://doi.org/10.1080/13604813.2011.568715>

Mehta, J. (2011). The Varied Roles of Ideas in Politics. In D. Beland & R. Cox (Eds.), *Ideas and Politics in Social Science Research* (pp. 23–46). Oxford University Press.

Michael, Y. L., Green, M. K., & Farquhar, S. A. (2006). Neighborhood design and active aging. *Health and Place*, *12*(4), 734–740. <https://doi.org/10.1016/j.healthplace.2005.08.002>

Mol, A. (2002). *The Body Multiple*. Duke University Press. <https://doi.org/10.1215/9780822384151>

Moulaert, T., & Garon, S. (Eds.). (2016). *Age-Friendly Cities and Communities in International Comparison*. Springer International Publishing. <https://doi.org/10.1007/978-3-319-24031-2>

Mullerat, R. (2009). *International Corporate Social Responsibility.* Kluwer Law International.

Mumford, L. (2016). *The Culture of Cities*. Open Road Integrated Media.

Nadobnik, H., Durczak, K., & Ławrynowicz, M. (2021). Temporality and the aging self. How subjective time is folding over its linear progression. *Journal of Aging Studies*, *57*(April 2020), 100933. <https://doi.org/10.1016/j.jaging.2021.100933>

North, D. (1990). *Institutions, institutional change and economic performance.* Cambridge University Press.

Novak, T., & Vute, R. (2013a). Spending leisure time and activities in the third period of life. *Anthropological Notebooks*, *19*(1), 35–44.

Novak, T., & Vute, R. (2013b). Spending leisure time and activities in the third period of life. *Anthropological Notebooks*, *19*(1), 35–44.

O'Connor, M. K., & Netting, F. E. (2011). *Analyzing Social Policy: Multiple Perspectives for Critically Understanding and Evaluating Policy.* Willey.

Olech, A., & Kaźmierczak, T. (2011). Modele partycypacji publicznej. In A. Olech (Ed.), *Partycypacja publiczna. O uczestnictwie obywateli w życiu wspólnoty lokalnej* (pp. 100–122). Instytut Spraw Publicznych.

O'Rand, A. M., Isaacs, K., & Roth, L. (2010). Age and Inequality in Global Context. In D. Dannefer & C. Phillipson (Eds.), *The SAGE Handbook of Social Gerontology* (pp. 128–136). SAGE Publications Ltd. <https://doi.org/10.4135/9781446200933.n9>

Orloff, A. S., & Palier, B. (2009). The Power of Gender Perspectives: Feminist Influence on Policy Paradigms, Social Science, and Social Politics. *Social Politics: International Studies in Gender, State & Society*, *16*(4), 405–412. <https://doi.org/10.1093/sp/jxp021>

Outila, M., & Kiuru, H. (2021). "Picturephone in My Home": Actor-Network Theory and Foucauldian Discourse Analysis on Northern Finnish Older Adults Starting to Use a Video Conferencing Service. *Journal of Technology in Human Services*, *39*(2), 163–192. <https://doi.org/10.1080/15228835.2020.1869670>

Pal, L. (2005). Case Study Method and Policy Analysis. In I. Geva-May (Ed.), *Thinking Like a Policy Analyst: Policy Analysis as a Clinical Profession.* (pp. 227–258). Palgrave Macmillan.

Parker, S. (2015). *Urban Theory and the Urban Experience* (Second). Routledge. <https://doi.org/10.4324/9780203122402>

Pasquallie, M. (2018). "Ons is die stam van die gemeenskap": rethinking old age and vitality in Nuwerus, Western Cape. *Anthropology Southern Africa*, *41*(2), 164–174. <https://doi.org/10.1080/23323256.2018.1476164>

Pe, Y., Gunawan, S., & Shieh, C.-J. (2014). Correlations between Social Engagement and Quality of Life of the Elderly in China. *Revista Internacional de Sociología*, *72*(Extra_2), 105–118. <https://doi.org/10.3989/ris.2013.08.15>

Perek-Białas, J., Ruzik, A., & Vidovićová, L. (2006). Active ageing policies in the Czech Republic and Poland. *International Social Science Journal*, *58*(190), 559–570. <https://doi.org/10.1111/j.1468-2451.2008.00655.x>

Phillips, J., Ajrouch, K., & Hillcoat-Nallétamby, S. (Eds.). (2010). *Key Concepts in Social Gerontology*. SAGE Publications: London, England.

Phillipson, C., & Estes, C. L. (2007). Critical Gerontology. In J. A. Birren (Ed.), *Encyclopedia of gerontology.* (pp. 330–336). Elsevier Inc.

Phillipson, C., & Scharf, T. (2005). Rural and urban perspectives on growing old: Developing a new research agenda. *European Journal of Ageing*, *2*(2), 67–75. <https://doi.org/10.1007/s10433-005-0024-7>

Pieliński, B. (2013). Instytucjonalizmy w analizach polityki społecznej. *Problemy Polityki Społecznej. Studia i Dyskusje*, *22*(3), 25–43.

Po-An Hsieh, J. J., Keil, M., Holmström, J., & Kvasny, L. (2012). The Bumpy Road to Universal Access: An Actor-Network Analysis of a U.S. Municipal Broadband Internet Initiative. *Information Society*, *28*(4), 264–283. <https://doi.org/10.1080/01972243.2012.689271>

Polakowski, M. (2012). *Polityka społeczna po 1989: Język, kontekst postsocjalizmui perspektywy rozwoju.* Friedrich-Ebert-Stiftung and Fundacja Międzynarodowe Centrum Badań i Analiz ICRA.

Poole, D. L., & Negi, N. (2008). Transnational community enterprises for social welfare in global civil society. *International Journal of Social Welfare*, *17*(3), 243–246. <https://doi.org/10.1111/j.1468-2397.2007.00528.x>

Pressman, J. L., & Wildavsky, A. (1974). *Implementation*. University of California Press.

Ranerup, A. (2008). for Public Policy Implementation The Case of Pension Reform. *Social Science Computer Review*, *26*(4), 428–445.

Rémillard-Boilard, S., Buffel, T., & Phillipson, C. (2020). Developing Age-Friendly Cities and Communities: Eleven Case Studies from around the

World. *International Journal of Environmental Research and Public Health, 18*(1), 133. <https://doi.org/10.3390/ijerph18010133>

Rezaeipandari, H., Ravaei, J., Bahrevar, V., Mirrezaei, S., & Morowatisharifabad, M. A. (2020). Social participation and loneliness among older adults in Yazd, Iran. *Health & Social Care in the Community, 28*(6), 2076–2085. <https://doi.org/10.1111/hsc.13018>

Ritzer, G. (2004). *The Globalization of Nothing.* Pine Forge.

Robertson, R. (1995). Glocalization: Time-Space and Homogeneity-Heterogeneity. In M. Featherstone, S. Lash, & R. Robertson (Eds.), *Global Modernities* (pp. 25–45). Sage Publication.

Robertson, R. (2013). Situating Glocalization A relatively autobiographical intervention. In G. S. Drori, M. A. Höllerer, & P. Walgenbach (Eds.), *Global Themes and Local Variations in Organization and Management* (pp. 25–37). Routledge.

Roe, E. (1994). *Narrative Policy Analysis: Theory and Practice.* Duke University Press.

Rose, A. M. (1962). The subculture of the aging: A topic for sociological research. *Gerontologist, 2*(3), 123–127. <https://doi.org/10.1093/geront/2.3.123>

Roudometof, V. (2015). The Glocal and Global Studies. *Globalizations, 12*(5), 774–787. <https://doi.org/10.1080/14747731.2015.1016293>

Sánchez-González, D., & Rodriguez-Rodriguez, V. (Eds.). (2016). *Environmental Gerontology in Europe and Latin America*. Springer International Publishing Switzerland.

Sanders, A. J. P., Hyldmo, S., Dini, R., Prasti, H., Ford, R. M., Larson, A. M., & Keenan, R. J. (2017). Guinea pig or pioneer : Translating global environmental objectives through to local actions in Central Kalimantan, Indonesia's REDD + pilot province. *Global Environmental Change, 42*, 68–81. <https://doi.org/10.1016/j.gloenvcha.2016.12.003>

Saunders, P. (1986). *Social Theory and the Urban Question*. Hutchison.

Sayes, E. (2014). Actor-Network Theory and methodology: Just what does it mean to say that nonhumans have agency? *Social Studies of Science, 44*(1), 134–149. <https://doi.org/10.1177/0306312713511867>

Schmidt, V. A. (2008). Discursive Institutionalism: The Explanatory Power of Ideas and Discourse. *Annual Review of Political Science, 11*(1), 303–326. <https://doi.org/10.1146/annurev.polisci.11.060606.135342>

Schmidt, V. A. (2010). Taking ideas and discourse seriously: Explaining change through discursive institutionalism as the fourth "new institutionalism." *European Political Science Review*, *2*(1), 1–25. <https://doi.org/10.1017/S175577390999021X>

Scott, R. W. (2014). *Institutions and Organizations*. Sage Publication.

Silverman, D. (2007). *Interpretacja danych jakościowych* (M. Głowacka-Grajewska & J. Ostrowska, Trans.). Wydawnictwo Naukowe PWN.

Simmel, G. (1950). The Metropolis and Mental Life. In K. H. Wolff (Ed.), *The Sociology of Georg Simmel* (pp. 409–426). Free Press.

Skórzyńska, A. (2018). We make up the rules as we go along? Projektyzacja, "bystre" miasta i widma emergencji. *Zarządzanie w Kulturze*, *19*(3), 233–256. <https://doi.org/10.4467/20843976zk.18.016.9470>

Skrzypek-Prawelska, G., & Jałocha, B. (2014). Projektyzacja sektora publicznego w Polsce—implikacje dla organizacji samorządu terytorialnego. *Zarządzanie Publiczne*, *27*(3), 273–284. <https://doi.org/10.4467/20843968ZP.14.023.2767>

Sławecki, B. (2012). Znaczenie paradygmatów w badaniach jakościowych. In D. Jemielniak (Ed.), *Badania jakościowe t.1* (pp. 57–88). Wydawnictwo Naukowe PWN.

Snopko, J. (2014). Public-Private Partnership and Hybrid Projects as an Effective Method for Financing Local Government Investment Projects. *Public Management*, *27*(3), 263–271. <https://doi.org/https://doi.org/10.4467/20843968ZP.14.022.2766>

Stake, R. E. (2008). Qualitative case studies. In K. N. Denzin & S. Y. Lincoln (Eds.), *Strategies of qualitative inquiry* (3rd ed., pp. 119–149). Sage Publications, Inc.

Star, S. L. (1991). Power, technologies and the phenomenology of conventions: On being allergic to onions. In J. Law (Ed.), *A Sociology of Monsters: Essays on Power, Technology and Domination.* (pp. 26–56). Routledge.

Strawbridge, W., Wallhagen, M., & Cohen, R. (2002). Successful aging and well-being: Self-rated compared with Rowe and Kahn. *The Gerontologist*, *42*, 727–733. <https://doi.org/doi:10.1093/geront/42.6.727>

Strumińska-Kutra, M., & Koładkiewicz, I. (2012). Studium Przypadku. In D. Jemielniak (Ed.), *Badanie jakościowe t. 2* (pp. 20–56). Wydawnictwo Naukowe PWN.

Sun, Y., Chao, T. Y., Woo, J., & Au, D. W. H. (2017). An institutional perspective of "Glocalization" in two Asian tigers: The "Structure–Agent–Strategy" of building an age-friendly city. *Habitat International*, *59*, 101–109. <https://doi.org/10.1016/j.habitatint.2016.11.013>

Suzuki, K., Dollery, B. E., & Kortt, M. A. (2021). Addressing loneliness and social isolation amongst elderly people through local co-production in Japan. *Social Policy & Administration*, *55*(4), 674–686. <https://doi.org/10.1111/spol.12650>

Swanton, D. (2011). Assemblage and Critical Urban Praxis: Part Two: Introduction. *City*, *15*(3–4), 343–346. <https://doi.org/10.1080/13604813.2011.610153>

Swianiewicz, P. (2016). Współczesne badania nad samorządem i polityką lokalną. In G. Gorzelak (Ed.), *Polska Gmina 2015*. Scholar.

Swyngedouw, E. (1996). Reconstructing Citizenship, the Re-scaling of the State and the New Authoritarianism: Closing the Belgian Mines. *Urban Studies*, *33*(8), 1499–1521. <https://doi.org/10.1080/0042098966772>

Swyngedouw, E. (1997). Neither global nor Local: "Glocalization" and the Politics of Scale. In K. R. Cox (Ed.), *Spaces of globalization. Reasserting the Power of the Local* (pp. 137–167). Guilford Publications.

Swyngedouw, E. (2004). Globalisation or "glocalisation"? Networks, territories and rescaling. *Cambridge Review of International Affairs*, *17*(1), 25–48. <https://doi.org/10.1080/0955757042000203632>

Swyngedouw, E. (2005). Governance Innovation and the Citizen: The Janus Face of Governance-beyond-the-State. *Urban Studies*, *42*(11), 1991–2006. <https://doi.org/10.1080/00420980500279869>

Szarfenberg, R. (2008). *Krytyka i afirmacja Polityki Społecznej*. Wydawnictwo Instytutu Filozofii i Socjologii PAN.

Szarfenberg, R. (2010). Jakość usług pomocy społecznej. *Problemy Polityki Społecznej*, *13–14*(41–58).

Szarfenberg, R. (2013). Perspektywy badawcze polityki społecznej—wprowadzenie. *Problemy Polityki Społecznej. Studia i Dyskusje*, *22*(3), 11–22.

Szatur-Jaworska, B. (2015). Polityka senioralna w Polsce—analiza agendy. *Problemy Polityki Społecznej. Studia i Dyskusje*, *30*(3), 47–75.

Szatur-Jaworska, B. (2016). Polityka społeczna wobec starzenia się ludności—konceptualizacja pojęć, ramy teoretyczne i aksjologiczne.

In *Polska polityka społeczna wobec starzenia się ludności 1971–2013* (pp. 67–105). Dom Wydawniczy ELIPSA.

Szatur-Jaworska, B., Błędowski, P., & Dzięgielewska, M. (2006). *Podstawy gerontologii społecznej.* Oficyna Wydawnicza ASPRA-JR.

Sztandar-Sztanderska, K. (2016). *Obywatel spotyka państwo. O urzędach pracy jako biurokracji pierwszego kontaktu.* Scholar.

Szulecki, K. (2011). Hijacked ideas: Human rights, peace, and environmentalism in Czechoslovak and Polish dissident discourses. *East European Politics & Societies*, *25*(2), 272–295.

Taylor-Gooby, P. (2018). Participation and solidarity in a changing welfare state. In P. Beresford & S. Carr (Eds.), *Social policy first hand. An international introduction to participatory social welfare.* (pp. 22–32). Polity.

Theiss, M. (2012). Trafna polityka lokalna? Przykład polityki społecznej wobec ludzi starych. *Problemy Polityki Społecznej*, *17*, 149–165.

Theiss, M. (2017). Wyjaśnienia lokalnej polityki społecznej. Podejścia i tradycje badawcze. *Polityka Społeczna*, *5–6*, 14–20.

Tittenbrun, J. (2014). *Concepts of Capital The Commodification of Social Life.* Routledge.

Tong, H., Lai, D. W. L., & Walsh, C. A. (2019). Formal Social Participation and Utilization of Community-based Services among Urban Elderly Chinese Living Alone in Shanghai, China. *Journal of Social Service Research*, *45*(4), 520–529. <https://doi.org/10.1080/01488376.2018.1481172>

Tsukamoto, T. (2012). Neoliberalization of the developmental state: Tokyo's bottom-up politics and state rescaling in Japan. *International Journal of Urban and Regional Research*, *36*(1), 71–89. <https://doi.org/10.1111/j.1468-2427.2011.01057.x>

Urban Assemblages. How Actor-Network Theory Changes Urban Studies. (2010). In I. Farías & T. Bender (Eds.), *Urban Assemblages*. Routledge. <https://doi.org/10.4324/9780203870631>

Urbaniak, B. (2018). Regional Senior Policy as a New Public Policy. *Przedsiębiorczość i Zarządzanie*, *XIX*(3), 93–105.

Wæraas, A., & Nielsen, J. A. (2016). Translation Theory "Translated": Three Perspectives on Translation in Organizational Research. *International Journal of Management Reviews*, *18*(3), 236–270. <https://doi.org/10.1111/ijmr.12092>

Wahl, H. W., & Gitlin, L. N. (2007). Environmental Gerontology. In J. E. Birren (Ed.), *Encyclopedia of gerontology.* (pp. 494–502). Elsevier Inc.

Walker, A. (2002). A strategy for active ageing. *International Social Security Review*, *55*(1), 121–139. <https://doi.org/10.1111/1468-246X.00118>

Walker, A. (2008). Commentary: The Emergence and Application of Active Aging in Europe. *Journal of Aging & Social Policy*, *21*(1), 75–93. <https://doi.org/10.1080/08959420802529986>

Wanchai, A., & Phrompayak, D. (2019). Social Participation Types and Benefits on Health Outcomes for Elder People: a Systematic Review. *Ageing International*, *44*, 223–233. <https://doi.org/10.1007/s12126-018-9338-6>

Wathen, M. V. (2020). A critical glocalization approach: attending to power in the innovation space. *Journal of Community Practice*, *28*(2), 144–159. <https://doi.org/10.1080/10705422.2020.1757543>

Weber, M. (1958). *The City*. Free Press.

Weber, R. P. (1990). *Basic content analysis*. Sage.

Wildavsky, A. (2018). *The art and craft of policy analysis*. PALGRAVE MACMILLAN.

Wincott, D. (2011). Ideas, Policy Change, and the Welfare State. In D. Beland & R. H. Cox (Eds.), *Ideas and Politics in Social Science Research* (pp. 143–167). Oxford University Press.

World Health Organization. (2002). *Active Ageing: A Policy Framework. A contribution of the second United Nations World Assembly on Ageing.* <http://www.who.int/hpr/>

Xiong, Y., Lu, Q.-C., & Hu, Y. (2020). Elderly Fitness-Oriented Urban Street Design: Case Study in Nanchang, China. *Journal of Urban Planning and Development*, *146*(1), 05019021. <https://doi.org/10.1061/(asce)up.1943-5444.0000547>

Yin, R. K. (1989). *Case Study Research: Design and Methods*. Sage Publication.

Yung, E. H. K., Conejos, S., & Chan, E. H. W. (2016). Social needs of the elderly and active aging in public open spaces in urban renewal. *Cities*, *52*, 114–122. <https://doi.org/10.1016/j.cities.2015.11.022>

Ziółkowski, M. (2004). Commodification of Social Life. *Polish Sociological Review*, *145*(4), 385–402.

Zybała, A. (2012). *Polityki publiczne. Doświadczenia w tworzeniu i wykonywaniu programów publicznych w Polsce i w innych krajach.* KSAP.

Zybała, A. (2013). *Państwo i społeczeństwo w działaniu. Polityki publiczne wobec potrzeb modernizacji państwa i społeczeństwa.* Difin.

Appendices

Appendix 1. The list of data sources

Table 15: The list of additional materials

	Title	Type of document	Source	Level	Dates	Length
1.	Statutes of the TRAKT Centre for Cultural Tourism (pl. *Statut Centrum Turystyki Kulturowej TRAKT*)	Formal document	<www.bip.poznan.pl>	Organization	Enacted on July 10, 2012	5 pages
2.	Organizational Regulations Centre for Older citizen Initiatives in Poznan (pl. *Regulamin Organizacyjny Centrum Inicjatyw Senioralnych w Poznaniu*)	Formal document	<www.bip.poznan.pl>	Organization	Enacted on November 27, 2020	4 pages
3.	Declaration on cooperation of mayors in the field of older citizen policy (pl. *Deklaracja Współpracy prezydentów miast w obszarze polityki senioralnej)*	Formal document	<www.bip.poznan.pl>	City	Singed on October 20, 2017	1 page

(Continued)

Table 15: (*Continued*)

	Title	Type of document	Source	Level	Dates	Length
4.	Older Citizens' Policy of the City of Poznan for 2017–2021 (pl. *Polityka Senioralna Miasta Poznania na lata 2017–2021)*	Formal Document	<www. bip. poznan. pl>	City	2017–2021	27 pages
5.	Older citizen package (pl. *Tytka Seniora)*	Informational document	<www. poznan. pl>	City	October and November 2019	150 pages
6.	Program of Older Citizen Days (pl. *Program Senioralni)*	Informational and pro-motional document	<www. centrum-cis.pl>	City	November and December 2019	75 pages
7.	Announcement of the open compe-tition No. 45/2021 for assigning the tasks of the City of Poznan in the area of activity for people of retirement age. (pl. *Ogłoszenie otwar-tego konkursu ofert nr 45/2021 na powier-zenie realizacji zadań miasta Poznania w obszarze działalności na rzecz osób w wieku emerytalnym.)*	Formal document	<www. poznan. pl>	City	Enacted on March 12, 2021	8 pages
8.	Act of April 24, 2003 on public benefit activity and volun-tary work (pl. *Ustawa z dnia 24 kwietnia 2003 o działalności pożytku publicznego i o wolontariacie*)	Formal document	<www. isap.sejm. gov.pl>	Country	Enacted on April 23, 2003	60 pages

Table 16: The list of interviews and event's observations

	Interviews	**Place**	**Type of social activity for older people**	**Date**	**Length**
1.	Interview with workers of the Centre for Older citizen Initiatives.	Centre for Older Citizen Initiatives.	Older citizen Clubs animation, city events for older people, promotion of event in Poznan, realization of Older Citizen Policy.	November 2019	36 min
2.	Interview with a museum worker at Porta Posnania ICHOT.	The Museum of Porta Posnania ICHOT	Tours of museum's exhibitions.		44 min
3.	Interview with a museum worker at The Museum of Applied Arts.	The Museum of Applied Arts	Tours of museum's exhibitions.	February 2020	30 min
4.	Interview with the foundation worker (interview granted anonymously).	Foundation's building	Reading club, writing club.		48 min
5.	Interview with a worker at the Centre for Older citizen Initiatives.	Online	Older citizen Clubs animation, city events for older people, promotion of events in Poznan, realization of Older Citizen Policy.	April 2020	45 min
6.	Interview with a worker at the Flandria Foundation.	Online	Language and sport activities.		30 min
7.	Interview with the founder of the *Green Group (NGOs* and the leader of the Centre for Local Initiatives.)	Telephone	Older citizen club, Memory Day.		74 min

(Continued)

Table 16: (*Continued*)

	Interviews	Place	Type of social activity for older people	Date	Length
8.	Interview with the founder of The Mill of Support Foundation.	Online	Integration of older citizen clubs, Engagement of older people into actions for others.		46 min
9.	Interview with the Director of the Centre for Older citizen Initiatives.	Centre for Older citizen Initiatives.	Older citizen Clubs animation, city events for older people, promotion of events in Poznan, realization of Older Citizen Policy.	May 2020	45 min
10.	Interview with a member of The Municipal Council of Older citizen Citizens.	Online	Consultation of city's actions for older people and co-organization.		81 min
11.	Interview with the founders of the Silver Years Foundation and older citizen Club.	Foundation's building	Older citizen Club, Open Concerts, Storytelling by older people in kindergartens.		80 min
12.	Interview with a worker at the Municipal Centre for Family Support.	Telephone	Animations of local community, among other older people.	July 2020	37 min
13.	Interview with older citizen activists.	Telephone	Leader of Older citizen Clubs, Volunteer at the Centre of Older citizen Initiatives, Member of The Municipal Council of Older citizen Citizens.		95 min

	Events observations	Place	Collected material	Date	
14.	Older People's Club Leaders' Forum (pl. *Forum Liderów Klubów Seniora*)	City Hall building	Field notes, Presentation of available financial support for older citizens' clubs.	September 2019	3 h
15.	Guided tour for older people titled *History of Certain Loves* (pl. Oprowadzanie dla seniorów pod tytułem *Historia Pewnych Miłości)*	The Museum of Porta Posnania ICHOT	Field notes.	October 2019	2 h
16.	VIVA Older Citizen Fair (pl. *Targi VIVA Senior!*)	Municipal Trade Fair in Poznan	Field notes, photographs, and leaflets.		6 h
17.	Meeting on air pollution in Poznan under the coal burning boiler replacement program (pl. *Spotkanie dotyczące zanieczyszczeń powietrza w Poznaniu w ramach programu wymiany pieców węglowych*)	Centre for Older citizen Initiatives	Field notes.		1.5 h
18.	Guided tours of the museum exhibition for older people (pl. *Oprowadzanie po ekspozycji muzeum dla seniorów*)	The Museum of Applied Arts	Field notes and photographs.		2 h

(*Continued*)

Table 16: (*Continued*)

	Events observations	Place	Collected material	Date	
19.	The debate of generations titled: *Is the development of new communication technologies the solution to human loneliness?* (pl. Czy rozwój nowych technologii komunikacyjnych jest rozwiązaniem problemu ludzkiej samotności?)	Adam Mickiewicz University Campus	Field notes and photographs.	November 2019	3 h
20.	Excursion of the Polish Tourist Country-Lovers' Society for older citizen citizens (pl. *Wycieczka Polskiego Towarzystwa Turystyczno-Krajobrazowego dla seniorów*)	Old town	Field notes and photographs		2 h

Appendix 2. Interview guide

Thank you for consenting to speak with me.

I wanted to let you know that, as agreed, our talk is being recorded; however, it will be included in the research anonymously, and the transcription will be submitted to you for review. Do you agree with this?

As part of our talk, I'd like to understand more about older people, which includes activities and initiatives for older people. In this regard, I have some questions for you. Of course, we may interrupt or skip any question at any time.

General questions

1. Who organizes events aimed at older adults?
2. What do you prioritize when constructing them? What is your goal? For example, disseminating knowledge and social activation.
3. Where did the idea for these activities originate?
4. How would you describe their organization?
5. How are they funded?
6. How do activities for older people vary from others?
7. What are the most visible changes for you as those who assist older people?

City Council of Older citizens

1. How does the City Older Citizens Council function?
2. On what regulations do you base the council's statute?
3. What activities do you take to support older people?
4. How do top-down directives/orders affect your job and actions?
5. Who do you partner with?
6. What prospects do you see for MRS's activities?
7. What new demands of older people are emerging?

Employee at the Older Citizens Initiatives Centre

1. What does social activity of older people entail?
2. How do top-down directives/mandates influence your work and decisions?
3. With whom do you collaborate?
4. What other opportunities for action do you see?
5. What new/old requirements of the older people are becoming apparent?

Employee at the Municipal Family Assistance Centre

1. Could you tell us how you got active with the older people in your neighborhood?
2. Could you tell us about planning an event to promote social activity among older adults?
3. Could you tell us about your collaboration with the older people?
4. Could you please tell us about your work with the Older Citizens Initiatives Centre?

Interview with a 60+ activist (creator of older citizens clubs and member of the City Older Citizen Council).

1. Could you please tell me about what you are currently doing for the older people?
2. Could you please tell me about an event that you organized or co-organized?
3. How did you arrive at the City Older Citizen Council?
4. How does the City Older Citizen Council work?

Appendix 3. Field notes

The Appendix includes samples of field notes taken during observations and interviews. I viewed the notes as interview transcripts, evaluating them using codes and categories. It was not possible to distribute all field notes because their large size prevents it. The chosen notes correspond to two events. First, the inaugural City Forum of Older Citizens' Club Leaders, which was set to take place at City Hall, and the second one, which was a guided museum tour for older citizens.

Older Citizens' Club Leaders Forum

The meeting took place in the White Hall, with around 50 people present, representatives and leaders of the Older Citizens' Clubs (OCC).
The clubs themselves have anywhere from a few to even several hundred members.
In February, a new Council of Older Citizens was elected, the IV term.
In this regard, its new chairman spoke, discussing the actions the council would like to undertake, which would concern older people and their participation in culture. He would like a special task to be included in grant competitions, namely the cultural engagement of older individuals, which could facilitate and popularise the

allocation of funds for such activities and lead to more such events. At the moment, one has to compete with large events like the Malta Festival. He would like culture to reach the outskirts of the city, where there has not been an opportunity to carry out such activities until now. In this regard, they will be looking for places for the operation of older citizens' clubs. Great hopes are associated with the BRACZ action (delivering books from the library), but also with schools that would lend their halls to Club members in the afternoons. An example of such a club is the one operating in Smochowice [the city district].

Next, Ms. M took the floor and presented the events and meetings in which older citizens can participate (see materials distributed at the meeting).

The next speaker was Mr. A, who encouraged the people at the meeting to run for the Neighbourhood Councils. He spoke about the significant financial opportunities of these councils and encouraged people to run for positions to have a greater influence on what happens and on the allocation of funds.

After him, the director of The Centre for Older Citizens' Initiatives spoke, also encouraging participation and saying that it provides an opportunity to secure funds for older people.

The issue of older citizens clubs lacking legal personality also arose, which prevents them from participating and applying for equal funding.

Next, Ms. M took the floor, presenting the topic of funding sources. Public funds can often be allocated to organisations mentioned in the Public Benefit Activity Act, such as NGOs, cooperatives, associations, etc., so to obtain funds, OCC must collaborate with them.

The exception is mini-grants, which are allocated for the activities of informal groups.

Ms. M encouraged the creation of ordinary associations, which would give older citizens the opportunity to independently apply for funds.

Parishes can also apply for public funds.

Neighbourhood Councils can also have funds for activities for OCC or similar initiatives, for example, the Neighbourhood Council on Sobieskiego [the city district], *which had no one to give the money to.*

On Witkacym (a municipal webpage where project competitions are announced), you can track competitions. Within the framework of open tenders, projects can be implemented throughout the year, so they can have a more continuous nature. On the other hand, Small Grants can last a maximum of 80 days.

Participants of the Forum report that the problem for them is precisely establishing cooperation with organisations.

The gentleman from OCC in Grunwald [the city district], *provided an example of their collaboration with a priest, thanks to which they obtain funds.*

Porta Poznań—guided tour for older peoples: The Story of Certain Loves.

The exhibition is part of Senioralni Poznań.[32] *I came early to arrange my entry and consent for the observation. The group gathered gradually, but all the spots were filled. Registration was required for the tour. You could see small groups, pairs of people who know each other and got together to go on the tour. While waiting for the guide, the ladies were signing up for other events.*

Some ladies were saying that they recently went on a trip to Montenegro and Albania and are now waiting for the next offers/discounts from the travel agency. It turned out that the ladies are still working—we are working retirees.

Porta Poznania ICHOT—the museum of the history of the beginnings of the Polish state—a public institution space, aimed at disseminating the history of the Polish state, used as an actor in the Senioralni Poznań program.

27 Ladies and 3 Gentlemen, midday.

The guide, while recounting love stories, compared the fate of Elżbieta Halszka to a soap opera, alluding to the tendency among older ladies to watch soap operas.

For the participants, equipment was available—an electric guide that helped those with hearing difficulties hear the guide better.

---

[32] It is an action, organized by city. For one-month various cultural institutions, but also private entrepreneurs establish a special offer for older participants.

Appendix 4. The stages of the analysis

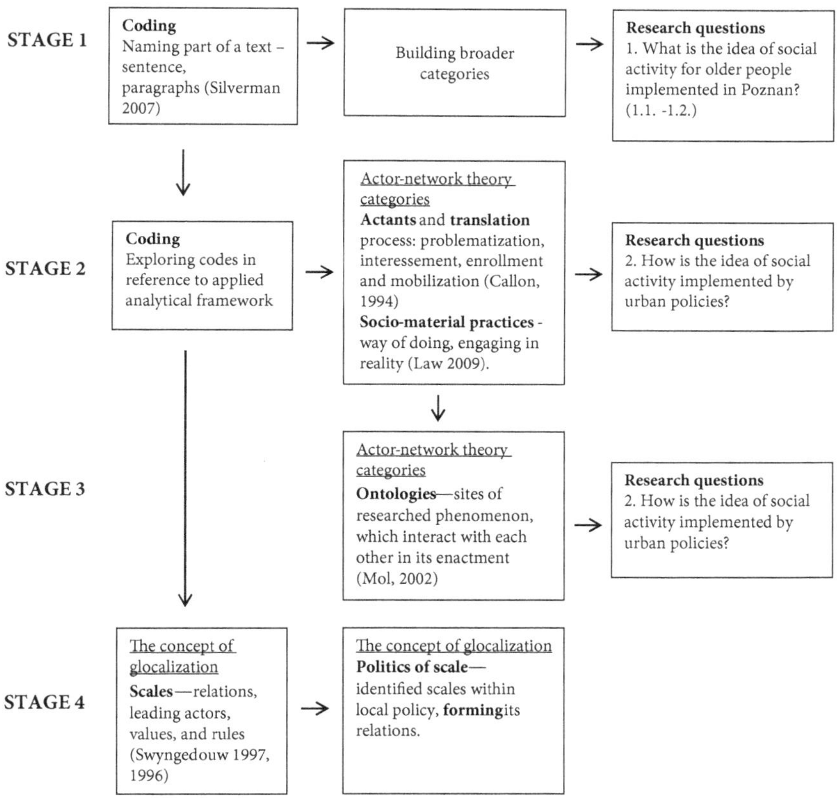

Figure 6: The stages of the analysis.

Appendix 5. An example of coding process in Atlas.ti

Table 17: An example of coding process in Atlas.ti

Interview transcription	Codes
Interviewer: ***And do they come to these other events or rather not?*** *Interviewee: Occasionally. If a workshop has to be paid for, no matter if it's 30 zloty or something, it's a step backwards, although I had a lady at a workshop (gardening in jars) which cost almost 150 zloty and there was no problem with that.*	ANT_t_enrollment_boundries
I say: maybe it's because Poznan is really doing so much for older peoples that you can choose an event either for symbolic money or even for free. Interviewer: **So, is it the case, then, that you can enter the foundation's premises from some hour to some hour every day, just like that?**	ANT_t_mobilisation_availability Practice_ creation of offer
Interviewee: Generally, I am on duty, they last from 9 a.m. to 12 p.m., and on Wednesdays and Fridays until 1 p.m., but it's not like someone just comes in for a coffee—although it happens some-times. Because that's not the point, the Foundation's Council decided that we rent the premises, because it's rented from the Foundation's funds, but it's not supposed to be a typical café, that's not the point, that wasn't the intention.	ANT_t_problematization_interests ANT_t_problematization_silent ANT_t_enrollment_boundries Practice_using space Practice_implementation of objectives

Polish Studies in Economics

Edited by Ryszard Kokoszczyński

Vol. 1 Wojciech Grabowski: Employee Stock Options, Payout Policy, and Stock Returns. Shareholders and Option Holders in Large U.S. Technology Corporations. 2012.

Vol. 2 Jan Jakub Michałek/Michał Brzozowski/ Andrzej Cieślik (eds.): The Relationship between Human Development, Exports and Foreign Direct Investments in Emerging Europe. 2013.

Vol. 3 Tomasz Żylicz: The Economics of International Environmental Cooperation. 2015.

Vol. 4 Juliusz Jabłecki / Ryszard Kokoszczyński / Paweł Sakowski / Robert Ślepaczuk / Piotr Wójcik: Volatility as an Asset Class. Obvious Benefits and Hidden Risks. 2015.

Vol. 5 Janusz Kudła / Konrad Walczyk / Robert Kruszewski / Katarzyna Kopczewska / Agata Kocia: Modeling Fiscal Policy in the European Union. 2015.

Vol. 6 Andrzej Cieślik / Jan Jakub Michałek (eds.): Liberalization of Transportation Services in the EU: the Polish Perspective. 2015.

Vol. 7 Katarzyna Metelska-Szaniawska: Economic Effects of Post-Socialist Constitutions 25 Years from the Outset of Transition. The Constitutional Political Economy Approach. 2016.

Vol. 8 Elżbieta Czarny / Andżelika Kuźnar / Jerzy Menkes (eds.): The Impact of the Transatlantic Trade and Investment Partnership on International Cooperation. 2017.

Vol. 9 Adam Czarnecki: Going Local? Linking and Integrating Second-Home Owners with the Community's Economy. A Comparative Study between Finnish and Polish Second-Home Owners. 2017.

Vol. 10 Adam Biela (ed.): European Questionnaire for Job Analysis (EQJA). 2018.

Vol. 11 Gabriela Grotkowska: Public-Sector Wage Premium in Poland. 2018.

Vol. 12 Piotr Dybka: What Determines International Competitiveness of the Economy? Evidence from Bayesian Model Averaging. 2022.

Vol. 13 Damian Bębnowski: The Importance of Constitutional Rules and Property Rights. The German Economy in 1990–2015. 2022.

Vol. 14 Wojciech Łątkowski: Projections of Demand for Care among the Elderly in Poland Including Health Status and Living Arrangements. 2024.

Vol. 15 Dominik J. Gajewski (ed.): VAT Gap in Poland: Policy Problem and Policy Response. 2024.

Vol. 16 Piotr Karaś: Money in Modern Social Encyclicals. 2024.

Vol. 17 Halina Nadobnik: The Idea of Social Activity for Older People – Local Policy Implementation. 2026.

www.peterlang.com

www.ingramcontent.com/pod-product-compliance
Ingram Content Group UK Ltd.
Pitfield, Milton Keynes, MK11 3LW, UK
UKHW020835290926
15470UKWH00004B/1365

9 783631 938188